SECRETS AND PRACTICES OF THE
FREEMASONS

© Patricia Bourin

About the Author

Jean-Louis de Biasi is a writer, lecturer and philosopher. He was initiated into Freemasonry in 1990 and raised in 1992. He was Grand Officer in France.

Some years later, he left Europe, and joined *Regular Freemasonry* in North America. He is a *Master Mason* and *Past Master*.

He currently belongs to several Grand Lodges F.A.A.M. in Canada and USA. He is also 32° in the Scottish Rite (S.J. USA—Valley de Washington), F.G.C.R., and Royal Arch Mason.

His philosophical and spiritual foundation is rooted in the Neoplatonic and Hermetic traditions and he is currently the Grand Master of the *Ordo Aurum Solis* and head of the *Kabbalistic Order of the Rose-Cross*.

He currently resides in Las Vegas, Nevada.

To Write to the Author

If you wish to contact the author or would like more information about this book, please write to the author in care of Llewellyn Worldwide Ltd. and we will forward your request. Both the author and publisher appreciate hearing from you and learning of your enjoyment of this book and how it has helped you. Llewellyn Worldwide Ltd. cannot guarantee that every letter written to the author can be answered, but all will be forwarded. Please write to:

Jean-Louis de Biasi
℅ Llewellyn Worldwide Ltd.
2143 Wooddale Drive
Woodbury, MN 55125-2989

Please enclose a self-addressed stamped envelope for reply,
or $1.00 to cover costs. If outside the U.S.A., enclose
an international postal reply coupon.

Many of Llewellyn's authors have websites with additional information and resources. For more information, please visit our website at http://www.llewellyn.com.

SECRETS AND PRACTICES OF THE
FREEMASONS

SACRED MYSTERIES, RITUALS AND SYMBOLS REVEALED

JEAN-LOUIS DE BIASI 32°

Llewellyn Publications
Woodbury, Minnesota

First Edition
Third Printing, 2013

Cover art: Celestial Moon & Sun: iStockphoto.com/Patricia Legg, Columns: iStockphoto.com/Viktoriya Sukhanova
Cover design by Kevin R. Brown
Editing by Tom Bilstad

Complete list of art credits is on page 290.

Llewellyn is a registered trademark of Llewellyn Worldwide Ltd.

Library of Congress Cataloging-in-Publication Data
Biasi, Jean-Louis de
  Secrets & practices of the Freemasons : sacred mysteries, rituals & symbols revealed / Jean-Louis De Biasi.
— 1st ed.
      p.   cm.
  Includes bibliographical references and index.
  ISBN 978-0-7387-2340-2 (alk. paper)
  1. Freemasonry—Symbolism. 2. Freemasonry—Rituals. I. Title. II.
Title: Secrets and practices of the Freemasons.
  HS425.B525 2010
  366'.12—dc22
                                                2010039531

Llewellyn Publications
A Division of Llewellyn Worldwide Ltd.
2143 Wooddale Drive
Woodbury, MN 55125-2989
www.llewellyn.com

Printed in the United States of America

Other Books by this Author

Masonic Spirituality
The Christian Qabalah
Masonic Esotericism
Sacred Magick
The Divine Arcana of the Aurum Solis

for PATRICIA

Acknowledgments

I would like to offer my grateful thanks to Carl Llewellyn Weschcke for enthusiastically embracing the publication of this book. His wisdom and experience were reflected in his excellent advice, the quality of his help in editing the text of the book, and his penetrating insight into all matters related to the publication of this work. These were a source of great inspiration and support to me.

It is awe inspiring to find such an innovative and active member of the publishing world taking the time to demonstrate his deep concern for the subject, meaning, and purpose of the books published by his company. Undoubtedly, Carl Llewellyn Weschcke is accomplishing a Great Work, in the most traditional meaning of this phrase. I wish to thank him very much for the living example he has provided for everyone whose work he has touched.

I would like also to offer my thanks to Linda Wheeler for her support and help in editing the last chapters of this book. Her work is a good example of the fraternity we share.

During a recent visit to the Masonic Lodge in Las Vegas, Nevada, I was privileged to meet Carl L. Banks, who is the current Grand Master of the Grand Lodge F & A.M. of the State of Nevada. I was very interested in the symbols he chose for his Grand Master's pin: the circumpunct and the two Saints John. He affably agreed to write the foreword of this book and to share the meaning of this fundamental Masonic symbol. Grand Master Carl L. Banks has been involved in Freemasonry since he was young. The work that he does is a manifest example of his knowledge of the Craft.

I would also like to thank Larissa Walkins, who helped me by researching the source of various artwork used in this book. Her insight and help were invaluable.

I would also like to thank the Ancient and Accepted Scottish Rite, Southern Jurisdiction, for authorizing the photos of the House of the Temple, which is one of the most dramatic Masonic buildings in the U.S.

Contents

List of Illustrations

FOREWORD

This foreword is written with deep gratitude to Jean-Louis de Biasi, a talented writer on the subject of Freemasonry, whom I am honored to have met during an official visit to a Masonic Lodge in Las Vegas, Nevada.

On my travels to various Masonic lodges as the Grand Master of the Grand Lodge of Nevada, my message has been based on "Pointing the Pathway by Rays of Light." My following comments are based on years of developing the symbolism behind my personal pin design for the purpose of this "Pointing the Pathway."

The customs of Ancient Craft (Operative and Speculative) Masonry are here discussed as they apply today, while still maintaining a deep appreciation and respect for the historical legacy dating back to King Solomon's Temple. It should be understood that Masonry is not a religion; all Freemasons do, however, have faith and a belief in a supreme being.

I come from a Masonic family; my grandparents and my mother and father were all active in their respective Masonic Appendant Bodies. I, myself, began as a member of the Order of De Molay[1], in 1948; today my membership transcends almost all of the Bodies in Freemasonry.

The concept for my pin design was based on the meaning of the Virtues of Freemasonry: Temperance, Fortitude, Prudence, and Justice; on the Tenets of Freemasonry: Brotherly Love, Relief, and Truth; and lastly, on the Symbolism of Freemasonry: Birth into the physical world, inherent need for light, and discovering the path in time to Eternity.

---

1. A youth organization affiliated with the Masons.

Historically, the "Point within the Circle," "The Circumpunct," has its origin in the solar system, both ancient and modern. It is a common astrological (and now astronomical) symbol for the sun. This image was also an alchemical symbol for gold, which was considered the most perfect of all metals. The alchemist looks upon it as the perfection of matter at all levels: the spirit, soul, and mind.

A goal of alchemy is to change base metals into gold. This objective certainly aligns itself well to Freemasonry, where the change of the base and crude state of one's personality into perfection is intended—from a man to a Mason by degrees.

In ancient times, before Christianity, the Greeks and Romans dedicated their temples and sacred objects to their gods. To the ancients, the Sun was the ultimate source of power and as they observed its course throughout the year, they determined regular seasonal patterns of warmth and cold, growth and decay. Eventually they came to personify and worship these seasonal changes, which became many of the gods of the ancient pantheons.

The point within the circle represents an individual brother; the circle is the boundary line beyond which we are not to suffer our passions, prejudices, or interests to betray us. In going around the circle, while we stay circumscribed within these due bounds, it is impossible to materially err.

Figure 1: Official pin of Nevada's Grand Master, Carl L. "Bud" Banks

With the Operative Mason's implements, it is possible to use a circle to construct a perfect square. No building can be built without a perfect square. Therefore, this circle is the first step in laying the foundation of the temple.

One such person, who embodied the Masonic ideals mentioned above, was Saint John the Baptist, who was noted for his devotion to God. It was said that he possessed the qualities of Christ, whose coming he foretold, which led to his beheading. So, this humble man, a surveyor by trade, through his strong teachings of devotion, was persecuted into martyrdom.

It became natural that the Craft Guilds of Masonry would adopt such a man as their patron saint, and he remained as such until about the 1500s, when Saint John the Evangelist was adopted by the Craft Guilds. This man had developed a legacy of enormous strength in mandating the cultivation of brotherly love.

These two Saint Johns became the men who stood beside and supported the two parallel lines denoting the solstices. These symbols predate the first Grand Lodge of 1717. The English dedicated their Lodges to the Saint Johns until 1813; since then, they have been dedicated to King Salomon. As Craft Masonry led to Symbolic Masonry, the two Saint Johns became known as the bookends of Freemasonry.

With this background, it is clear that the Masonic Feasts of Saint John the Baptist on June 24 and the Feast of Saint John the Evangelist on December 27 are, by no coincidence, occurring with the Solstices. These two dates occur at the time of the Summer solstice and the Winter solstice, times when the Sun reaches its greatest northerly and southerly declination.

With this history, the attempt has been made to bring my pin design into the meaningful experience that a Freemason has as he receives his degrees to become a Master Mason.

When looking at the pin, John the Baptist appears on the left, and Saint John the Evangelist appears on the right. The experience that a Mason receives in the three degrees when visualizing the meaning of this pin can always offer him the tools for rebuilding the temple within his heart, according to the Masonic moral teaching, where one may falter but also repair his mind and soul.

M. W. Carl L. "Bud" Banks
Grand Master F. & A. M. of Nevada

*Figure 2: Executive Chamber of the Supreme Council
33rd Degree Southern Jurisdiction, in the House of the Temple
(House of the Temple, AASR-SJ, USA)*

INTRODUCTION

Why Freemasonry?

Is it possible to say something new about "Ancient and Accepted" Freemasonry today? Freemason or not, are there any individual practices you can use immediately for personal benefit? Are these Masonic ideas fundamentally useful in meeting the challenges and problems of everyday life?

The answer to these three questions is YES!

The book you have just opened is going to help you understand the true inheritance this Masonic initiatic tradition gives to all of us. It will lead you from the birth of the ancient Egyptian and Greek mysteries to the discovery of the essential role of this initiatic brotherhood in the world today, and *especially in the United States of America.*

As mentioned in Dan Brown's novel, *The Lost Symbol,* there are few countries in the world where Masonic ideals have had such a fundamental role as during the founding of the United States. Freemasonry was present and rooted in the founding texts, the symbols, and the very architecture of the new republic to give it all its power.

The Lost Symbol reveals to us a secret history and geography that marks Washington DC with its footprint, giving to this city an aura and an egregore shining worldwide. The city of Washington was laid out according to Freemason ideals and beliefs. The symbolic center of this city, the National Mall, is known in all countries. It runs from the dramatic obelisk of the Washington Monument on the west to the United States Capitol Building on the east, with national museums and memorials on both sides. The White House is directly north of the monument, and the Lincoln Memorial and the reflecting pools to the west just behind the monument. The Jefferson Memorial is to the south.

Built to commemorate George Washington, the first president and "father of his country" and a Freemason, the Washington Monument is the world's tallest stone structure and the world's tallest obelisk, standing 555 feet 5⅛ inches high. The cornerstone was laid in an elaborate Masonic ceremony on July 4, 1848, the aluminum capstone was finally set December 6, 1884, and the completed monument was dedicated on February 21, 1885. It was the world's tallest structure until 1889, when Paris' Eiffel Tower took that title. The Washington Monument, and the geography of Washington DC, play a key role in *The Lost Symbol*, as does the mythology of Freemasonry.

It is rather necessary to say that an extraordinary gift was given at America's founding by a line of Freemason initiates, entrusting to the new nation the future of their beliefs and idealism. But, as Dan Brown said in his novel, this gift does not belong to the past. It is something living and unique, providing inspiration to the nation through its most difficult periods of history, and Freemasons acted according to this noble ideal.

What exactly is Freemasonry? Freemasonry is known as, according to Masonic texts, "a beautiful system of Morality veiled in Allegory and illustrated by Symbols." Also called "the Craft," Freemasonry is a wonderful worldwide movement of fraternity, tolerance, and philanthropy. Altruism is not always an easy virtue to express individually. People are focused on their own difficulties, problems, or pain. Most of the time, it is difficult for us to forget our personal feelings and consider those of other people. Sometimes it is even difficult to go beyond challenges of religion, culture, age, color, status, and profession to remember that every human being has fundamental rights to life, liberty, and happiness; to the freedom to practice his or her beliefs; and to have access to education, wellness, and opportunities for self-development and growth.

It is only too human, too natural, to focus on immediate personal needs. To surmount this reaction, humanity's leaders understood a long time ago that it is necessary to live by laws and ideals conceived with the vision of an ever more glorious future. Then, a kind of competitiveness occurs, helping each person to become better and to remember that this work must be constant.

Freemasonry represents and demonstrates this principle. It helps every initiate to work on one's self to become better and to put the good of all before his or her own needs. Freemasonry shows to the world that an action like that is possible between brethren, and also between them and those who are not initiated but are in need. Then it is seen that this effort is accessible to every human being and is actually intrinsic to our continued advancement.

Even more, Freemasonry's longevity reveals that this way is an essential key to survival and progress. There is not an epoch when it would be more important than the others. Human nature has been the same, whatever the period of history. Today, technological powers increase the dangers of human errors, and the stakes have become total and planetary. Any sectarian deviance or expression of intolerance is immediately felt worldwide. You begin understanding that your individual acts may result in unlimited repercussions. See, for example, the problem of climate change and the case for climatic modifications, and observe the divisions between those who resist the obvious need for action and those who accept the challenge of taking corrective action. The characteristics of the human being I described before are always the same. Freemasonry has no claim to find answers to all these questions, but the consequence of its teachings and its rituals makes the appropriate answers appear. Here is a manifestation of the extraordinary power of this tradition to give an understanding of what is right, and to make you capable of putting it into practice and using it in every moment of your life. These ideas are essential, and they constitute the moral pedestal of Freemasonry and its philanthropic action.

To most, the rituals and private customs of this brotherhood have long seemed strange. The symbols used in Masonic myths do not seem always useful in relation to the ambitious and important role I've foreseen and described. What relationship can exist between being initiated in a very strange ceremony, invoking strange and exotic names that may not be understood, and those Masons known as Shriners? Why would these Shriners wear such colorful and fanciful clothing if the goal is to find inner simplicity and learn to be a better person? Well, Freemasons operate many of the world's greatest charitable organizations. The best known is the Shriners, with their circuses, their colorful parades, and their work on behalf of physically challenged children through the Shriners Children's Hospitals. Lesser known is the fact that each Shriner must be a Freemason before being becoming a Shriner.

Of course, appearances can be misleading. Rituals perpetuated carefully, inherited from ancient traditions, are not always what they seem to be. Dan Brown's *The Lost Symbol* shows very well that the history of the brotherhood doesn't start or stop at the time of the master-builders of the cathedrals in Europe as the Masonic mythology says.

Even if the most visible symbols refer to it (the square, compass, level, rule, etc.), many of them are really more ancient.

You must look in the ancient places where the first civilizations of humanity appeared. It is symbolically (or actually) necessary to walk on the rich lands of Chaldea, mysterious Egypt, intellectually stimulating Greece, the glorious enlightenment of the Italian Renaissance, and empowering Elizabethan England to understand how the ancient initiations have been perpetuated. It is necessary to "visit" these ancient temples and open secret and sacred books to begin to discover the true origin of Freemasonry.

The relationship between Freemasonry and symbols is fundamental. It has been known for a long time that the mind's powers, rediscovered today, are the central concerns of the initiates. Ritual processes are the visible manifestation of the invisible world as understood by the ancient adepts of these traditions. Their inner experience of the different realities of the world and their perception of hidden powers of the psyche allowed them to create efficient transformative practices. What is now called noetic science has long known that you use only a little part of your mind's powers. Most of these innate abilities remain unawakened and undeveloped. The ancient adepts knew this reality and, without the obstacles experienced in our culture and our time, they used these abilities and organized a specific process for their development. But just like any tool, this knowledge can be used for weal, or it can be used for woe.

It is for this reason that the moral commitment of the initiate is key. This morality must imperatively be linked to the development of your hidden abilities. For centuries, this rule remained central in any initiatic society.

You can imagine that such training cannot be made in a single step. It is necessary to reveal the truth gradually through progressive training. It is for this reason that degrees were developed, allowing us to practice in complete safety. Supervision by experienced initiates validated this quality of transmission. In fact, the teaching received, which opens our consciousness, cannot be limited to the present life. This is only a visible exterior, an envelope that contains much more. The perception of our unearthly and invisible spirit shows us inevitably that the strongest existential anxiety of humanity is the fear of death (or more precisely, the belief in interrogation and review of life after death).

The ancient initiates did not provide only a philosophical essay on the different hypotheses you can make on this life after death. Knowing how those processes work in our mind, they created ritual practices, allowing us to have a real experience of this state of consciousness, without having to die physically. The goal was to put a foot on "the other side" and, with this experience, erase the common anxiety we all have and replace it with knowledge. These processes were secretly transmitted. Amid the wonderful encounters with many different ancient cultures, the city of Alexandria in Egypt became the birthplace for the Hermetic Tradition, one of the major traditions that later gave us Freemasonry. It is Hermeticism that developed this deep respect for every religion, seeing in each of them an aspect of the supreme truth. It is Hermeticism that transmitted the understanding of ritual structure and explained how to use it.

In any initiatic tradition, there are group rituals and practices, as well as individual ones. This is also the case in Freemasonry. The initiations can create in the candidate a particular state of consciousness. This is an important step. But after that, it is the progressive practices that allow him to learn how to manipulate these "inner vibrations" and then to advance in using these inner powers. This knowledge is less known and rarely given out. Surprisingly, Dan Brown's novel refers to it often and you can believe that, perhaps, the author intuitively has perceived important realities of this tradition.

Every period of history gives different challenges. Those problems we are living through now give us the opportunity to accept the ways they work on us and take our destiny in hand.

The work in this book, while explaining the most significant elements of Dan Brown's *The Lost Symbol*, will allow you to actually experience this initiatic transmission. It is time to move beyond historical and philosophical speech and give you the opportunity to act. The rituals known as the Scottish Rite contain in themselves practical and ritual keys immediately useful for people initiated or not. I will provide you with several opportunities to begin your own journey through the mysterious staircase, giving you enlightenment and control of your life here and now!

These two aspects, philanthropic and initiatic, will immediately give you a wonderful key to know divinity (inside and outside), to truly practice tolerance, and to become more and more capable of using your very real innate abilities.

chapter one
THE MASONIC TRADITION

The Mythical Spirit

Any initiatic, spiritual, or religious tradition is rooted in one or several "founder myths." Basically, this type of myth is the story of the origin and the foundation of all that follows: explanations, interpretations, and rituals. However, in our modern consciousness, myths are mostly considered as fiction or as fictional accounts of history.

On first examination it is difficult to know what meaning and purpose the story of the founder of a religion or an existent fraternity can have. Of course, if the founding story is imaginary and not real, this question has no importance. On the contrary—for the person who believes the story to be "real"—it is for him or her the expression of the truth because it is perceived to come from a supreme power. If there is a contradiction with other statements of history or science, the believer has to give the greater credence to the myth.

The myth is important in itself because it gives meaning to life. Its role is to try to answer the question "why" from a spiritual perspective, while it is the role of science to answer the question "how." The modern belief that myth is "unreal" is wrong and simply misses the point that there is more than one reality. Myth presents one kind of reality and science presents another kind, and it is important to see them separately, just as it is important that you separate church and state. History shows the fallacy of government and politics dominated by religious ideology that always imposes its certitude to have the "one and only definitive truth," which then leads to the elicitation of violence on behalf of the "one true god." So you must determine for yourself whether such a myth is useful or not, its real nature, and how should you make use of it.

To be able to answer these fundamental questions, it is necessary to discuss the nature of the human thought process.

Perhaps it will seem surprising, but the modern "mind" differs from what it was some centuries ago. We've mutated. Of course, your brain is fundamentally identical to that of earlier people. It works like always and its hidden and visible faculties are nearly the same. However, the major difference is the appearance and establishment of rational thought. The development of philosophy and the progressive popularization of its way of reasoning, followed by the progress of science, changed your mode of thought.

I can say that modern man has surrounded his original consciousness with a kind of outer shell of rational consciousness. A conflict followed between what I can call the mythical consciousness and the rational consciousness. The foundation of modern society is based on science and technology. The principles are clear, comprehensible by all, and reproducible. It is what gives modern society its strength. If you want to use something like a tool in daily life, it does not lead to a philosophical debate on the reality of this object. You put a dish in the microwave and turn it on. You pick up the phone and speak to your correspondent far away. There is no doubt with this process and you proceed with confidence.

But it is very different when the concern is spiritual or religious. The stories presented in the sacred books refer to another world radically different from that perceived with the rational mind. Our ancestors living at the time when most of the sacred books were written did not see their world the same way you do. "Reality" was not reduced to what is visible and measurable. It was not limited to what is verifiably seen; instead, everything was perceived as real in spite of a different nature: gods, men, animals, etc. were equally real. It was not amazing to see a divinity manifesting among them. Their use of plants as medicine was as natural as the action of prayer. The world was permeable to any influence, and wasn't divided into several strictly independent levels.

And thus there are many cases where the founding stories calling for faith seem in contradiction with scientific certainties. A believer living in our time has a choice to make that seems irreducible: abdicate the faith or reject science. The consequence is a conflict you see regularly in our society, for example, in the debate between creationism and evolutionism.

All that is a consequence of confusion between two realities: one visible and the other invisible. But this split is recent. It was created unconsciously and people now tend to define themselves as believers in faith or in science, and think they can, simply speaking, have their faith on Sundays and live in the real world the rest of the week. Others find no conflict. It is possible to simply recognize phenomena as involving one reality or another. But, as in a dream with a special message, you accept that there are times when one reality does cross over to another while recognizing that the laws of each apply.

In a spiritual and initiatic tradition such as Freemasonry, the notion of reality is not a problem, because there you are in the world of myth. It is important to understand this definition, because the absence of a clear understanding of this point will lead us to surprising aberrations. You can have an example of that if you go into a bookstore. If you are looking for books about the "immortal gods" (sometimes called "ancient gods"), Egyptian, Greek, Nordic, etc., they are generally in the category "Mythology." If you are looking for books about Christianity, Judaism, or Islam, they will be in the category "Religion." You can speculate about in which category you'll find books about animist or polytheist religions such as the Hindu or Santeria religions. As for Freemasonry, you will most likely find it in either "History" or "Philosophy," but probably not "Myth" or "Religion."

The true function of myth has been forgotten and its stories are perceived as legend, or as fictional tales. I have to give a new definition of myth to communicate why it can be useful to us. Any myth is a founder story (about the founder, whether historical or legendary) that has giving meaning to life as its goal. The word *meaning* indicates that the myth shows the moral values of your life, speaks about your origin, and gives you the direction in which you must go in pursuit of your greater purpose. This is the first step and function of the myth. Consequently, it does not matter if the myth contradicts the apparent reality in which you are living. In fact, the goal of the myth is not to explain *how* the world works, but *why* it works. Since the time of the ancient Greeks, science has developed to answer this question of how. Answers can vary according to new discoveries. The results of science remain correct until they are challenged. On the other side, the myth does not have to evolve because its object is the eternal part inside us, our inner consciousness or unconsciousness (in Jung's definition). Questions on the meaning of life are exactly the same today as one thousand, two thousand, or three thousand years ago.

It is necessary to see the myth as a story linking two things very intimately: (1) facts coming from your mind, and (2) inspiration from the deepest parts of your consciousness capable of answering your existential questions. It is also necessary to realize that your perceptions can interpret or understand something in a completely different way at the same time. A fire, for example, may seem to appear spontaneously, or a whirl of wind will appear to a contemporary mind as a simple meteorological phenomenon. For the believers, on the contrary, this manifestation will be divinity revealing its presence for a precise purpose.

For centuries, initiatic traditions (and sometimes religious traditions) defined these two aspects by using the words *esoteric* and *exoteric*. The first corresponds to an invisible plan that can be felt by the use of symbols. The second, exoteric, will be literal and visible. It is the one I called historical. The sacred books are composed in the same way and I will speak about this point later in this book. Even if the creation of these books is close to the myth, they imply a presence of the divine that is not systematic in the myth.

It is now important to learn how you can understand the myth, to be able to clearly perceive its meaning, and, more importantly, to assimilate it. You have to bring the myth inside you, revealing its meaning and modifying your vision of the world and your life. This is the only way the myth will be able to have influence on your way of seeing life and your role in society, as well as your destiny after death.

Myth does not concern the intellectual aspect of your mind. It concerns a part called the *imaginary*[1] *realm* of human beings. When a mythical story is told, you must enter into a special state of consciousness, closer to the one of your ancestors before the appearance

---

1. You must become aware that *imagination* and *imaginary* are different things. "Imagination" is always composed of different elements that are already present in your mind. This mental combination of these elements is really very close to the ability to create. Our imagination helps us to anticipate our actions and to see the consequences of those actions. Imagination is also a rich source of illusion, including fantasies, fancy, etc. In summary, I may say that imagination is a part of your mind that is not naturally controlled. The "imaginary realm" is very different. In general terms, anything that is "imaginary" is imagined, and therefore unreal. In the common parlance, the imaginary realm is a fantasy, something that only exists in your imagination, in your mind. However, there is something beyond the popular and commonly understood notion of this term *imaginary realm*. Though it may be difficult to understand at first, the imaginary realm is not as fanciful and fantastic as most people believe. The imaginary realm is a real function of the mind and it is different from your personal use of imagination. The imaginary realm is a part of your mind that is open to the higher dimensions of the universe. In order to move through these different planes, you must access this realm, this function, through the use of meditation or through ritual practice using the esoteric symbols and the myths connected to them. In other words, you use your imagination to move through the imaginary realms and to thus interact with the invisible planes.

of the rational and scientific mind. It is necessary to put your rational thinking on hold and become as a child listening to a mysterious history without any doubts regarding the reality. As you will see later in the book, reading the story aloud gives a real existence to the story, which the child intuitively feels. With a little insight you will be able to understand the symbols of the story. But it is not necessary to begin the analysis before deeply living the myth. What is necessary is to feel it in the most intimate parts of your body and soul, in your inner consciousness.

Freemasonry has several founder myths. Some of them are well known: the myth of its origins, the master-builders, and Hiram's myth. The structure of the myth of the cathedral's builders is different than the myth of the origins or the one of Hiram. But all three are myths and can be understood through your inner consciousness. The ancient origins to which Freemasonry refers belong to a time of the myth, a moment when the perception of historical reality was not the same as it is today.

The historical and symbolic analyses that can be developed are very important, but are not on the same level. You will see that a little farther along. But let us not forget that the myth does not need proofs, whatever type they are. Proofs are not necessary to perceive the meaning and values of the myth.

The Original Myth of Freemasonry

At the beginning of speculative Freemasonry in the eighteenth century, pastor John Anderson wrote a strange story. Deeply rooted in the first books of the Bible, the story explains the origins and the founders of this fraternity. This story is the heart of contemporary Freemasonry and reveals many elements of its real origins and goals.

As in the ancient oral times, let us tell you the epic story of the Craft (Freemasonry).

At the beginning of time was the first being, father of all humanity. Biblical tradition gave him the name of Adam, the original man, and put Eve beside him. Created just as the representation of God, the Grand Architect of the Universe, Adam received, engraved in his heart, the knowledge of Liberal Sciences, particularly geometry. Grateful to his creator, he transmitted his knowledge to his sons, Cain and Seth. Using his knowledge of the Craft, the first son created the most ancient cities. He became the prince of the first half of humanity. Seth, the second son and less educated than his brother, became the first farmer and taught his descendants the divine sciences of geometry and of masonry.

It is in this epoch that dramatic and extraordinary constructions were under-taken. The memory of other architectural realizations was orally transmitted in the first populations.

In these ancient times, God was in constant interaction with men. One day, God asked Noah, the ninth son of Seth, to build a big ark to protect Noah and his family from an imminent disaster. The ark was constructed according to the rules of geom-etry and masonry.

It was the way in which Noah and his three sons, Japhet, Shem, and Ham, all three true Masons, transmitted this traditional knowledge through the flood.

Then they decided to glorify God by building a huge and marvelous city mani-festing God's glory on earth. Over several years, they used their knowledge to build a colossal tower in the center of the city. They worked without pause, raising the construction higher and higher to the sky. A huge number of workers was organized and equipped with science, allowing uninterrupted work.

Seeing their work, God did not react as they expected. God hadn't asked them to manifest their skills like that. His anger increased in front of what he considered as a mark of human vanity. Then God decided to interrupt this demiurgic work. He introduced confusion into their minds, making them unable to understand each other. Until then, all had been the heirs of the same family and spoke the same lan-guage. Suddenly, hundreds of different languages appeared. Eager that the secrets of geometry and masonry would not disappear, and to be able to prove their status as initiates, the Master Masons created signs, gestures, and simple words belonging to the ancient original language. Then they scattered in the world, leaving this marvel-ous city, and built new kingdoms and new buildings in Chaldea, of Egypt, and many other regions.

In these new kingdoms, upon the Tigris and Euphrates rivers, there flourished many learned priests and mathematicians known by the names of Chaldeans and Magi, who preserved the good science, geometry, as kings and great men encouraged the Royal Art.

The Royal Art was brought down to Egypt by Mitzraim, the second son of Ham, about six years after the confusion at Babel, and after the Flood. The ancient noble cities, with the other magnificent edifices of that country, and particularly the fa-mous pyramids, demonstrate the early art and genius of this civilization.

The ancestor Masons went through all known lands. They raised the most beautiful temples, honoring the Eternal God in all divine forms he had in the countries where they were.

About 268 years after the Confusion at Babel, Abram was called out of Ur of the Chaldeans, where he learned geometry and the arts that are performed by it, which he would carefully transmit to Ishmael, to Isaac, and to his sons by Keturah; and by Isaac to Esau and Jacob, and the twelve patriarchs: nay, the Jews believe that Abram also instructed the Egyptians in the Assyrian learning.

Many years passed. Civilizations developed. Wars devastated countries followed by periods of peace, during which the Masons built both in stones and bricks. Then Moses, having learned the science of the Egyptians, guided his people out of Egypt into the arid desert of Sinai. It was there that the god of his people revealed to him the laws, which would guide the tribes of Israel. In his texts and commandments, God revealed to him the plans for the glorious tent that was to contain the Ark of the Covenant and allow the manifestation of the Eternal. Revealing for the first time to men the perfect plans of the temple, allowing the divine epiphany, Moses became the first General Master Mason. I could say the first Grand Master of Freemasonry. He was the first king of Jerusalem and transmitted the teaching of Egypt to his people, linking it to the divine revelation he'd received. The sublime knowledge of Masonry was saved. Before dying, Moses installed the first lodge and taught his followers the charges, orders, and signs that he received.

The people of Israel built cities, fortresses, and buildings. Years passed until there appeared a wise king, taught by the traditional knowledge. This king of peace, an architect himself, undertook to build the temple that would allow honoring the god of its people. He recruited many workers in the neighboring regions. Adoniram worked in the mountains of Lebanon. Solomon dealt with Hiram king of Tyre, who sent his masons and carpenters and gave him the wood of cedar that was necessary for it. But Solomon also asked Hiram, to authorize the most accomplished of his masons to go to Jerusalem in order to supervise the construction of the temple.

For seven years and six months, all worked according to the instructions of Solomon and Master Hiram. At the end of this fantastic work, a meeting point of the human and divine, as the Grand Master of the Lodge of Jerusalem, King Solomon solemnly dedicated the temple. This ceremony took place in the presence of the

Grand Master of the Lodge of Tyr, King Hiram and Hiram Abif. Since this time, all the Masons are under the protection and assistance of the Grand Architect of the Universe.

Many artists employed for this construction, under Hiram Abif, after it was finished dispersed themselves into Syria, Mesopotamia, Assyria, Chaldea, Babylonia, Media, Persia, Arabia, Africa, lesser Asia, Greece, and other parts of Europe, where they taught this liberal Art to the freeborn sons of eminent persons, by whose dexterity the kings, princes, and potentates built many glorious edifices, and became the Grand Masters, each in his own territory, and were emulous of excelling in this Royal Art.

But several hundred years after its consecration, the sacred beauty of this temple increased the jealousy of other monarchs. The Grand Monarch Nebuchadnezzar invaded Jerusalem and burnt down the Temple. Understanding progressively his error, he learned the mysteries of architecture from the masons and architects that he had taken to his city of Babylon. With this education, he developed his city and conceived wonderful gardens, which became one of the seven wonders of the world. He became the Grand Master of the Masons of his country.

In later years, Cyrus, the king of Persia, conquered Babylon and many other nations. It was with Cyrus's decree that the Israelites were allowed to come back to Jerusalem and rebuild their temple. And Cyrus having constituted Zerubbabel, the son of Salathiel the Head, or Prince of the Captivity, and the Leader of the Jews, the Israelites returned to Jerusalem and began to lay the foundation of the second temple. This temple was even more marvelous than the first. Even the people of other religions admired its splendor that seemed incomparable.

Then the Royal Art of Masonry was transmitted in Greece. It was after this transmission that the finest buildings of this country were constructed. Pythagoras contributed greatly to the learning of geometry. Architecture, religious, civil, and military art expressed in all countries the genius of these people and their inheritance. The research into proportions expressing the best balance and harmony raised human realizations of a divine ideal, glorifying the soul.

Many famous names contributed to the development and teaching of divine geometry and the art of Masonry. But it was under the reign of Ptolemeus Philadelphus (Grand Master of the Masons), the best protector of Liberal Arts and builder of the famous library, that the Craft came back to Egypt. He ordered the construc-

tion of another wonder, the tower of Pharos or lighthouse of Alexandria. Let us not forget to name the remarkable buildings of Sicily and the presence of the scientist Archimedes.

The Roman Empire, present throughout the Mediterranean world and continental Europe, transmitted this knowledge of architecture. The size of its architectural buildings demonstrates this inheritance in all architecture, religious or civil. Vitruvius was undoubtedly the father of all architects of our time.

Nor should it be forgotten that painters and sculptors were always recognized as good Masons, as much as builders, stone-cutters, bricklayers, carpenters, joiners, upholders, or tent-makers, and a vast number of other craftsmen that could be named, who perform according to geometry and the rules of building. And then the noble science geometry was duly cultivated, both before and after the reign of Augustus; even until the fifth century of the Christian era, Masonry was held in great esteem and veneration.

After centuries, the secret teachings were transmitted to the architects of the medieval and gothic religious buildings.

From Noah to Egypt, from Alexandria to medieval Europe, this mysterious, magical, and almost divine "Art of Geometry," which I call the Craft, was given in the secrecy of the lodges. Heirs of the ancient demiurgic secrets, the contemporary Freemasons always learned how to build the temple. As for an outward realization in the past or as today an inner work, the goal is the same: to allow the manifestation of the divine in our world.

From the Secret Stone to the Sacred Temple

You may wonder what you have in common with these master-builders and this magnificent myth. Contemporary Freemasons are not necessarily Christians or Jews. You need to ask what practical value a myth such as this one, so rooted in the biblical text, can have for you.

As I said before, any myth has universal consequences. It uses symbols and archetypes present in different cultures and that is why such a myth can transcend historical and anecdotal matters. It is necessary to see through the myth, much as you look at a landscape through a dusty window. The dust and dirt, and visible defects in the window glass, are part of what you see. However, you know that the view through the glass of the window is something different than directly seeing the landscape. Both the landscape and the image through the window glass each have their own reality, but the one you are looking for in the myth is the primary source located in the landscape, not that seen through the window. That's how you must see the myth I tell. I will not explain right now the nature of the symbols and their relationship to the ritual. To give light to this tradition that lives today in the lodges, I have to be able to go beyond the surface of the story. For that, it is necessary to separate the wheat from the chaff and to try to understand what the ancient masters wanted to tell.

The Masonic model of the master-builders of the Temple is interesting, but in all honesty it seems completely anecdotal, like a delightful fairy tale from your childhood when you played at building sand castles. It is very entertaining to choose a few simple objects and symbols and then imagine that they might contain a great secret.

Now let me take a different perspective and ask these questions: *Is it seriously possible to imagine that universal secrets are hidden behind a square, a compass, or a rule? Can you really believe that Freemasonry set up a worldwide conspiracy among the master-builders of cathedrals? What would be the reason?* It may seem difficult to follow Dan Brown's logic and believe that this noble fraternity, which continuously repeats an old-fashioned ritual, is capable of leading us to the discovery of an immemorial secret linked to the nature of God.

You are facing a problem if you want to go behind the veil of appearances. The relationship between the master-builders' guilds of the Middle Ages and Freemasonry is well established. However, you can see clearly presented in *The Lost Symbol* novel, as in the foundation myth, that moral requirements are present. And once again it's easy to see that a moral attitude has few things in common with the worker who builds a temple or a house. The honesty you would expect from a house builder would be honesty in relation to the contract signed. But to know if this worker has an inner spiritual morality is something different. Common sense clearly shows us that Freemasonry is something different, on another level. Considering the number of direct or indirect allusions to esoteric and spiritual traditions, there's no doubt that I am speaking of this higher dimension. The presentation of Freemasonry you can see in the tradition and in the novel is this:

For the first step, you can just listen to the subtleties expressed in the novel, especially about the origins of stonemason guilds. But one of the fundamental points of the novel is not directly about the worker, but the material he uses—in other words, about the nature of the "stone." In the whole Western esoteric tradition, the nature of the stone is central. But not just any stone; it is the one used in alchemy. This aspect is expressed in the tradition of the philosopher's stone, an alchemical substance that could transmute lead into gold and even confer immortality to its owner.

Alchemy has principally two appearances: the one called the internal, and the second called the external (plant and mineral) alchemy. For now I am speaking about the internal or spiritual alchemy, which looks for the hidden stone within in order to work on it.

The short description of the philosopher's stone doesn't say enough about the true essence of the stone, but its myths bring us back to an ancient time in the Middle East, at the origin of humanity. The original myth gives us an indication of the origin of the revelation, God, but seems not able to go further. However, the traditional texts have not been lost. One of them reveals an essential key for understanding the search for the philosopher's stone, which will become the cornerstone on which you will raise the temple. Then you will be able to analyze more precisely the hidden characteristics of the Masonic initiation ritual and understand why Freemasonry can be so useful and yet so subversive.

Plotinus, one of the Masters of the Neoplatonic Hermetic Tradition (which I will define precisely later), wrote a set of these traditional texts, called the *Enneads*. The sixth book of this group of texts is titled *Beauty*. In this text, there is an amazing passage:

> *And this inner vision, what is its operation? [. . .] But how are you to see into a virtuous soul and know its loveliness?*
>
> *Withdraw into yourself and look. And if you do not find yourself beautiful yet, act as does the creator of a statue that is to be made beautiful: he cuts away here, he smooths there, he makes this line lighter, this other purer, until a lovely face has grown upon his work. So do you also: cut away all that is excessive, straighten all that is crooked, bring light to all that is overcast, labor to make all one glow of beauty and never cease chiseling your statue, until there shall shine out on you from it the godlike splendor of virtue, until you shall see the perfect goodness surely established in the stainless shrine.*[2]

---

2. Plotinus, Enneads, *First Ennead*, Book 6:9.

What Plotinus shows us here in a wonderful way is that you are this stone. It is necessary to turn your vision inside you, to be interiorized, to look for the Beauty. If it does not appear immediately, it is necessary to act and begin to work on the raw stone that you are, to cut it, to fashion it as the cutter or the sculptor is doing, in order to obtain a perfect stone illustration of your moral improvement. I am speaking here about the real work of the cutter, but the moral aspect is now explicit. It is necessary to work "until there shall shine out on you from it the godlike splendor of virtue, until you shall see the perfect goodness."

You can find this idea of Beauty also in the Bible, but not really with the same meaning. Beauty is often connected to woman (principally her face), sometimes to God, and also to the nature of man before he was banished from heaven's garden, as you can read in this quotation from Ezekiel:

> "The word of the Lord came to me. He said: Son of man, sing this sad song about the king of Tyre. Say to him, 'This is what the Lord God says: You were the perfect man so full of wisdom and perfectly handsome. You were in Eden, the garden of God. [. . .]
>
> 'Your business brought you many riches. But they also put cruelty inside you, and you sinned.
>
> 'So I treated you like something unclean and threw you off the mountain of God. [. . .]
>
> 'Your beauty made you proud. Your glory ruined your wisdom.'"[3]

Without debating the goodness of God, you can see in this quotation that Beauty is the expression of the divine world and the essence of man when he was in the Garden. Once banished and exiled, the king's beauty is no more than mere external beauty. So, it is very important to know which stone Plotinus was talking about. The hermetic principles expressed by Dan Brown indicate that it is the hidden stone of the philosophers (alchemists).

The practice of the sculpture will give you an interesting indication. To carve a statue in a block of stone, you have two possibilities: (1) impose a form on to the stone, or (2) feel the statue that lives inside the block and cut the stone to liberate the figure that is

---

3. Ezekiel 28:11–19.

already inside to appear. You reveal it. So, the goal is not to create a figure with the stone, but to realize the inner truth and beauty you have to unveil, and bring it to light.

This is what Plato says clearly. (Let us remember that Plato can be considered as the founder of philosophy. His bust is in the House of the Temple, which is the heart of the Scottish Rite in Washington DC.) In his famous text *The Republic* he writes:

Figure 3: Bust of Plato in the Library of the Scottish Rite, Washington DC (House of the Temple, AASR-SJ, USA)

The soul, I said, being, as is now proven, immortal. [. . .] Her immortality is demonstrated by the previous argument, and there are many other proofs; but to see her as she really is, not as we now behold her, marred by communion with the body and other miseries, you must contemplate her with the eye of reason, in her original purity; and then her beauty will be revealed, and justice and injustice and all the things which we have described will be manifested more clearly. Thus far, we have spoken the truth concerning her as she appears at present, but we must remember also that we have seen her only in a condition which may be compared to that of the sea-god Glaucus, whose original image can hardly be discerned because his natural members are broken off and crushed and damaged by the waves in all sorts of ways, and incrustations have grown over them of seaweed and shells and stones, so that he is more like some monster than he is to his own natural form. And the soul which we behold is in a similar condition, disfigured by ten thousand ills.

[. . .] How different she would become if wholly following this superior principle, and borne by a divine impulse out of the ocean in which she now is, and disengaged from the stones and shells and things of earth and rock which in wild variety spring up around her because she feeds upon earth, and is overgrown by the good things of this life as they are termed: then you would see her as she is, and know whether she

has one shape only or many, or what her nature is. Of her affections and of the forms which she takes in this present life I think that we have now said enough.[4]

Here is the secret stone I spoke about, the stone that is inside us since immemorial time, the stone you can feel without knowing it: the secret stone is the soul! You should not be surprised that Dan Brown makes a digression in his novel about the subject of the reality of the soul in your body. Its existence explains why the question of life after death is mentioned in the novel. Of course, the author doesn't write a lot about this notion, but it is implicit in *The Lost Symbol*. You must now understand what it says about your destiny and the meaning of your existence.

But before that, it is important to notice that this notion has been present in Freemasonry since the creation of this fraternity in its speculative constitution. The Masters who created Freemasonry used the myths of their culture, but introduced significant elements of its true origins to help us to find them. Among the fundamental elements of Freemasonry you can find that of "Beauty." Written in the most ancient Masonic instructions of the eighteenth century, we find the following statements:

> Q. What supports your Lodge?
> A. Three great Pillars.
>
> Q. What are their names?
> A. Wisdom, Strength, and Beauty.

A Masonic writer, Dr. Samuel Hemming, wrote in his *Lectures*, adopted by the Grand Lodge of England in 1813: "Our institution is said to be supported by Wisdom, Strength, and Beauty, Wisdom to contrive, Strength to support, and Beauty to adorn. Wisdom to direct us in all our undertakings, Strength to support us in all our difficulties, and Beauty to adorn the inward man."

Finally, you can see that the two other pillars of Freemasonry are also present in the *Enneads* of Plotinus. They are always used in the same perspective, to emphasize the essence of soul and the moral qualities that must be linked to it. For wisdom, Plotinus said:

---

4. Plato, *The Republic*, Book 10.

For, as the ancient teaching was, moral-discipline and courage and every virtue, not even excepting Wisdom itself, all is purification.

[...] And Wisdom is but the Act of the Intellectual-Principle withdrawn from the lower places and leading the Soul to the Above.[5]

And for Strength he wrote:

If all this be true, we cannot be, ourselves, the source of Evil, we are not evil in ourselves; Evil was before we came to be; the Evil which holds men down and binds them against their will; and for those that have the strength—not found in all men, it is true—there is a deliverance from the evils that have found lodgment in the soul.[6]

So it is clear here that these elements present from the birth of speculative Freemasonry are fundamental in order to understand the true objective of the Craft.

It is necessary now to see why this secret stone, the soul, is imprisoned in you, what you can deduce from this situation, and what the Masonic way can propose to perform the inner work.

It is also necessary to go deep inside your own self to find the solution and listen to the way of the ancient Masters who left these indications for you.

According to the Neoplatonic tradition (to which Plotinus belongs), your being is composed of two parts: the first is spiritual and invisible, and the second is material and visible. Of course, the ancient philosophers and initiates went further than this duality, but it is this duality that is fundamental. The soul is undying and belongs to the divine world; on the other hand, the body is material and belongs to the physical world. There is no need to go back to the beginning with the insolvable question of the emergence of an undying soul. It is enough to believe it was with the first impulse of the Great Architect of the Universe that souls appeared in the upper planes that I call the divine realms.

In its evolution, the soul was embodied in the physical envelope. That means that the soul descended through the different veils of the cosmos represented by the ancients as the zodiac and the seven traditional planets (Saturn, Jupiter, Mars, Sun,

---

5. Plotinus, *Enneads*, *Second Ennead*, Book 9:6.

6. Plotinus, *Enneads*, *Second Ennead*, Book 8:5.

Venus, Mercury, and the Moon). Going through each of these levels, the soul was not transformed. The soul remained what it was, but was surrounded by more and more dense envelopes, much as shellfish and other concretions covered the statue thrown in the bottom of the sea in the example given by Plato. So there is no moral sin in this descent, but only a consequence of the progression of soul.

So, you are in a situation in which your soul lost its original clear vision. Now your soul must try to see through the dense veils of character and influences it received. As Freemasons say, you are in the darkness and looking for the light: the shine of the ideal, harmonious, and divine world. You are trying to return to the place you came from.

This is the reason why Freemasonry asks you to believe in a supreme being and at the same time not to claim a specific faith. Freemasonry is religious in the most etymological meaning. Understanding this ancient doctrine, its founders knew that it was necessary to remember this ancient origin. At the same time, it was important not to be locked in temporal and political religious dogmas but to be free to pursue one's own spiritual vision.

It is necessary to remember your divine origin and to feel the inner desire coming from the soul. The ancient masters said this desire is felt very deeply in the heart of your soul and comes from an unconscious memory of the world that is really yours. You keep in your inner being a picture of what you saw there and how you lived. This is the place where you will return after your death, after the disappearance of your physical body. The Neoplatonist says you will not stay in this divine world but will come back to this material world where you learn by experiment, by trial and error. The ancient initiates knew and taught what they called the metempsychosis (reincarnation), undoubtedly a long time before the Far East even began speaking about it.

But without going so far, your characteristic of being dual, both spiritual and material at the same time, calls for you to move aside the veils of the illusions of this world to express as best you can the divine light you have inside you. As Plotinus said, you must take the tools of the sculptor and cut away those crusts surrounding you to reveal the divine statue of your soul.

You must work on your secret stone in order to reveal it to yourself and to the world. This is the first step of the Masonic work and the first act of a sculptor. This perfect stone, your soul, is at the same time the cornerstone of the temple. It is from it and on it that we will be able to lean in order to build the temple.

In the text of the Gospels you can read this sentence credited to Jesus: "I can destroy the temple of God and rebuild it in three days."[7] Without any doubt, the temple of this text is your own being. The nuance is important and it is necessary to emphasize it. The goals of Freemasonry are to build, to organize order above chaos and not the opposite. The purpose can't be to reject, banish, or criticize. You must choose, purify, order, and build. As I just pointed out, these purposes can be established upon the cornerstone, from the desire of your soul.

As you saw in the founder myth of Freemasonry, the building of the Temple of Jerusalem consists of two parts: the material one with the magnificence and the beauty of the Temple, but also the subtle part that is the presence of the divine. It means that the beauty of the Temple expresses the beauty of the divine. This law common to all Master architects and builders in all epochs gives us a fundamental key of the Freemasonry Order: the sacred temple can't be built without the help of the physical elements that constitute it!

Your body must not be rejected or considered as a curse or obstacle. On the contrary, from its origins Freemasonry taught that the body is a blessing for the soul. Your physical envelope can express by its acts the inner beauty of the soul, which is divine. Freemasons are not monks living with the secret desire to leave the world and be in a place far from everything. Freemasons live and work in this world because they know that, like the body, the physical world is the best and most beautiful way to express the divine that is inside us and in the universe! For that, the inner work and the construction of our temple according to the rules of beauty and harmony based on moral commitments are the fundamental elements.

Here is the basic rule of the temple, heart of the Masonic code: learn continuously to be better! Thus can be built the sacred temple.

But, like every master-builder and architect, you must discover and learn the divine laws of harmony, beauty, wisdom, and force. These laws are present in the Masonic symbols and in all worship in all ages. However, your understanding of the laws is not immediate because, as I said before, your vision is obscured by the veils of illusion. Therefore it is necessary to move forward for a while on the other side of the veil (or mirror) in order to catch sight of the divine plan, the afterlife. It is necessary that, in this unique moment and these specific conditions, someone takes your hand and helps you

---

7. Matthew 26:61.

to cross this threshold. With this help you will be able to understand and accomplish your destiny. This step is the initiation!

The ancient Platonic, Neoplatonic, and Hermetic philosophies organized this process, which you can find partly in Freemasonry. The Master Initiate must give a helping hand to the apprentice (or companion) and help him or her to symbolically step across the doors of death. To philosophize is to learn to die, said Socrates, the master of Plato. To philosophize is to liberate the soul and to allow it to see beyond, to perceive the other plan. To be initiated is to learn how to die.

But it's important not to make a mistake in thinking that it would be necessary to commit some strange suicide in order to learn this secret. It is absolutely the opposite. Every Western initiate of this tradition always forbade suicide, because as I said, the temple you erect is here and now. It is your physical body and the body of the society. You learn by living your term of life, and fulfilling your life's purpose.

The initiatic process, on which I will speak further, gives this privilege: make the inner experience of contact with the soul and with the other side of reality. It is from this instant that you will understand how to rebuild the temple. The secret of the initiation and of the master-builder (as for a shaman) is to see the temple destroyed, razed to the ground, and to know which is the stone that you will be able to use in order to rebuild the temple.

Then it was obvious that this myth of death and resurrection had to be at the heart of Freemasonry because it constituted the heart of the initiatic quest. The inspiration was that of the Egyptian traditions. So appeared the myth of Hiram, the eternal master-builder, dying at the hand of ruffians, experiencing chaos and destruction, to come back to life and rebuild the temple, its body on the cornerstone of his soul hidden in the depths of the ruins. Revived Hiram is revived Osiris, and it is what these two myths will show us.

From Hiram to Osiris

Some years after the creation of speculative Freemasonry in the eighteenth century, there appeared a new founder story, the Hiram Abif myth.

As I said before, a myth is intended to reveal the meaning of existence and you can understand now why this is connected with the existence of the soul. The consequence of that is the question of your life on earth. As you have realized, the secret of life is hidden in death. This association was created progressively, at the same time through ritual and speech during the Freemason's initiation. This revelation constituted the structure of the third initiation. Although Masonic rituals can be slightly different according to the story of each country, the myth of the death of Hiram remains practically identical in each of them. It was published again and again, even outside the secrecy of the lodges. Famous figures were interested in it. The French poet Gerard de Nerval is one example. The structure of this history is interesting to know and as you will see the major symbols will be connected to the Ancient Mysteries.

You saw in the first myth of this fraternity how Solomon, son of David, organized the construction of Jerusalem's Temple devoted to the Grand Architect of the Universe. After thirteen years of uninterrupted work, the Temple was completed and Solomon hired Hiram of Tyre, son of a widowed woman of the tribe of Nephtali and of a Tyrian worker named Ur. Hiram the Wise cast bronze with a wonderful ability. His science had only his intelligence as equal. He made two bronze columns each forty-eight cubits high, and cast separately two capitals of five cubits and put them on the top of the two columns. They were raised in the atrium of the Temple: Hiram called the one to the right Boaz; the one to the left was called Jakin. Then he made a sea, or cauldron, of circular cast iron forty cubits in diameters and five cubits high. This cauldron was surrounded with support in the form of consoles, placed in groups of ten at intervals of one cubit. Finally, this cauldron was put down upon twelve oxen. Three oxen were looking north, three west, three south, and three east. All these sculptures, and many others of the same type, were created to adorn the inside of the Temple.

The workers were under the authority of Hiram and organized in three classes: Apprentice, Fellow-Craft, and Master. The wage was shared according to the class. The apprentices gathered to be paid beside column B, the fellow-crafts by column J, and the masters in the heart of the Temple. Fifteen fellow-crafts, seeing the temple almost finished and not having obtained the initiation as Master, because their time was not accomplished, decided to extort by force the secret words, signs, and grips from Hiram. Their purpose was to be able to mask their level and obtain the wage of the Masters. Twelve of these companions thought about probable consequences of this bad deed and abandoned the project. Three persisted and decide to attack Hiram, to get the passwords and the secret signs of the Masters. These three workers knew that he came in the Temple every day at midday while the workers rested. They went to the three doors of the south, west, and east.

To leave the Temple, Hiram had to go to the eastern door. The first ruffian who was there stopped him, asking for the word of the Master. Hiram answered that he could not give it to him like that. It was necessary first that the fellow-craft should finish his training. Only then would he be able to have an increase of wage, and the secret word of the Masters could be given to him in the presence of the kings of Israel and Tyre. These two kings and Hiram had made an oath to give this word only when all three were united. Displeased by this answer, the fellow-craft stabbed the master with a ruler through his throat.

Hiram then ran away toward the door of the south, where he found the second ruffian who asked the same thing. Courageously, Hiram still refused. His adversary hit him violently with a square on his left breast.

Staggering, Hiram ran toward the western door, where he faced the third ruffian. Refusing once again to reveal the secret of the Master, the bad fellow-craft hit Hiram on his forehead with a mallet and killed him outright.

The three murderers realized they had just committed a senseless crime. They took Hiram's corpse away and buried it on the mountain. When Hiram failed to appear on the construction site, Solomon investigated, without success. Twelve companions who suspected the truth put on white gloves and white aprons as signs of their innocence and went to inform Solomon of their misgivings.

Solomon sent the twelve companions in search of the master Hiram. Thinking that the secret word of the Master had probably been stolen before his death, they decided that the first word that was pronounced upon finding Hiram's body would become the

Figure 4: Masonic representation of Hiram's grave

new Master's word. The companions travelled for five days without discovering anything. Solomon then chose nine masters to continue the search instead of the twelve companions. Exhausted by the searching, one of them stopped to rest on a small hillock. He saw that the dirt had been recently moved. Calling the brothers, the nine started to dig. After a while, they began to see Hiram's body. Without touching the body of the master, they closed the hole and planted a branch of wattle. Then they went back to inform King Solomon of their discovery.

Some of the masters were ordered to return to the grave and recover the corpse. Having taken away the dirt, the masters saw Hiram's body and recoiled in terror. The murder had happened nine days before and the body was already in full decomposition. They screamed and this sound became the secret word of the Master.

One of them tried to raise the corpse, gripping the forefinger of the right hand while saying, "Boaz," but it was impossible to move it. Another gripped the major finger of the right hand, saying, "Jakin." He didn't have any success either. A third one gripped the right wrist of the corpse and raised it by grabbing it by five different points and pronouncing the new secret word of the Masters.

When they went back, Solomon organized a splendid funeral for Hiram. He was put in a tomb under the Temple of Jerusalem and they put there a triangular gold medal, on which was engraved the ancient sacred word. After the death of the master, the brothers looked after his mother, who was widowed. She lived to a very old age in the city of Tyre.

Hiram's myth became central in Freemasonry. Many moral and symbolic elements are attached to it. But as you were shown in the paragraph before, it is the mysteries of death and the afterlife that gives the myth its accuracy.

Let us remember that the temple is your own body. The first and essential philosophical message is to realize that your destiny is death. The existential anxiety that has been inside you since your birth can find its solution only in a deep acceptance of this inevitable fact. The message given by the myth is the existence of an eternal spiritual presence in your being. It means that the death of Hiram is not an absolute and final disappearance. It is only about the death of the physical body. After several days, the Master can be raised from death, resurrected and whole. Freemasonry considers this act as a main one. This part is short in the story of Hiram in comparison to the complete episode, but it gives its name and its nature to the 3rd Degree. This Master's initiation received the evocative name of "Raising."

In itself, the myth gives less information on this mystery of death and revival. If you focus on what is essential, you can see that revival is not the result of Hiram's will. He can rise only with the help of other masters. So it's something different than Jesus, who rose from death on his own as the Christian myth claims.

Here the symbolic act manifesting Hiram's revival is the instant when he is raised by the masters with the help of the five mysterious points. So he goes from the horizontal position (earth and material) to the vertical (mind and spiritual). I am speaking here of a fascinating group of archetypal symbols that illustrate a timeless action. The most esoteric and spiritual aspects of Hiram's myth were considered for a long time as secondary. But this story about the mysteries of life and death is closely linked to the Ancient Egyptian Mysteries. To go further and to be closer to the heart of Freemasonry, it is necessary to go back to the source. It is what many Freemasons did, turning their research to the black earth of Egypt. It is also what the first ancient Greek initiates did. This is very well shown in the life of the man who is known as the founder of a very important school in the history of the Western initiatic traditions: Pythagoras. This master is mentioned in the ancient texts written by the Christian Qabalists of the Renaissance and by the modern founders of Freemasonry.

In *Life of Pythagoras*, written by the initiate Iamblicus, you can read that Pythagoras "sailed to Sidon, being persuaded that this was his natural country, and also properly conceiving that he might easily pass from thence into Egypt. Here he conversed with the prophets who were the descendants of Mochus, the physiologist, and with others, and also with the Phoenician hierophants. He was likewise initiated in all the mysteries of Byblos and Tyre, and in the sacred operations that are performed in many parts of Syria."[8]

It is interesting to emphasize the names of the cities in which Pythagoras was initiated because they are very important in the Masonic myth. These cities were also significant places in which Phoenician, Greek, Egyptian, and Hebrew worshipers were in contact. It was naturally from there that Pythagoras boarded to Egypt. Then, "he spent therefore two and twenty years in Egypt, in the adyta of temples, astronomizing and ge-

---

8. Iamblichus, *Life of Pythagoras*, trans. by Thomas Taylor, (Watkins, 1818), p. 7.

Figure 5: Bust of Pythagoras in the Library of the Scottish Rite, Washington DC (House of the Temple, AASR-SJ, USA)

ometrizing, and was initiated, not in a superficial or casual manner, in all the mysteries of the Gods . . ."

All you can find to confirm this is that, as the novel *The Lost Symbol* claims, the birth of the Freemasons' Tradition can be found in Egypt. But to suggest it or claim it is one thing; to demonstrate it is another. Although it is not possible today to see a direct report from this ancient civilization, you can have confirmation of it in another way: myths and symbols. The archetype of the death of the Master Mason I just described has its origin in one of the aspects of the symbolic act of the resurrection of the god Osiris. The illustrations of the raising of the pillar named Djed, symbolizing the revival of the god-king, are well known.

This first indication reveals a very close connection between these myths. From the reading of this story, it is clear that it was used as the foundation of Hiram's myth. The Osiris myth was retold by the Greek writers and especially Plutarch in his book *Isis and Osiris*:

Ra, the creator of all things (on whom I will speak again further), becoming old, chooses the son who had to succeed him: Osiris.

The new sovereign reigned over the earth of men with his sister-wife Isis. Osiris represented the goodness of his kingdom and was the expression of this harmony.

But Set (Typhoon under his Greek name), jealous of his brother, tried regularly to kill him with different traps and tricks. But all were foiled by the vigilance of Isis.

One day Set hired seventy-two accomplices to finally reach his aims. Having secretly measured the precise length of the body of Osiris, who was a tall giant from seven to eight cubits in height (about sixteen and a half feet), Set asked for a wonderful box, remarkably decorated, and ordered that it should be brought into the middle of the feast. At the sight of this box, all guests were astonished and delighted with its beauty.

Then, laughing, Set promised he would give it to the one who, by trying it, would fit it exactly. In turn, all the guests tried it, but none of them found it to be his size. Finally Osiris laid down in it and it was the right size. Immediately, all the guests ran to close the lid. Some closed it with nails, while others sealed it with some well-blended lead. When this operation was ended, the box was thrown into the river, where it was carried away to the Mediterranean Sea.

At this news, Isis cut off part of her hair and wore a dress of mourning.

Sometime after, Isis was informed that the box was taken by the sea to the foot of a tree (a Tamarisk), which flourished near Byblos. [9]

This tree had grown to the point of including the sarcophagus of the god inside its trunk. The king of the country, amazed to see the vigor of this tree, ordered it cut to make a column to support the roof of his palace.

Isis did not find a way to obtain the body of her husband, Osiris. She was lamenting, sitting on the edge of a fountain, when she met the maidservants of the queen. She was hired to the court of the king. There she became the babysitter of the royal baby. To feed him, she put her finger in his mouth instead of her breast. During the night, she plunged him into the fire to burn away from him what was mortal and give him immortality.

But one day the queen came to see the baby at the time when Isis was purifying him in the fire. Afraid, she took the child, depriving him of immortality.

Then Isis revealed her royal nature and demanded that they extract the divine sarcophagus, which was inside of the column of wood. Then she anointed all the parts of the box with perfume and wrapped it with a fine linen cloth. The remaining

---

9. This very ancient Phoenician city is today on the coast of Lebanon. It was from this city that cedar wood was sent to Egypt and it was where King Solomon obtained the wood for the Temple of Jerusalem. It is also from the Phoenician city of Tyre (south of Byblos) that the architect Hiram was sent to Jerusalem.

It is very interesting to note that, according to the writer Philon of Byblos (either Philo or Herennius, 64–141) Byblos, the city where the sarcophagus of Osiris was found, had a reputation as the most ancient city of the world. Today, this idea is still supported by many experts. Even more revealing, Byblos is the place where the god Thoth is said to have invented writing. Let us be not surprised either that this city became an important place of Osiris' worship. As I noted, it was also there that Pythagoras came before going to Egypt.

Figure 6: Masonic representation of an Egyptian goddess with the blazing pentagram.
One of the main symbols of the Egyptian Masonic rituals.

fragment of the column became an object of veneration for the inhabitants of Byblos,
who put it in Isis' temple.

Going back to Egypt, Isis hid the sarcophagus and the body of the god in the
marshes of the delta of the sacred river. When she was alone, she opened the sar-
cophagus and embraced Osiris, crying.

One night when Set was hunting under moonlight, he discovered the place where
Isis had hidden the body. He recognized the body of Osiris, cut it into fourteen pieces,
and dispersed them throughout valley of the Nile. Finding out about this act, Isis
took a small boat made of papyrus and began to search all along the Nile.

After a long quest, Isis found all parts of the body of Osiris except his penis. In
fact, immediately after cutting it off, Set had thrown it into the river and a fish had
eaten it. To replace his member, Isis made a fake one (the phallus) with the aid of
silt and saliva. Anubis, the god with a jackal head, who supervises the mummifi-
cation of the dead, put all the pieces together and tightened them with the aid of

bandages. Isis took the appearance of a milan (a bird of prey, like an eagle) and, agitating her wings above the body, she gave again the breath of life to Osiris, who was thus resurrected.

In other versions of the story, the resurrection of the god is sometimes the consequence of his mother Nut, and sometimes by the pity of Ra, who hired the god Thoth to give life to Osiris with his magical abilities. In other texts, the despairing cries of Isis and Nephthys helped Osiris to be resurrected. There are pictures of both goddesses waving their large wings above the dead god to give him the breath of life.

Isis then had sexual relations with Osiris and conceived a child, the young Horus, the god with the hawk's head. Isis hid him in the Nile's tidal swamps to avoid Set finding and killing him. Later, when Horus was an adult, he reclaimed the throne in his own right, and avenged the murder of his father Osiris.

You will find this myth later in this book, because it is undoubtedly the text that inspires the story of the revenge for Hiram's death. It will be one part of the important High Degrees of Freemasonry following the 3rd Degree's myth.

The founder myths give us precious indications of the relationship between these two traditions. It is interesting to point out that the concept of initiation finds its origin in Egypt and continues, later, in Judaea. You can see here a fusion of two elements, the master-builders and the Egyptian religion, as well as the initiations that had their origin there.

As I said at the beginning of this part, the consciousness of the men of the eighteenth century was Christian. Even if they were heirs of ancient esoteric and spiritual traditions, it was difficult for them to imagine a tradition without the words of the religious culture they had received since their birth. So this explains why a Christian education and the Bible were the filters through which the ancient tradition was seen.

chapter two

DISTRICT OF COLUMBIA: MASONIC LIGHT OF ANCIENT EGYPT

Just as Dan Brown writes in *The Lost Symbol*, Egypt is the birthplace of what constitutes the structure of Masonic initiation. It is in this country that we find the original meaning of most of its essential symbols. Others will be discovered in the initiatic Schools of Mysteries, which inherited different parts of its teachings and practices.

This reference to Egypt allows you to understand some of the information given in the novel, as well as its connection with the founding of United States and its capital, Washington DC.

The American Pyramid

Origin of a Symbol

It's not a plot spoiler to reveal that one of the main elements of *The Lost Symbol* is the pyramid, completed or not. Dan Brown is correct when he writes that the pyramid is one of the most famous and significant symbols of Egypt. Moreover, the Great Pyramid of Giza was on the list of the Seven Wonders of the World[1] created by the Greek Herodotus in the fifth century. It is likely that these famous pyramids were the result of symbolic observations by the ancient priests and architects.

---

1. The Seven Wonders of the World chosen by Herodotus were: (1) the Great Pyramid of Giza; (2) the Hanging Gardens of Babylon; (3) the Statue of Zeus at Olympia; (4) the Temple of Artemis at Ephesus; (5) the Mausoleum of Maussollos at Halicarnassus; (6) the Colossus of Rhodes; and (7) the Lighthouse of Alexandria.

Before pyramids began to be raised in the North of Egypt, the dead were buried in the Valley of the Dead at Thebes. This valley was located west of Thebes, the sacred city that was for a long time the capital of Egypt. Beyond the city there are mountains that are vaguely pyramidal in shape, more clearly revealed as the Sun sets at night. As told in Egyptian stories, when the solar bark disappears on the western horizon, it begins its progression through the world of darkness and the dead, reemerging the next morning in the east. Thus we see that the pyramid is the perfect symbolic representation of the sacred mountain under which the bodies of the deceased were buried, to wait for the rising of day on the other side of the earth.

The first pyramids rose progressively above the burial tombs underground. In the beginning they were simple buildings of a single step called *mastabas*, used for the worship of the dead. These buildings covered the well that gave access to the tomb. Later, successive levels of decreasing size were stacked on the primitive mastaba, following the Sumerian model.

The first Egyptian pyramid was created for King Zoser by the architect Imhotep, who became the model for the Master of the Masonic Egyptian rituals. Pyramids remained close to the temples and were used as chapels for worshiping the pharaoh god buried under this sacred artificial mountain. It is difficult to know if the first pyramid had six levels or seven, but it is plausible that the initiates associated it with this significant number that was already the model for most of the ziggurats in Mesopotamia.

The Egyptian pyramids are also the expression of a very important symbolism, that of the Sun, the god Ra. Since time immemorial, light was linked to the awakening of consciousness and to the spiritual world. It was natural to consider that darkness and heaviness belonged to the material world as symbolized by the cave, which was used many times to show this opposition to the light. On the other hand, light is insubstantial, higher, and seems to emanate from the highest point of the sky, from the Sun that brings life to the world.

Usually the rays of the benefactor Sun are not clearly visible. When the sky is veiled by clouds, you can't perceive the ethereal blue, symbol of the highest planes of mind.

When the clouds open partway and the Sun's rays shine through these openings, you can see a wonderful representation of the pyramid made of light.

Several drawings from the famous alchemical book *Mutus Liber* illustrate very well this phenomenon and this form. Then the pyramid becomes the materialization of the rays of celestial energy. It is fascinating to imagine that this radiance, before quite invisible, becomes the representation of the union of God and the world.

Progressively, this primal form was simplified and linked to the representation of the Sun's rays giving life as realized in the Egyptian pyramid with its smooth and bright sides. This building remained for all Western people an expression of perfection and harmony. The simplicity of its shape and the purity of its lines demonstrate the wisdom of the ancient masters. Geometric symbols derived from this form continue the power of this original divine representation.

The two essential symbols making up the pyramid are the square and the triangle. The square represents the surface of the base of the pyramid, which is very often orientated according to the north/south axis. Of course, the symbol of the square and of the number 4 were linked to the four elements codified by the ancient masters (earth, water, air, and fire). The four cardinal directions (north, south, east, and west) were also linked to it. This is why these buildings were very often oriented according to these principles. These symbols and forms are universal.

From Egypt to the District of Columbia

The sentence "the pyramid is a map" is a recurring theme of *The Lost Symbol*. Although presented in a novelized manner, these words reveal very interesting information connected to the design of Washington DC and, more precisely, the District of Columbia. As shown in the original maps, the District of Columbia is a rare example of a perfect square exactly orientated on the four directions. The Masonic Tradition has many examples in which human-designed buildings incorporated inner and archetypal symbols. Sometimes these representations rise from the unconscious mind of the architect, suggesting the form of a new building or city. Usually the architect tends to link this unconscious impulse to his knowledge and culture, and to his goals. In the case of the U.S. federal capital, you should know that several Freemasons participated in the project, and it is clear that the symbolism of this tradition was manifested in the most important elements. This symbolism was also used to represent and manifest their purposes and ideals. Although I will speak of this later in this book, it is important to know that to accomplish and manifest ideals in the world requires a tangible, physical component. Architecture and the resultant building is a means of such material realization that continues to project those ideals in the minds of the people. As you saw in the myth of the

Tower of Babel, it is for this reason that we can link Masonry to the demiurge—seeming to take a form from nowhere and nothing, through which the builder creates a divine work. This is an important aspect of Masonic initiation.

The square formed by the District of Columbia can be seen as the base of an invisible pyramid in contact with the ground. Its center is exactly the center of the city of Washington. Precisely, this center is on the Mall and is marked by the Jefferson Stone. This representation shown on a map is very significant, but when you consider the dimension chosen for the District of Columbia, you can see that the choice is also very symbolic.

The side of the square of the great Pyramid of Giza, the model of geometric accomplishment, has a 0.143132-mile dimension. If you multiply this dimension by 70, you get the exact size of one side of the District of Columbia, that is to say 10 miles. Considering the deep significance of this Egyptian building for the architects and master-builder Freemasons, this source of inspiration becomes obvious. The numbers chosen are meaningful. The number 70 corresponds in Hebrew to the letter Ayin (ע). You remember that words and letters of this language were often used by the Freemasons, trying to link their work to their founder myth. Any letter of the Hebrew alphabet also constitutes a word and has significance.[2] The letter Ayin means "divine providence, eye, fountain of wisdom, and the ability to find wisdom." The Qabalistic tradition says that the right eye is turned to the transcendent light of God, while the left eye looks at the world from the celestial sphere. It is very interesting to see the relationship between this meaning of Ayin and the intentions of the Founding Fathers. They tried to work under protection of divine providence and used the power of wisdom to build the new nation.

If the number 70 is reduced to 7 by addition (70 ⇨ 7 + 0 ⇨ 7), the symbolism is also very rich. The most ancient reference that was used throughout the centuries is that of the seven traditional planets. They were, for the ancients, the visible manifestation of the seven most powerful divinities. The Neoplatonic and Ogdoadic Traditions chose the Chaldean ascending sequence, which puts the Sun at its center (Moon, Mercury, Venus,

---

2. In the Latin language, a letter is not a word. Thus A is written with just one letter, A. In Hebrew, as in other ancient languages, a letter is a word composed of other letters. For example, the letter Ayin (ע) is also a word composed of three letters Aleph (א)—Yod (י)—Final Noun (ן). As Hebrew is written from right to left, you obtain for this example: Final Noun (ן)—Yod (י)—Aleph (א), and so ןיא = ע = Ayin. So this word (letter) has several meanings that relate to its etymology and its uses in the sacred texts of Judaism. This is the way you can give a meaning to the letter.

Sun, Mars, Jupiter, and Saturn). This succession is used in most versions of the Qabalistic Tree of Life in which planets are attributed to the Sephiroth.

From the time of the Chaldeans, it was well known that the lunar month is divided into four parts, each composed of seven days. These seven days were allocated to seven divinities very early on. In the Greek system, the seven divinities are Helios, Selene, Ares, Hermes, Zeus, Aphrodite, and Kronos. Vowels were also linked to these divinities (I, A, O, E, U, H, final A). Hebrew Qabalists made similar attributions.

This assignment of planets and vowels points out a will to link the earth with the cosmos, introducing balance and harmony, and maintaining order above chaos. Finally, if the divinities that correspond are represented with their attributes in the space delimited and in the most important places of power, buildings, etc., then their influence will be even stronger. You will see that this is really the case in each of the major buildings of Washington.

As I have just said, the dimension of the base of this invisible pyramid formed by the District of Columbia is ten miles on each side. The number 10 is an extremely important number in the Western Tradition. You will see that in the symbol of the triangle seen on the face of the pyramid. This regular form of the Egyptian pyramid naturally became the symbol of the descent of the light emanating from a unique celestial point seen from its summit looking towards the base of it (the world). Considered in another sense, it is also the symbol of the return one must accomplish, going from the multiplicity to the ultimate unity (see the signification of the letter Ayin mentioned before).

The triangle (constituting the sides of the pyramids) is one of the essential geometric shapes of Freemasonry. It was used over many centuries by several cultures before being used as one of the founder symbols of this brotherhood. Outside of Egypt, the triangle is a central symbol of the Pythagorean Mysteries. Without considering now the important mathematical theories that came from Pythagoras, it is interesting to note that the number 10 (called the Divine Tetraktys) was represented with its triangular and pyramidal shape. For Pythagoras, this number was undoubtedly one of the most important mysteries and under its protection the oaths of the brotherhood were pronounced: "By the one who gave in our souls the Tetraktys, source of the eternal nature."[3] Porphyrius wrote, "They introduced Pythagoras among their Gods and when they had to

---

3. Pythagoras, *Golden Verses*, §47–48 and Jamblique, *Pythagoras' Life*, chapters 150, 162.

pronounce a solemn oath, they began to do that under the protection of the Tetraktys."[4] The Tetraktys was for the Pythagoreans the Decade obtained by the addition of the first four numbers. The result is a pyramidal representation, as you can see below.

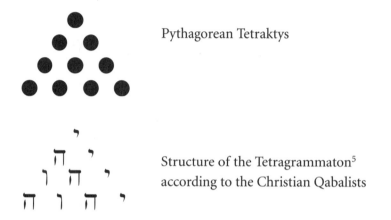

Pythagorean Tetraktys

Structure of the Tetragrammaton[5]
according to the Christian Qabalists

So the size of the ten-mile square chosen for the District of Columbia is very significant.

As shown by several studies, the shape and the proportions of the Great Pyramid of Giza generate a powerful subtle and invisible energy. Several studies done with BioGeometry demonstrate the powerful energy of its shape. Everything in nature has shape, and every shape generates a specific energy. The impact of geometrical shapes on human energy has always been a reality known by the initiates of the Ancient Mysteries. They used this knowledge in religious and sacred buildings to generate special energies to activate precise states of consciousness. It was the same for some traditional religious tools. Thus, a pyramid shape can have a real and powerful effect. In the case of the District of Columbia, the proportion was kept to maintain the quality of energy the founders wanted to use in the establishment and organization of the new country. Divine providence, linked to the intuition of wisdom, guided those who were chosen to act in this special area in order to develop the country according to the founders' principles.

---

4. Porphyre, *Pythagoras' Life*, chapter 20.

5. The Tetragrammaton is the name of God in the Torah. This word is composed of four letters: Yod ('), He (ה), Vav (ו), He (ה). This name is considered by tradition as unpronounceable by someone not an initiate. The high priest of Israel was the only one to be able to pronounce this word in the heart of the temple once a year.

But to activate this special and energetic building, it was necessary to give it a real existence. Since the most ancient times, such energies have been created in the same way, by raising stones (or buildings) and by "planting" them in the ground. It is the process used by the ancient people of Europe to create sacred areas that did not need an architectural superstructure. Stone markers put in special places were used to generate invisible power in this space, then surrounded. The character of the energy was the consequence of the shape, the position, and the number of the stones. You can find examples in several structures of traditional ancient people even as old as the megalithic period. Examples can be seen in Carnac (France), Stonehenge (England), and many other places.

These traditional rules were used in the District of Columbia, during the planning of this particular area. The square was delimited by forty stone markers, planted in the ground on a very regular sequence.[6]

Beyond the activation of the power I just spoke about, the significance of the number chosen (40) gives a special meaning and effect to this realization. In the Hebrew Qabalah, this number corresponds to the letter Mem (מ).

Mem, the letter of "water" (Mayim), symbolizes the fountain of divine wisdom. This flow goes from the top of the Qabalistic Tree[7] (Keter, the "crown") to the second sphere (Chokmah, "wisdom"). This letter Mem is the thirteenth letter of the alphabet. The number 13 is well known in the Qabalah because the addition of the letters composing the words *one* (Echad) and *love* (Ahavah) are equal to thirteen.

The form of this letter is also interesting. Mem can be seen as a summary of creation. The base of the letter represents the primordial ocean, without form and substance. Above it you see the form of the vault of the sky and the Yod, which represents the spirit of God. This original flame was above the waters. It is from this union that the Book of Genesis shows the creation of the whole universe. You can find another original story connected to the same archetypal symbol. In the sacred myths of ancient Greece, there, too, was a primordial ocean. The sky above was named Ouranos. One day, Cronos, the god of time, cut off the penis of Ouranos and some drops of blood and sperm fell in the ocean. Aphrodite, goddess of beauty and love, was born from the union of

---

6. See this website about the District of Columbia's boundary stones: http://www.boundarystones.org/.

7. The Sephirotic Tree or Tree of Life is a symbolic representation of the cosmos and the being represented by a group of ten spheres (power centers) connected with paths (streams of energy). One of the practices of this book is connected with the Tree of Life.

these two substances and the salt water. This reminds us how important beauty is in the Freemasonry ideal and philosophy.

This myth has an equivalent here. The powers of the forty stones stuck in the ground manifested in the creation of the young republic. It is interesting to note that the number 40 is feminine and liquid, and that the name *Columbus* was changed to the feminine form *Columbia.*

As you now understand how these powers were utilized to help the rise and development of the country, you should also realize that it will be possible to use them with special processes and practices. This will be discussed in the last part of this book. Let us note finally that the energy generated by this preparation of the area can be changed if some of the stone markers are destroyed or moved. Alas, that has been the case for some of them. Considering the invisible effect of these forty stones, it would be important for our era to raise and to restore all of them to their original positions (or at least a substitute of the stones stuck in the ground). Then the energies could be regenerated in order to give more power to the symbolic center of the United States and help its leaders manage the difficult times of this beginning of the twenty-first century.

The Sacred Triangle

The Masonic symbol of the triangle I mentioned before is also called a "delta," according to the representation of the Greek letter (Δ). In architecture, you can see this triangle on the pediment of the Greek and Roman classical temples. As research has demonstrated, proportions have a substantial importance. Without going further into these archaeological and geometric principles, you should remember how important the triangle and other symbols were in their pre-Christian origins.

The ancients (Platonists, Neoplatonists, Pythagoreans, writers like Plu-

Figure 7: The sacred delta in the center of the ouroboros, symbol of eternity

tarch, Vitruvius, etc.) wrote a lot about the geometric and symbolic value of the triangle. In several Eastern traditions, the Triad (3) is a mysterious number. It is the representation of the attributes of the supreme being, because the triangle unites the properties of the two first numbers, Unity and Dyad. The different trinities we can see in different places and times gave to this symbol an important theological meaning. This was also the case in the Western Tradition with trinities like Isis, Osiris, and Horus; Zeus, Poseidon, and Hades; the Three Fates (goddesses of life and destiny); the triple Hecate; and in the Father, Son, and Holy Spirit.

The main official Washington buildings were constructed according to the classical models, and their facades often reveal the presence of this symbolic triangle on the pediment. At the beginning of *The Lost Symbol*, Dan Brown invites the reader to be prudent with the numerous deductions made possible by the alignment of the streets of any city of the world. However, there are some fundamental geometric structures that are very significant when they can be associated without contradiction. The is the case with the triangle I am talking about. It does not require much imagination to see a precise triangle between the Capitol Building, the White House, and the Jefferson Memorial. This triangle is formed by Pennsylvania Avenue, Maryland Avenue, and the north/south line between the White House and the Jefferson Memorial. Some authors have tried to superimpose on Washington's map the symbols of the square and the compass as universal symbols of Freemasonry. Of course, it would be possible to link the two avenues (Pennsylvania and Maryland) to the branch of the compass. However, it is completely arbitrary and extremely difficult to find any square in the map.

The triangle I am speaking about is oriented on the central axis east/west and is much more obvious. I will explain more about it later in the book. The geometric center of this triangle is one of the important energetic points of the Mall and I will give you an example in the last part of this book. Dan Brown's novel mentions the Great Seal of the United States many times, with its incomplete pyramid and shining triangle upon it with the eye in the center, as it is found on the U.S. one-dollar bill. Dan Brown links this eye to a solar symbol called the *circumpunct*, the circled dot or circle with a point at its center, which is an ancient symbol of the Egyptian god Ra. Freemasonry, following Christianity and pre-Christian traditions, often used the delta with the central eye.

It is correct that the origin of the symbolic divine eye (or *oudjat*) can be found in Egypt. In the ancient myths, the eyes of Horus represented the Sun and the Moon. According to this story, Set, representing the nocturnal force, fought Horus and pulled out his lunar eye. Thoth recovered it later and gave it back to Horus, restoring the order of the cosmos. You should easily understand why the triangle is often put at the East of the Masonic temples, associated with the representations of the Moon and the Sun.

The temple is the sacred place in which initiations can be performed. Several important symbols representing the cosmos compose this space. They give power to the area and allow the initiate to understand the philosophical and spiritual message. It is also with their help that the nature and true origins of this initiatic tradition will be found.

Origins and Symbols of the Masonic Temple

According to myth, the architecture of a Masonic temple has its origin in the Temple of Solomon and the lodges of the operative freemasons (the builders) built beside the cathedrals. It does not require much research to realize that this claim is superficial and does not explain the important symbolism of Masonic temples. While many of the elements have a Hebrew origin, most of the architectural elements belong to other sources. The same is true for the function of the temple itself.

The Temple Building

First of all, it is necessary to know that Solomon's Temple follows the general structure of the Egyptian, Phoenician, and Mesopotamians temples. Both pillars, often mentioned in Freemasonry teachings, are the two columns of the entrance named Jakin and Boaz. They have no architectural function and were present on both sides of the entrance to the Jerusalem Temple. You can find their description in the Bible, in the Book of Kings, and 1 and 2 Chronicles. In Masonic temples, these pillars are generally surmounted respectively by an Earth's globe and a celestial globe. In some countries, their design is very close to the Bible's text, but generally their design varies according to the general style of the temples. There are very good examples of this in the wonderful temples of New York and Philadelphia. In each of these, the main architectural styles of the Western Tradition are represented, from Egypt to the modern epoch. It is always difficult to limit the analysis of a Hebrew word because this language can be the subject of long and complex interpretations. However, the Hebrew names of these pillars can cast some light on their meaning.

The pillar Jakin (יכין) is derived from the word *Jehovah* and the verb *establish*, and traditionally means "God will establish His House."

The pillar Boaz (בעז) is derived from the prefix *in* and the word *strength* and traditionally means "in strength." A little further study connects these pillars to the pillars of the Qabalistic Tree. The first one is associated with the idea of mercy and the second one with severity.

It is obvious that these pillars were inherited from the obelisks of the Egyptian Tradition, which were in front of the entrance of the temple. These pairs of stone columns also stood at the entrance of many oriental sanctuaries such as Khorsabad, Tyre, and Hieropolis. Today in Freemasonry, they are generally located inside the temple and function as useful symbolic elements for meditation and teaching purposes. However, you can sometimes find these pillars on the outside, as in front of the Masonic Hall in Montreal, Canada.

The layout of the temple corresponds to ancient standards. The points in common with the Egyptian temple are significant: the shape is a rectangle (called by Freemasons a "long square"); a lowered ceiling as you approach closer to Naos, the Sanctuary of the Most Holy; the darkness of the place, with areas providing strict physical separation from the external secular world. The orientation of the temples in Egypt differs from those we know today that are symbolically orientated along the west/east axis. In Egypt, it is often the sacred Nile River that determines the orientation of the temples.

In both of these examples, the Egyptian sanctuary and the Temple of Jerusalem, the temple is considered to be the residence of God on earth, the place where divinity manifests. As a result, this place is forbidden to laity. Only the priests can penetrate into the temple and only the pharaoh (or his representative such as a grand priest) can enter in the Naos, the Inner Sanctuary of the Most Holy. This place for divine manifestation results from such factors as the temple's special architecture, the presence of divine statues and consecrated ritual objects, and specific rituals. I am speaking here about a real manifestation of divinity and not just a symbolic one.

So it is clear that these temples had a different function and purpose than the Masonic temples today. The teachings and other minor ceremonies were performed in peripheral chapels or rooms similar to contemporary classrooms.

We can see that there was a time in the past when the purpose of the temple changed. Symbols and rituals provide precious clues, useful and important to consider. Two important initiatic traditions provide the key to understanding what a Masonic temple really is. These traditions are Pythagorism and Mithraism. Let us consider places where rituals and initiations linked to the mysteries were performed. You will see that these ceremonies constitute the true origin of the Masonic brotherhood.

In 1917, a Pythagorean underground basilica from the first century, located near the famous Porta Maggiore, was discovered in Rome. This basilica is oriented west/east, and composed of three naves and a square, or atrium. It is interesting to note that the throne of the Master is in the east, facing west and toward the initiates, who would gather in this place. Stucco and mosaics decorated the whole interior. Oil lamps illuminated the place. The floor is a mosaic composed of black and white tiles. Black tiles surround the room and stop on both sides of the throne of the Master.

Let us note that this black and white mosaic became a standard of the Masonic temples, although no indication can be found in the Bible or in the founder myths. Instead, its origin in the initiatic Pythagorean Mysteries is clear. In the Pythagorean basilica, the atrium (the small room at the entrance) included a basin where the members of the order washed their hands, face, and feet before entering the temple. Pythagoras said, "Put first your right shoe on, but wash first your left foot." Iamblicus explains that the initiate could only enter the temple with his right side and never with his left. Pythagoreans considered the right as solar, positive, odd-numbered, and divine while the left was lunar, negative, even-numbered, and an emblem of dissolution. You do not find such basins in Freemasonry, but some ancient esoteric Masonic rituals mention the necessity of purifications prior to ritual. It is also the case in some initiatic Rose-Cross Orders, which I will discuss later. However, the distinction between left and right sides is clearly used in the contemporary Masonic tradition and is the origin of special codes used in the gestures, signs, and ritual movements that every member must memorize. Again, the origin of these Masonic traditions is clear.

There are fewer records of the movements used and positions taken by the Pythagoreans during their studies and initiations. Decorative stuccos give some interesting elements of rituals and myths, but further discussion is beyond our purpose here.

Mithraism, the initiatic tradition that spread throughout the Roman Empire, gives us some very interesting architectural elements, which the Masonic lodges inherited. Mithraism was one of the rare initiatic traditions that was exclusively masculine, another interesting point shared with Freemasonry.

Unlike the rare Pythagorean temples, many Mithraeums have been found. These archeological remains give us a precise record of their architecture and strikingly different details about the members of the assembly.

First of all, these temples are also rectangular. They always have two higher parts on both sides of the axis of the temple, on which the brothers are seated. Seating in today's Masonic temples is exactly the same. The vault is in general semicircular, to represent the celestial arch. Other architectural details linked to the initiations, such as a well containing the water necessary for the purifications, are, of course, present.

As you can see, the Masonic temple has the same architectural structure as these ancient temples. The purpose of the temple is the same in the past and today: to give knowledge and an inner experience through ritual and symbols.

Specific Temple Buildings

THE "SANCTUM SANCTORUM"

Dan Brown's novel gives us the opportunity to see temples that are different from the basic and most common plan just described. As I have shown you, the plan of most Masonic temples comes from antiquity and the cults of mysteries of Mithras and Isis. Archaelogy shows that in the past there were different temples according to the tradition, the country, the divinities, and the purpose. It's obvious that the temples for oracles like Delphi, Didyma were different from a temple dedicated to Asclepius. The purposes are different and the temples are different. It was the same regarding the treasure spent to build and beautify the building. The most important symbols are constant, but others can be added, and the beauty of the building increased according to the finances and the number of worshipers. It's exactly the same process today for religious or initiatic buildings.

Some magical or religious temples, sometimes called oratories, are unique. In such cases the design and dimension depend on the knowledge and finances of the owner. Of course, if it is in an initiatic tradition, the buikding will be structured on traditional and ancient principles, as were the temples described by Dan Brown in *The Lost Symbol*.

An interesting description given in *The Lost Symbol* is Mala'akh's subterranean temple. Here the temple is devoted to bad intentions and purposes. Nevertheless, a temple, even for black magick, is built according the rules of symbolism. Its Sanctum Sanctorum is a twelve-foot square. This temple must recreate the order of the cosmos through its occult and spiritual structure. In fact, here the very symbolic number 12 is associated with the number 4, the square. It's necessary to represent first the material world. The number 4 is used for that. The temple is oriented according to the four directions, and the square increases the power of the four elements in this cube. The twelve-foot dimension creates the connection between the representation of the material world (the square) and the celestial world (the zodiac).

Seven divine powers regularly cross the sky: the seven planets manifesting the seven divinities (remember that in this practice, the Sun and the Moon are considered planets). They are the Sun (Helios), the Moon (Selene), Mars (Ares), Mercury (Hermes), Jupiter (Zeus), Venus (Aphrodite), and Saturn (Cronos). These are just the seven traditional planets visible to our natural vision. The Sun, the Moon, and the planets travel through the zodiac according to the celestial rules of astrology or astronomy. As you saw before, these planets are sometimes painted on the ceiling of the temple.

To materialize and concentrate the energy of the planets, Mala'akh installed in the center of this temple a stone altar, seven by seven foot square. In order to increase the power, Mala'akh utilizes a very ingenious process sometimes used in the past, but rarely in this manner.

The theory of correspondences gives many attributions to the planets. The first one is the daily cycles and sequences of the seven celestial bodies. Progressing from local sunrise to sunset, the daylight duration is divided into twelve periods. This is the same for the twelve hours of the night. It is obvious that these planetary hours are different each day, but today it is very easy to calculate. The first hour of the day is the same as the day. For example, on Sunday, the first planet that gives his power at sunrise is the Sun (Helios), followed by the Moon (Selene), Mars (Ares), Mercury (Hermes), Jupiter (Zeus), Venus (Aphrodite), and Saturn (Cronos). The same will continue according to the chart on the next page.

Each planet is associated with a very important group of symbols like colors, numbers, letters, sounds, plants, sacred names of divinities, spirits, etc.

For the magus, the goal is to learn these different traditional correspondences and use them in a ritual to attract the appropriate powers. But to re-create and concentrate all these seven powers, you need to activate each one consecutively. An ingenious magical tool is a light above the altar composed of seven colors that change according to the planetary hour. The names given in the novel are some of the magical hours connected to angels, divinities, etc. For example, the novel says the hour of Yanor is blue. According to the *Heptameron*, Yanor is the name of the second magical hour, Nasnia the name of the third magical hour, and Salam the name of the last (12th) magical hour of the night. As you can see in the chart, the spelling of the names is not exactly the same.

		Sunday	Monday	Tuesday	Wednesday	Thursday	Friday	Saturday
Day hours	1-Yayn	Sun	Moon	Mars	Mercury	Jupiter	Venus	Saturn
	2-Janor (or Yanor)	Venus	Saturn	Sun	Moon	Mars	Mercury	Jupiter
	3-Nasnia	Mercury	Jupiter	Venus	Saturn	Sun	Moon	Mars
	4-Salla	Moon	Mars	Mercury	Jupiter	Venus	Saturn	Sun
	5-Sadedali	Saturn	Sun	Moon	Mars	Mercury	Jupiter	Venus
	6-Thamur	Jupiter	Venus	Saturn	Sun	Moon	Mars	Mercury
	7-Ourer	Mars	Mercury	Jupiter	Venus	Saturn	Sun	Moon
	8-Tanic (or Thaine)	Sun	Moon	Mars	Mercury	Jupiter	Venus	Saturn
	9-Neron	Venus	Saturn	Sun	Moon	Mars	Mercury	Jupiter
	10-Jayon (or Yayon)	Mercury	Jupiter	Venus	Saturn	Sun	Moon	Mars
	11-Abay (or Abai)	Moon	Mars	Mercury	Jupiter	Venus	Saturn	Sun
	12-Natalon (or Nathalon)	Saturn	Sun	Moon	Mars	Mercury	Jupiter	Venus
Night hours	1-Beron	Jupiter	Venus	Saturn	Sun	Moon	Mars	Mercury
	2-Barol	Mars	Mercury	Jupiter	Venus	Saturn	Sun	Moon
	3-Thanu	Sun	Moon	Mars	Mercury	Jupiter	Venus	Saturn
	4-Athir (or Athor)	Venus	Saturn	Sun	Moon	Mars	Mercury	Jupiter
	5-Mathon	Mercury	Jupiter	Venus	Saturn	Sun	Moon	Mars
	6-Rana	Moon	Mars	Mercury	Jupiter	Venus	Saturn	Sun
	7-Netos	Saturn	Sun	Moon	Mars	Mercury	Jupiter	Venus
	8-Tafrac	Jupiter	Venus	Saturn	Sun	Moon	Mars	Mercury
	9-Sassur	Mars	Mercury	Jupiter	Venus	Saturn	Sun	Moon
	10-Aglo (or Agla)	Sun	Moon	Mars	Mercury	Jupiter	Venus	Saturn
	11-Calerna (or Caerra)	Venus	Saturn	Sun	Moon	Mars	Mercury	Jupiter
	12-Salam	Mercury	Jupiter	Venus	Saturn	Sun	Moon	Mars

These differences come from the various translations. It is the same for the colors, the planets, the part of the day, etc. Thus, you can imagine that black magick is performed on Saturday during the 11th hour of the night. This day is under the influence of Saturn/ Cronos, the god who ate his children according the ancient texts.

This part of *The Lost Symbol* continues with the descriptions of the different symbols and magical tools used in this black magick operation: the fumigations, knife, etc. I will speak later about these items.

The villain of the novel calls his special place the "Sanctum Sanctorum," which means literally "Holy of Holies." This expression was used for the most holy place in the ancient Solomon's Temple and in fact this expression is universal and religious. The Sanctum Sanctorum is used generally in a religious context to describe the place where divine powers can be manifested. This is also the case for the magical temples.

While the structure of a magical ritual like this one is very close to that used in white magick, the purpose is very different; some of the symbols and tools are used in a different way.

THE HOUSE OF THE TEMPLE

As noted previously, the temples used in Freemasonry can be very different depending on their purposes. The famous one called the House of the Temple is located at 1733 Sixteenth Street NW, in the District of Columbia. This monumental building has been the national headquarters of the Supreme Council 33rd Degree, which is the governing body of the Scottish Rite in America, since 1915. The cornerstone was laid in 1911 and the building was completed in 1915. Its architecture is an adaptation of the famous mausoleum at Halicarnassus, one of the Seven Wonders of the Ancient World.

The architect of this temple was John Russell Pope, well known for his other works connected to our subject such as the Jefferson Memorial. This building is a major contribution to American architecture, which employs the simplicity and grandeur as an example of the classical form in America. But more than a wonder of architecture, this building is one of the world's most famous contemporary symbolic buildings that is nonreligious. It is important to note that the word *temple* is never used in Freemasonry with a religious meaning connected to a purpose of worship. A temple like this one is a sacred and symbolic place used to raise the inner and unconscious level of the mind to a high spiritual level. The power of the symbols connected together can create a real impact on us, and something happens. Generally, the temples are formed with one major

Figure 8: House of the Temple, Washington DC
(House of the Temple, AASR-SJ, USA)

room and some smaller rooms. It is very rare to find a whole building that can be considered as a temple in itself. This is the case of this unique construction and it is the reason why the choice of this building for use in *The Lost Symbol* is such a good one, considering all these elements.

This is not the place to study and explain each symbol of this building, but some observations can be interesting. Of course, it could be strange to choose a mausoleum as a sacred temple. Freemasonry is not associated with necromancy. But, as I said, the purpose here is symbolic and, as Dan Brown writes, its identity as a mausoleum increases the focus on the initiatic process. Initiation, in the practice of classical philosophy, is the study of going through the gate of the invisible world. According to the initiatic teachings, this process is the same as the experience of death. In initiation and in special practices, the experience can be a living and inner realization leading to modification of one's perception of the world. The connection between the building and this intimate and essential experience constitutes a very powerful reminder.

Figure 9: Entrance door of the House of the Temple, Washington DC.
Beautiful use of an old Mithraic symbol.
(House of the Temple, AASR-SJ, USA)

The building harmoniously associates such different styles as classical Greek architecture and Egyptian statutes and designs. The ancient model of the Mausoleum is another connection with Freemasonry. It is interesting to know that this "Wonder of the World," located in the city of Bodrum, was built around 353 BCE by the wife and sister of the king, who asked the king for the best architects and sculptors of her time (Satyrus and Pythis as architects, and Scopas of Paros, Leochares, Bryaxis, and Timotheus as sculptors).

Of course, the House of the Temple is not an exact replica of the Mausoleum, but from the outside the proportions and appearance of the building are very close.

It is interesting to make an additional remark about King Mausolus. One of the distinctive signs of this king, which can be found on coins, is one star (or sun) with eight branches. This sign and this symbolic number are an important indication of the ancient tradition that would lead to Freemasonry. Also, let us point out the representation on the front doors is one of the important Mithraic symbols: a head of lion holding a circle (or a snake) closed in its mouth.

Besides having different and very interesting rooms and a remarkable library, the first one opened to the public in Washington DC, this magnificent building also contains a gigantic chamber named the Temple Room. It is surrounded by huge windows with the glass shading up from a deep orange at the bottom to a pale yellow at the top, symbolizing the increasing light (knowledge) that the initiate will receive. Crowning the center of the window is the double eagle, symbol of the Scottish Rite. Around the walls is a sentence inscribed in bronze letters on black marble, saying: "From the outer darkness of ignorance through the shadows of our earth life, winds the beautiful path of initiation unto the divine light of the Holy Altar."

In the center of this room, a wonderful altar made of black and gold marble is engraved with golden Hebrew letters from Genesis 1:3, saying: "God said, 'Let there be light' and there was light" (ויאמר אלהים יהי אור ויהי אור).

The light of illumination, insight, and education is central in the Scottish Rite. This is the symbolic light of the lighthouse of Alexandria, which Freemasonry received in inheritance and keeps high in the sky to illuminate humanity. Different sacred books are put on top of this sacred altar to show again one of the most important messages of this fraternity, that the immortal and eternal divine manifests its presence under different veils and appearances.

One hundred feet above this altar, an oculus open to the sky allows the light of day to illuminate the room or the starry sky of night to veil the top of this symbolic structure, which is a pyramid. It is interesting to see that, as in the ancient Mausoleum, the top of this sacred building was built in a pyramid shape. In the ancient Mausoleum, a sculpture of a horse-drawn carriage was put on top of the pyramidal roof. Here this sculpture was replaced by an oculus, which allows light to enter the temple. You can find the same architectural principle in the Pantheon in Rome.

This whole building raises this fraternity to one of the leading lights of contemporary initiatic traditions, and can really be seen as a pure symbolic jewel.

The Square

In Mithraism and Pythagorism, the square (atrium) is a room located at the entrance of the temple and was used by members to dress in their ritual clothes, to accomplish the purifications, and to store the ritual tools, perfumes, and other items necessary for rituals. It was a place for preparation, a transition between the secular world (outside) and the sacred space (inside). It was the same in early Christianity because it was forbidden for noninitiates to have access to the temple. The heart of the sacred building was always restricted to the initiates. All this is retained in contemporary Freemasonry. It is often in this special place that pillars or commemorative markers are built.

The Vault

The symbolic model of the vault in a Masonic temple is a starry arch. Undoubtedly this kind of arch comes directly from Egypt. It appears in temples and in some tombs with the representation of the goddess Nut, her body painted on the ceiling with stars spangled on the whole surface. Later, this starry arch was also the model for all Mithraeum ceilings. Generally, the shape of the vault is an arch in order to represent the sky. The color of the background is generally deep blue spangled with gold five-branched stars. Christian buildings used this symbolism from the fifth century. We also see that some ceilings in ancient Egypt included zodiacs. This is an important element that I will discuss later for Washington DC.

The Altar

In the ancient temples, there were several types of altars. Some were located outside the temple and in front of it, while others were located indoors. Generally, it was their function that defined the altar's position in the temple. Some were used for offerings, burning incense, etc. The one located in the Naos (the most hidden and secret room of the temple) was used as a portable chapel containing the consecrated statue of the god.

In Mithraism, an altar in stone was put on the central axis of the temple and in its central point, although it was sometimes located in a position closer to east. There is not absolute certainty about its usage, which could be different depending on the ritual. However, we observe that the Masonic altar takes the same place in a temple and is not the pedestal of any statues. On the Masonic altar we find the sacred book, the square, and the compass. Oaths are pronounced on this altar and it is very plausible that this was also the case for Mithraism.

The shape of the ancient altars was not unique but the most common were circular and cubic. The Masonic altar follows the same rule as the Mithraic temple and is cubic. Two very beautiful examples can be seen in the House of the Temple that is at the center of Dan Brown's novel. The first one is in a small temple located at the first level and the other one is in the Big Temple, the place used for the climax of the novel.

The East

In the Pythagorean basilica, the place of the Master was higher than the floor of the temple and located in the east. The first Hermetists recommended praying in the morning facing east, the place where the light flows to the world and its beings. In Mithraism, the *tauroctony* was also put in the symbolic east of the temple. And in contemporary Masonic temples, the east is very often symbolic. It is not always possible to build a temple well oriented and in this case the orientation is symbolic. It is important to see that the east of the temple is always the part that is the most important and sacred. The four directions (real or symbolic) are also connected to the four elements. In the Masonic temple, as in both initiatic traditions I am discussing, the Worshipful Master is in the east. It is also on this wall that you can see the representations of the divine, often represented with the symbol of the triangle. In its center we can find different symbolic representations of the Great Architect of the Universe, such as the circumpunct, the letter *G*, an eye, etc. We see that the place of the Master in the east, channeling the divine light, is absolutely different than the function of this direction in Egypt or in the Temple. In these two cases, you can find in the most sacred place of the temple the manifestation of God, giving his light and blessings to the priest and, through him or her, to everyone. Nobody can replace the light. So you can see that the meaning differs. Freemasonry seems closer to the ideology of the Ancient Mysteries than contemporary religions.

The Elements

Around the sixth and fifth centuries BCE, the Greek philosophers began to study the structure and dynamics of the living world. Pythagoras, heir of the Egyptian traditions, considered that the world resulted from some mixture and combination of four primordial elements, earth (▽̶—solid state), fire (△—imponderable substance), air (△̶—gaseous state), water (▽—liquid state), and a fifth principle, aether (⊕—mind, or spirit).

Philolaus, a Pythagorean initiate, very clearly synthesizes this structure of four elements, saying that there are five bodies in the sphere: fire, water, earth, air, and the circle of the sphere, which is the fifth. The five-pointed star (the pentagram), which the ancient Greeks called a *Pentagrammaton* or *Pentalpha*, was a sign of recognition to

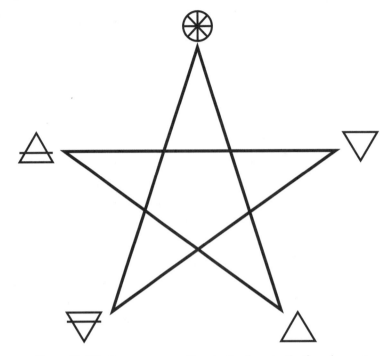

Figure 10: The Pentagram and its attributions to the five elements

the Pythagoreans. Plato used these ancient representations and connected them to special geometric symbols. Earth was linked with the cube (three-dimensional figure of six equal square sides), air with the octahedron (three-dimensional figure with eight sides), water with the icosahedron (three-dimensional figure with twenty sides), and fire with the tetrahedron (three-dimensional figure with four sides). Plato put the dodecahedron (three-dimensional figure with twelve equal pentagonal faces) in correspondence with the whole, the world, because it is the solid that resembles most closely a sphere. In another passage of Timeus, Plato identified four important orders in nature: Gods and the celestial orb (fire), the winged animals (air), the animals of the earth (earth), and the aquatic animals (water).

A part of the famous text of the *Corpus Hermeticum* introduces this topic of elements as seen through the alchemy filter. Initiatic traditions used this text to link the four elements to the four directions, which did not have any religious roots.

In short, all traditional representations (hermetic, astrological, alchemical, etc.) show that the foundation of the initiatic progression is composed of four elements that constitute us and can be symbolized by the Pentagrammaton (the Tetragrammaton with the letter Shin added). So, as I said, they are the four traditional elements (earth, water, air, and fire) and aether (or mind) that overcomes them.

Elements	Earth	Water	Air	Fire	Aether (Cosmos for Plato)
Symbols	▽	▽	△	△	⊕
Platonic solids	Cube (or Hexahedron)	Icosahedron	Octahedron	Tetrahedron	Dodecahedron
Description of the platonic solids	Composed of 6 faces.	Composed of 20 faces	Composed of 8 faces	Composed of 4 faces	Composed of 12 faces
Greek letters	Gamma	Delta	Rho	Pi	Theta
Hebrew letters		Mem	Alef	Shin	

The Sun and the Moon

The Sun and the Moon have important symbolism and appear from the beginning of Freemasonry on the east wall of the temples. Their position is not absolute, however, as you can also find them in the opposite position.

At first, you can believe that this use of the Sun and the Moon could come from Christianity. In Christian iconography, these two bodies are linked to the death of Christ on the Cross at the top of Golgotha through interpretation of the Gospel of Matthew 27:45: "At noon the whole country became dark. The darkness continued for three hours." Luke states in 23:44–45: "It was about noon, but it turned dark throughout the land until three o'clock in the afternoon, because the Sun stopped shining." The Christian iconographic tradition started with these texts.

A very interesting illustration can be seen in the Cloisters, in New York's Metropolitan Museum. We see seven red flowers in the center of two columns, one black and one red. At the top of these two columns, we see two circles and a face in the center of each one. This is a very rare ancient representation from the Coptic Tradition (Egypt). The connections are rich and complex. The two figures can be linked to the early Mithraic and Greek Traditions. In fact, if we go back earlier, we can see that these symbolic representations of the Sun and the Moon can be found in the initiatic Ancient Mysteries.

Figure 11: Ancient representation of Mithra and the ox sacrified

Again, the best source can be found in the Mythraic Mysteries. These representations are precise and systematic. In the east of the Mithraeum you can find the classical representation of Mithras killing the bull. He is always surrounded by the Sun and the Moon. It is exactly as was used from the beginning in the Masonic temples.

You can also find this presence in nature. Occasionally, you can see both the Sun setting in the west as the Moon rises in the east. Let us not forget that stars were considered to be divinities, in this case the two divinities Helios (the Sun) and Selene (the Moon).

The Chamber of Reflection

In his novel, Dan Brown reveals a very interesting secret room in the temple, the Chamber of Reflection. This place is not well known in those lodges using the Emulation's Rite and York's Rite, which together make up the majority of lodges around the world. However, this symbolic place is actually Masonic, but better known and used in European Masonic rituals (Scottish Rite, French Rite, Egyptian Rites, etc.). The beginning of

V. I. T. R. I. O. L.

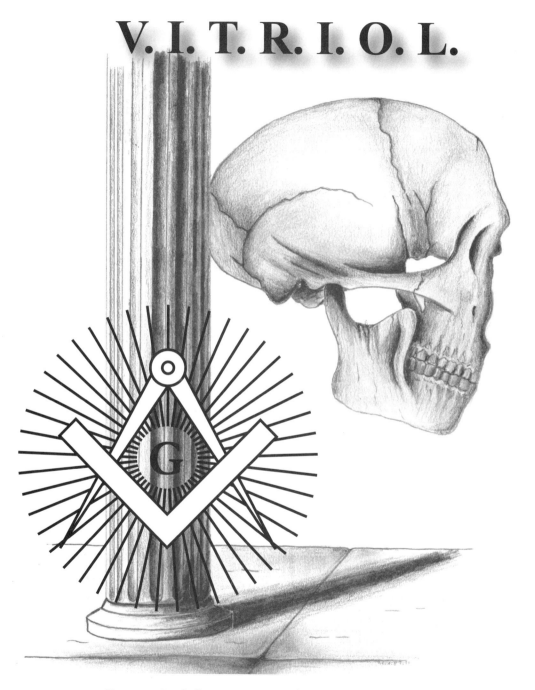

*Figure 12: Symbolic representation of the Chamber of Reflection
subject by the author of this book*

the use of this chamber was around 1789, and it was the result of esoteric Freemasons eager to use all the processes and initiatic symbols of Western tradition.

In *The Lost Symbol*, Dan Brown tells us that the Chamber of Reflection is a place of meditation and introspection, intended to generate a special state of consciousness in the initiate. It is organized just like a darkened cave in which one can find a human skull and bones. This decor can increase the level of fear and generate speculations in one's mind. The traditional representation seen here is generally painted on the walls of this underground room.

This chamber represents the heart of the primordial earth. It is not rare that it is organized as a tunnel and sometimes even dug in the ground. This is the case of the one described by Dan Brown in the depths of Washington's Capitol Building. The cell in which is hidden the Chamber of Reflection has the number SBB XIII, symbolic reference to the thirteenth card of the Tarot of Marseilles, representing death.

It is in this place that the candidate is locked up before his initiation, to allow him time to meditate on the mysteries of his own existence and, therefore, on death.

There is no biblical source for this place. It is more likely alchemical symbolism and a ritual linked to the ancient Mystery Cults, especially Mithras and Isis. The ritual tests of Mithraism began with a meditation in a kind of well, in the presence of human remains. Such a well can be seen in the Mithraeum at Carrawsburg in England. As Tertullian[8] said, candidates for the initiation were locked up in sepulchers sealed and then reopened and tied with the intestines of chickens. Sometimes they made a pretence to the candidates that they were going to be thrown into a gaping abyss.

In the mysteries of Isis in the Roman Empire, often the temple included a small building located at the entrance of the area, generally in the northwest. A door opened onto a staircase that led to an underground room. It is completely plausible that the candidate was driven into this place before his initiation, as if his body had gone down into a tomb to live a symbolic death. These initiatic caves could be real or artificial. Pausanias, a geographer of the second century CE, tells that he went down a narrow path of a cave used for the initiations.

We can see a relationship between this dark place with two symbolic elements of the world and the body, which I will come back to in detail a little further on.

---

8. Quintus Septimius Florens Tertullianus (Tertullian) (160–220 CE) was a prolific and controversial early Christian author.

For the ancient initiates, the world in which we live is a distorted and delusional representation of the spiritual world. Plato said that the world can be compared to a cave in which one would be chained since birth, without the possibility of seeing external reality, which is the divine world. The goal of the initiation is to help us to realize this situation and to point out the way, allowing us to come back to reality. I can say this is the same for one's body, which can be seen as a cave, a tomb, in which one's soul would be a prisoner.

The Chamber of Reflection linked these different elements to allow us to live this inner experience. Then we would be capable of understanding that this ascension to the One, the Beauty, and the Right is the main goal of our initiation.

The Hidden Masonic Temple of Washington DC

There are many theories about the layout of Washington DC. Most of them are related to the special interlacing of the streets. They infer a complex group of symbols, sometimes distorted as people tried to connect them to the Western initiatic tradition and Freemasonry. Whatever the truth of these theories, undoubtedly the creators of this city used symbolic elements of their tradition to dedicate and to invigorate the capital of the United States.

The traditional origins of the main architectural elements of a Masonic temple will help us to understand the design of the city. Since earliest times, the only way to build and respect the tradition is to begin with a delimitation of the space. As you saw before, it was made by the shape, proportions, and orientation of the District of Columbia.

The second step is to build the space of the temple itself, organizing the main elements that constitute it. Of course, this will be a very important part of the energetic activation. Let us not forget that the function of the Masonic temple is to allow a bond to appear between the brothers, and so at the same time an action in the city, and affecting all levels of the human being.

The Masonic temples built according to the ancient traditions are usually closed, covered places. They re-create the order of the cosmos, and are a representation of the macrocosm (the world) in the microcosm (the space of the temple). But considering their role in society, the temple is not always closed and secret. Sometimes Freemasons practice their ritual meetings outside, in nature for example, where the elements that were merely symbolic until then can access all their power.

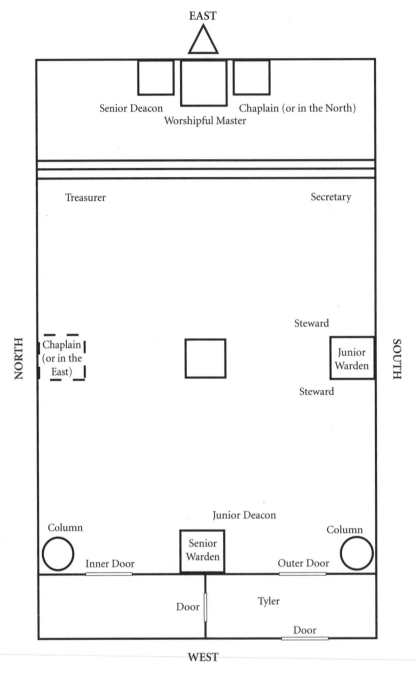

Figure 13: Masonic Lodge

The rectangle of a Masonic temple is orientated east/west. In English Freemasonry, the three major officers sit in the east, west, and south. They are the Worshipful Master of the Lodge (east), the Senior Warden (west), and the Junior Warden (south).

In other cases, the north also has an officer. It is not always the same. It can be the Tyler, the Chaplain (he can sit also to the left of the Master), or even an empty chair. However, on the symbolic level, this position in the north is important because it marks the last direction of the lodge and assures its balance and existence on the material plane. The three major officers constitute the trinity, which gives its radiance, and the fourth point gives stability to the lodge.

The Master ("Worshipful Master" is his honorary title) of a Masonic lodge is the highest ranking of all lodge officers and is elected by the members of the lodge. The Master sits in the east and directs all of the ritual, ceremonies, and business of the lodge. He is similar to a president of any other organization. The symbol he wears is the square.

The Senior Warden is the second in command among the lodge officers. You can compare his duty and function to a vice-president who can work in the place of the Master in case of absence. The Senior Warden sits in the west. The symbol he wears is the level.

The Junior Warden is the third in command of the lodge. He sits in the south. He is responsible for the brethren while the lodge is at ease or having refreshments. The symbol he wears is the plumb.

More important than these official functions and duty, each officer of a lodge has an esoteric function connected to his symbolic position. As the lodge is the representation of the cosmos, each position has a real and effective power on the invisible level. It is this second function that provides the spiritual authority behind the rituals and the initiations, the spiritual and esoteric aspects necessary to really act on these two levels.

As noted previously, the fourth point or direction, north, is not always connected to a visible officer. If the Tyler is there, he can maintain the contact between the inner lodge and the outer world. If the Chaplain is there, he assumes the contact between the inner lodge and the spiritual and higher levels. Both positions show that this direction is important to root the lodge and give a kind of energy different from the Master. The Chaplain opens the book of the sacred law and pronounces the invocations. It's not necessary that the Chaplain has a real function, as in a church. It may be more important to give this charge to the initiate, to bring more awareness of the invisible power of the ritual work and his connection to the divine.

Looking at the layout of the lodge and the symbolic functions of the officers, we realize something very interesting. This symbolic universe of the lodge represents a goal of fraternity, a will to create a new world regardless of differences. Everyone has a symbolic function and duty, is elected to his position, and must act for the good of everyone. Their positions in the temple allow us to receive the invisible influences that help us to really accomplish our purpose.

The center of the federal capital was created as a special and symbolic place, but not as a church. This place is sacred but not in the sense of a religion. The symbols used by the Founding Fathers were Masonic. To complete the symbolic map, it was necessary to represent and create the heart. If I transpose the layout of a temple on to the heart of the federal capital, you realize immediately that a beautiful synchrony created a roofless Masonic temple within a rectangle orientated according to the traditional rules. The throne of the Master is in the east, well located in height. This is the Capitol Building, where the power is really to be found.

Even more symbolic, it is to this direction that all brothers and sisters of the American nation turn, putting their right hand flat upon their heart to listen to the oath pronounced by the new president. It is exactly the same ritual that takes place every year in all Masonic lodges. Gestures, the place of the president during his oath of office, and his symbolic authority are demonstrations of this intention to consecrate the one who was elected. The president puts his hand on the sacred book to pronounce his oath in the presence of a chaplain.

The space of the lodge is represented according to the precise proportions of the temple by the three other directions, which are the White House (north), the Jefferson Memorial (south), and the Lincoln Memorial (west).

The central altar that can be found in every lodge exists and its position was precisely chosen by Thomas Jefferson. This cube with a pyramid shape at the top is exactly located in the center of the cardinal axis, with each side measuring two feet. Like any lodge altar, this altar has symbolism and a very important function. I will explain in the last part of the book the different practices connected to it.

Both the two pillars generally located in the west of the temple are absent, but in their place you see statutes of peace and war, located on both sides of the Lincoln Me-

Figure 14: The Capitol

morial. They are completely similar from the point of view of the Qabalistic symbolism of the two pillars.

The two buildings of the Supreme Court and the Library of Congress are very well connected to the other officers of the east. You will have the opportunity later to see important connections between the Tradition and the Library of Congress.

The obelisk is slightly to the east of the Jefferson Stone. This is the position in a Masonic temple where a shining five-pointed star is often suspended from the ceiling. The Pentagrammaton includes in its center the initial *G*, the manifestation of the divine.

The presence of water is also complete here. The Potomac and its tidal basin are in the place where, according to the tradition, the purifications would take place.

The starry arch is represented by the goddess Nut herself, symbolized by the forever flying starry flag during the day. The symbolic triangle that I mentioned before between the Capitol, the White House, and the Jefferson Memorial is, of course, east-oriented, in the direction of the most important place of this symbolic group.

Figure 15: The Capitol

One can really be amazed to understand this whole area constituted by the District of Columbia and the Mall of Washington DC. All of it was created to allow communication between the higher levels of energy and the necessity for the young republic to develop its power, influence, and radiance. The Masonic ideals, which are very similar to those established by the Declaration of Independence, are continuously empowered through the material reality of this architectural construction, as was its intention.

chapter three
THE WIDOW'S SONS

Egypt: The Hidden Widow of Freemasonry
Alexandria: Birth of the Ancient Mysteries

THE HERMETIC SCHOOL AND THE ANCIENT MYSTERIES

It may seem strange to look to the past—usually thought of as prescientific, non-empirical, and archaic—in order to understand the present. It's just as strange and even amazing to imagine that scientific discoveries can come from the ancient traditions. So it is extremely useful to see if this supposition is true, and to understand the characteristics of this knowledge, and of course, where we can find it.

In *The Lost Symbol*, Dan Brown says that ancient knowledge was spread across time, secreted away in thousands of books; this knowledge originated from the ancient papyrus scrolls of the Egyptians and even the clay tablets of the Sumerians. Yet despite the diverse sources, the texts all say the same thing; these secrets of ancient knowledge can be unlocked. This seems almost contradictory. The first one shows that ancient knowledge cannot be found in one single place. The second shows that these secrets can be found in the venerable writings on the same subject, and all coming from the same source: east of the Mediterranean basin.

This notion illustrates the feeling that has existed for centuries in Western culture, that this region was the early origin of important moral and spiritual ideas as well as the beginnings of technological and scientific knowledge. This part of the world is not far from where human beings first appeared.

The ancient Greeks, eager to be initiated into this ancient wisdom, came to Egypt, and many of these seekers did receive a part of this heritage and its secrets. They used what they received, but they also respected what was called secret. It's for this reason you find so few explicit Greek writings on those rituals and mysteries.

The priests of ancient Egypt did not look upon these Greeks seeking the Ancient Mysteries as equals. The gods had transmitted sacred knowledge to the Egyptians in their temples the seekers had to receive these mysteries in ceremonies more religious than philosophical. We should not expect to find in ancient Egypt any rational analysis of their magical and religious practices, nor will we find their gods and goddesses in classifications logical to our modern minds. The distinction between reason, science, and religion was not as strict as today.

As the centuries passed, Egypt was invaded several times and many Greeks and other foreigners began to live in this country. Alexandria, the city founded by Alexander the Great, progressed into a very important center for spiritual, religious, and scientific studies. It is in this period of history, called the Ptolemaic[1] period, that a real exchange of ideas began between initiates from different cultures—Phoenician, Greek, Chaldean, Jewish, Egyptian, etc. Until this time, Egyptian initiates were what I could call "elitist," looking at other cultures as inferior and without interest. Following the will of Ptolemeus Soter the First, an honest and balanced man, the city of Alexandria began to illuminate the whole world. No doubt that the protection of Alexander the Great, buried in the city, was effective in this issue.

During this difficult time for Egypt, some priests met regularly with religious people and initiates of other faiths then living in Egypt, principally in the north of the country. New interpretations of ancient local traditions rose from this exchange, integrating the best of each. Links were established on different religious, initiatic, philosophical, and scientific levels. An amazing example of this benevolent collaboration came about through the meeting between an Egyptian priest, Manethon, and the Greek priest of Demeter, Timoteus. From their theological debates arose a new divinity named Serapis, whose image of a divine and noble old figure carrying on his head a basket/grain-measure symbolizing his agricultural character was undoubtedly a fusion between Osiris-Apis and Demeter. This god was often associated with Isis and Harpocrates, and

---

1. The Ptolemaic period began with the reign of Ptolemeus Lagos, faithful companion of Alexander the Great, and lasted until the end of Egyptian Empire (from 323 to 30 BCE).

was present in Isiac worship and mysteries throughout the ancient world. A Serapeum was built in Memphis to accommodate this new god. Nearby was a semicircular auditorium surrounded by statues of Greek philosophers who had come to study in the Egyptian temples. Among these figures were Solon, Thaleus, Plato, Eudoxus, and Pythagoras. Greeks identified Harpocrates with Asclepius, and patients came to sleep in his temple in order to receive dreams of healing guidance.

At this time, Alexandria was a city where everyone freely prayed and worshiped the gods of their choice. Greeks frequently went to Egyptian temples and the Egyptians freely reciprocated. Besides their own feeling for one or another divinity, it was often the deity's recognized "rulership" (purpose or function) that determined their choice.

Please note that the tradition I am talking about in this book is not religious. Its philosophy is not opposed to religion per se, but it does not use the dogmatic and theological approach, nor the sacraments found in some religions.

The contacts between different cultures in Alexandria during the Ptolemaic period went further than simple religious discussion. Greeks brought with them a rationalist and analytic way of thinking almost unknown to the Egyptian Tradition. From this connection between wise adepts and initiates, a completely original school was founded on the Hermetica (Hermetic texts) and, more precisely, on the famous Emerald Tablet.

As the French scholar Françoise Bonardel once wrote: "Hermeticism was autonomous regarding Christianity and independent regarding the initiatic societies it organized. In fact Hermeticism would have gathered all along the centuries of Western history, a family of minds first of all eager to work on overtaking all forms of dualism. It would be characterized by some sort of feeling, tolerance allowing one to receive different ways of spiritual realization." The uniqueness of the Hermetic Tradition is this determination and desire to link reason and intelligence, and to progress toward a free spirituality. In spite of the loss of very important texts in the destruction of the famous Alexandria library, a real philosophical corpus is still available to us—including the *Corpus Hermeticum*, the *Chaldaic Oracles*, and various theological and philosophical treatises belonging to this school.

Later, this philosophical and spiritual tradition was organized around the Greek Academy of Plato and its work. Masters of the academy kept these inner teachings from Egypt alive for many centuries. Today it is called Neoplatonism, but the heirs of Plato did more than just perpetuate his teaching, codifying and organizing it into a complete system called *Religio Mentis*, the "religion of mind." For us today, following the work of

Thomas Aquinas and the German philosophers, philosophy can be seen as mostly an abstract and purely mental practice.

Hermetic philosophy, however, is not a pure mental abstraction with no other purpose than to examine the essence of things and beings. The practice of this philosophy cannot be separated from spiritual life and the search for the divine. Reason linked to spiritual and symbolic practices allows this progress in a stable and balanced way. Of course, Hermetic initiates did have a religious practice, but their intellectual studies were not necessary for popular religious practice.

We can view initiation in two ways:

1. The first consists of progressive training and practice of philosophy. It is mostly mental and links in a balanced way reasoning, visualization, and meditation. You will learn more about that in the practical part of this book.

2. The second corresponds to specific rituals that I specifically call the *Mysteries*.

It is evident that Hermetists who practiced the first way received at the same time one or more initiations to the mysteries. At that time, no initiation was considered superior to another and it was common to be initiated into several divine mysteries. We see this in Apuleus' writings: "I was initiated in Greece to most of the religions. Symbols and gifts were given to me by priests and I keep them piously. There is nothing extraordinary, nothing prodigious here . . . there are many religions, several ritual practices, a large variety of ceremonies which I studied for love of the truth and as duty for the Gods."[2]

These "mystery cults" are very close to some Masonic rituals, but have to be differentiated by the common religious practice. The mysteries transmit hidden, esoteric knowledge to a small number of people sometimes chosen for their moral qualities. They use different spiritual and ritual practices relating to the sacred geographical places that perpetuate them. These same processes further encouraged the development of the hidden powers of the human being, helping one to understand one's essence and the way toward the full possession of one's potential.

Dan Brown in *The Lost Symbol* explains that the ancient knowledge hidden in these texts enabled practitioners to access and control powerful, almost magical, abilities that lie hidden within the mind. Such powers were too dangerous to be wielded by the uninitiated, and hence the mysteries were only disseminated to a select few by the masters,

---

2. Apuleus, *Apology*.

whom they believed could handle and control this newfound power with skill and morality. An analogy can be made to the use of fire. In the correct hands, fire is a beneficial and advantageous tool when used for cooking food, warming a house, etc. In the wrong hands, fire can be used as a murderous weapon or as an instrument of torture.

It is for this reason that the Ancient Mysteries or initiations were intended to keep the initiatic process, understanding, and knowledge secret. These secrets were given only under very different and solemn oaths. Most of our present knowledge came from initiates who betrayed their oath, often after being converted to Christianity. Clement of Alexandria (chief of the Theological School of Alexandria in the second century CE) wrote: "Not only Pythagoreans and Plato hide most of their dogmas, but the Epicureans confess themselves that they have secrets and they do not allow everybody to handle the books where these teachings are written. On the other hand, following the Stoics, Zenon wrote some treatises which they do not give easily to read to their followers."[3] In the same way, Iamblicus wrote: "The Pythagoreans kept for themselves the most important and the most understandable of their dogmas, forbade giving them to exotericists, and teaching them without writings, as divine Mysteries, to their successors."[4]

These Ancient Mysteries were organized in different schools dedicated to specific divinities. The word *Mysteries* comes from the Latin *mysterium*, and from the Greek *musterion*, meaning in this context "a ritual or a secret doctrine." An initiate who had experienced such mystery was a *mystos*, an "initiate." They constituted the esoteric aspect of rituals and popular beliefs.

It is really only those mysteries that can be called "initiatic groups," like those of Eleusis, Bacchus, Samothrace, etc., that are of interest to us here in the discussion of Freemasonry.

However, Hermetic philosophy is not something radically different from the practice of the mysteries. It is a teaching developed from the Thoth-Hermes revelation and transmitted by the initiates to the mysteries. Mircea Eliade wrote: "Differently than private groups governed by a hierarchic power, initiatic rituals, and progressive revelation of a secret doctrine, Hermeticism, just as alchemy, implicates simply some texts revealed, transmitted, and interpreted by a *master* to a few followers well prepared. [...] You should remember that the revelation contained in the big treatises of the *Corpus Hermeticum*

---

3. Clement of Alexandria, *Stromata*, V, 9.

4. Iamblicus, *Life of Pythagoras*.

constitutes the supreme gnosis, the esoteric science allowing salvation. The simple fact to understand and assimilate is the same to an 'initiation.'"

This idea is very well illustrated by the prayer opening the *Commentary on Plato's Parmenides* by Proclus: "I pray all Gods and Goddesses to guide my mind in this study that I have undertaken—to kindle in me a shining light of truth and enlarge my understanding for the genuine science of being; to open the gates of my soul to receive the inspired guidance of Plato; and in anchoring my thought in the full splendor of reality to hold me back from too much conceit of wisdom and from the paths of error by keeping me in intellectual converse with those realities from which the eye of the soul is refreshed and nourished."[5]

The student should deeply study the texts of the tradition he received as this training is the fruit of a long solitary learning, but it would be wrong to stop there. It is clear that the philosophical study as conceived by Plato following Pythagoras is in direct relation to mystical currents such as Pythagorism and Orphism. It is useless trying to divide these heritages, because the similarity of these doctrines is obvious.

At its beginning, Hermeticism put the emphasis on philosophical study rather than on ritual work. Mystical revelation manifests itself as the result of this inner practice linking meditation and philosophical analysis. The practitioner of this form of asceticism progresses towards the state of contemplating the One, going from phantasms of the material world to the clarity of the world containing the first principles.

It was between the second and sixth centuries CE that this particular form of spirituality was established. Among those who structured this tradition were Plotinus, Iamblicus, Plutarch, Syrianus, Proclus, Damaskios, and others. Initiatic rituals, some separate from Hermeticism, were in harmony and had direct interaction.

From the beginning, this spiritual and mystical path was placed under the protection of Thoth-Hermes, an all-knowing and omnipotent god. The appearance of the founder god of this tradition is the subject of a very symbolic myth, which can be viewed in relation to Dan Brown's *The Lost Symbol*.

In this story of creation, the world originates as one formless primordial ocean, a primitive chaos with only the primordial powers present, represented by four pairs of personified divinities. According to the Egyptian Tradition, every divinity was symbolically represented in both a human and an animal form: the body was human while the gods had a frog's head and the goddesses a snake's head.

---

5. Proclus, *Commentary on Plato's Parmenides I*, trans. by Glenn R. Morrow and John M. Dillon (Princeton University Press).

Then the eight divinities (the divine *ogdoad*[6]) began organizing and balancing each other, bringing order to chaos. A primordial hillock appeared in the center of the sea and a lake was formed on this island.

An ibis (one of the symbolic forms of Thoth) appeared gliding above this shining island, alighting on the top of the hill and laying an egg. The egg cracked and Ra, the Sun-god, appeared in a blazing light. Going up to the sky, the blaze of this first sun illuminated the whole universe.

Then the members of the divine ogdoad appeared in their visible aspect and went to the lake. Performing a magical ritual together, they made a lotus flower from the water. The flower opened in a shining light and gave birth to a female being.

This goddess then rose in the air and united with Ra. Thoth was born from this union, the first divine birth and the founder of the initiatic tradition. For this reason, the ogdoad was sometimes called the "souls of Thoth." It was on this first sacred hillock, center of the world, that the city known by the Greeks as Hermopolis or by the Egyptians as Khemenou ("City of the Eight" or "Eight Cities") was built.

Therefore it was there that the Hermetic (Ogdoadic) Tradition was really born.

Since the most ancient times, Thoth was considered as a lunar god. It is very interesting to see this symbolic relation between Thoth and the appearance of Ra rising out of the ibis' egg. It is undoubtedly for this reason that, as the Moon owes its light to the Sun, Thoth's authority rises from his work as secretary and adviser to his father, Ra. You find this connection to the east in most of the Masonic temples, in representations of both the Sun and the Moon.

It was Thoth who brought language and science to men. Thoth governed worship in the temples, sacred rituals, as well as the texts that composed them. Esoteric wisdom was his attribution.

With Isis, he represents the magical aspect of rituals and practices. The invisible action of symbols used in rituals was taught by Thoth and it was he who taught Isis the magical formulas that allowed her to revive her husband Osiris.

Knowing the possible relationship between the Isis-Osiris story and Hiram's myth, we can see how the action of Thoth can be hidden behind the resurrections of the deity and Master Hiram. It is Thoth who plays an important function in life after death, where he is

---

6. A group of eight. This number of 4 + 4 is a symbol you can find as a footprint or signature throughout the story of the Tradition.

at the same time psychopomp and judge of the dead. As possessor of secret formulas of resurrection, Thoth is the one who allows the transition from life to death and from death to life.

As you may know, it is the word, written or pronounced, that contains the divine power that is creative in itself. The central position of the secret (and lost) word in Freemasonry comes directly from this origin. Progressively, Thoth will be connected to the god Hermes, giving birth to the figure of Hermes-Trismegistus under the aegis of whom this tradition was perpetuated.

One of the main intentions of the Hermetic initiation was to restore unity, putting humans back into their ordained function as mediator between the material world and the divine. The vocation of Thoth-Hermes is therefore to assist humanity in this work, which Freemasonry synthesizes into this sentence: unite what is scattered. From multiplicity and chaos, the goal is to recreate a unity of order and harmony, which has been lost to us both inwardly and outwardly.

One of the important consequences of this Hermetic doctrine is the refusal to divide knowledge into different parts. Hermes leads the initiates toward unification of opposites with the ability to exchange one's own perspective for that of another, thus welcoming the difference between people in respect of their essence. Hermeticism is the intuition of this unity in every initiate's action. But, at the same time, Hermetists know that it is impossible to have a real definition of the divine. The initiate knows that exclusion and dogma are opposite to this balanced path to unity.

It is for this reason that Hermeticism is so modern today and so important despite its ancient origin. It is this Hermetic ideal, reflected in the principles developed in eighteenth-century Europe as the "Philosophy of the Lights," that Freemasonry and the Founding Fathers of the United States understood, transmitted, and accomplished in the constitutional birthing of the nation.

THE PROPHECY

Hermetic, Egyptian, Greek, and Roman schools of the mysteries were developed during antiquity with the Egyptian city of Alexandria as their intellectual and spiritual center. This book is not the place to recount the entire extraordinary history and destiny of this city. However, its spiritual and initiatic schools, as well as its famous library, remain undying landmarks for Hermeticism and the mysteries.

The deities of fate are always very efficient in their creation of fortuitous symbolic chance occurrences, which I would name *synchronistic*. The coherence of a group of symbols is traditionally seen as the manifestation of such synchronism. The same is true, as you will see, with some very significant names of United States cities.

The city of Alexandria, Virginia, first known as Belhaven, was named in honor of John Alexander, who in the late seventeenth century bought from Robert Howison the land on which the city now stands. The first settlement was made in 1695, and Alexandria was laid out in 1749 and incorporated in 1779. This place was not chosen by chance, because Shuter's Hill[7] was the very spot once proposed by Thomas Jefferson as the ideal site for the nation's capitsl. Shuter's Hill was also the actual site in Alexandria, Virginia, for the Masonic memorial to President George Washington built in the shape of the Alexandria, Egypt lighthouse.

In fact, the Capitol was constructed more to the north and was included in the symbolic Mall of Washington. However, such a symbol could not remain without symbolic meaning. Chance acted once again, and it was on February 22, 1910, that a meeting was organized at the Alexandria-Washington Lodge for the purpose of forming an association to plan and build a suitable memorial to President George Washington, the Freemason. The representatives of the twenty-six U.S. Grand Lodges approved the erection of the memorial and formed the George Washington Masonic National Memorial Association. Ten years later, the concept of the colossal building was approved.

The site selected was located on land with which General Washington was familiar and gives a prominent place for a symbolic building. As you can read in *The Lost Symbol*, the Masonic memorial to George Washington was built to symbolize the intellectual ascent of humanity, from the most basic to the most complex, in its choice of Greek columns and architecture, and was directly inspired by the Pharos lighthouse in Egypt's Alexandria.

Uniting both cultures of the past, this monument also included some elements of the Parthenon's architecture.[8] The inside of this building contains temples, meeting rooms, and, of course, a rich library.

On the website of the George Washington Masonic National Memorial you can read that "George Washington did not ascend into greatness simply by his intellect, but

---

7. This hill was named after an early Alexandria resident named Shuter.

8. The Parthenon is the well-known temple built on the Acropolis in Athens, Greece. A perfect replica of this sacred building can be visited in Nashville, Tennessee. It is another manifestation of the Tradition on United States soil.

through his deep morality, his profound spirituality and devotion to country."[9] These are the real Masonic virtues that were always linked to the expression of *Religio Mentis*, manifesting the Hermetic spirit.

This building was very well designed to represent and manifest this Alexandrian ideal. Of course, it is the memorial of a famous man, but it is well known that tradition is always composed by leaders who put values and heritage above their own needs and desires. They are modest before the responsibility placed upon them. George Washington did not seek to be the first president, but his friends urged him to accept the position and his feelings of duty and loyalty to the work still to be undertaken encouraged him to accept this historic role.

This broad acceptance of morality was always very important in the Hermetic Tradition and in Freemasonry. This search for virtue and its personal necessity in rising toward the divine, cultivating the most sacred values, was present at all times. This moral demonstration of fidelity regarding responsibility placed upon the individual and the collective consequences is one of the pillars of Freemasonry. One aspect of the founder myths that best explains this principle is the figure of the widow. She appears several times in Hiram's myth, as well as in Isis' myth. Hiram is called in the Bible "a widow's son of the tribe of Naphatali."[10]

In *The Lost Symbol*, we can see this aspect of the widow myth, although it less used in the English-speaking countries. In other countries, we can quite literally hear these famous words when a Mason is looking for some help: "Is there no help for the widow's son?"

Later in the novel, this subject is directly connected to one of Freemasonry's origin myths, Hiram's murder.

The first Freemasons, called the Adonhiramite Masons, tell the story that they looked after the mother of Hiram after the death of their master. Being all brothers, they were naturally called "the widow's sons." Today, Freemasons refer to themselves as "widow's sons" because they are the descendants of this first mythical brotherhood. This expression became in some countries a synonym for the Freemasons. The widow's story is seen in Masonic art containing death's symbolism. It was also the basis for the

---

9. http://www.gwmemorial.org/
10. 1 Kings 7:14.

casual clothing of the Freemasons that can be seen during some meetings, which emphasizes sobriety and seriousness.

Next, I can reveal a little more of this story and go back to a source almost forgotten. As usual, it is clear that this expression is symbolic and hides another reality. It is interesting to explain who really the widow is. She may be only a symbol illustrating the necessity of collective moral requirements to build a better man and society. But at the same time, she is a memory of a more ancient teaching from a tradition that was veiled in order to be perpetuated. It is a familiar phenomenon among initiatic traditions and one should not be surprised to find it here.

Before the light of Freemasonry could shine in the world and participate in the founding of the United States, the light of the original tradition, just born in Alexandria, Virginia, had to increase. There were signs pointing out that the ancient land of initiation would see important events that would change forever the nature of the relationship between the spiritual and the divine world. Among the sacred Hermetic texts there is a book, of which only the Latin translation was saved. The title is the *Asclepius*. It contains valuable teachings on cosmology, the essence of God, destiny, cycles of the world and life, theurgy, etc. In the ninth part of this book, we can read an amazing prophecy linked to a beautiful explanation of the way Egypt was considered by the initiates.

Trismegistus said:

Dost thou not know, Asclepius, that Egypt is the image of Heaven; or, what is truer still, the transference, or the descent, of all that are in governance or exercise in Heaven? And if more truly [still] it must be said—this land of ours is Shrine of all the World.

. . . The time will come when Egypt will appear to have in vain served the Divinity with pious mind and constant worship and all its holy cult will fall to nothingness and be in vain.

For that Divinity is now about to hasten back from Earth to Heaven, and Egypt shall be left; and Earth, which was the seat of pious cults, shall be bereft and widowed of the presence of the Gods.[11]

---

11. In Latin we find the same meaning: "*E terris enim et ad caelum recursura diuinitas linqueturque Aegyptus terraque, sedes religionum quae fuit, <u>uiduata</u> numinum praesentia destituetur.*"

And foreigners shall fill this region and this land; and there shall be not only the neglect of pious cults, but—what is still more painful—as though enacted by the laws, a penalty shall be decreed against the practice of [our] pious cults and worship of the Gods—[complete] proscription of them.[12]

. . . For Darkness will be set before the Light, and Death will be thought preferable to Life. No one will raise his eyes to Heaven; the pious man will be considered mad, the impious a sage; the frenzied held as strong, the worst as best."[13]

Beyond its prophetic dimension, this important text reveals different keys that can shed more light on the sacred mysteries and the initiates, for the initiates were the authors of this text.

Here we discover a very interesting idea: the earth (as the temple) can be the representation of heaven, the spiritual world. Egypt was considered in that way and temples were built in precise and symbolic places in order to help the manifestation of invisible divine powers. Gods and goddesses welcomed every day in temples represented the presence of heaven in the world. As the above quotation says, "This land of ours is Shrine of all the World." Once again this is the manifestation of the powerful Hermetic motto quoted again and again: "As above, so below."

The Lord's Prayer says: "On earth as it is in heaven . . ."

"As above, so below." This well-known sentence takes on a new and very interesting aspect. The microcosm is the temple. The macrocosm can be the earth itself. As below, so above. This is what the Egyptians wanted to do with their sacred land. The process is the same for the temple and for the initiate's body, which is also a temple. The divine power is invoked in order to be manifested.

But the prophecy tells of a time when this close relationship between heaven and earth would be interrupted. The gods would leave the earth and go back to the sky. And so the earth became widowed of the gods. The intimate relationship that joined them and which allowed this descent of the divine and the rise of the soul was lost. The earth was widowed of the benevolent and constant presence of the divine. The prophetic message was given, but the only ones who fully realized its importance and decided to perpetuate this teaching were the Hermetists, from whence came the Freemasons,

---

12. *The Perfect Sermon, or the Asclepius*, trans. by G. R. S. Mead. Part 9:24.

13. *The Perfect Sermon, or the Asclepius*, trans. by G. R. S. Mead. Part 9:25-2.

the widow's sons. They are really the sons of the earth, which became widowed by the disappearance of the gods, and without the gods' divine presence became unbalanced, a condition that still continues today. It is also the earth that constitutes our own physical bodies and which lost vision of the inner presence of the divine, as we are reminded by the Hermetic motto just quoted, and by the alchemical injunction of the Chamber of Reflection, VITRIOL (a Latin acronym for "Visit the interior of the earth and rectifying [i.e., purifying] you will find the hidden stone").

The second part of the prophecy describes the appearance of a power that will forbid practices, worship, studies, etc., on which was based until then this balance between sky and earth. It uses expressions that are today common in the Masonic language, "Darkness will be set before the light, and death will be thought preferable to life." Facing the start of these religious restrictions, the initiates wisely chose to keep this tradition of living mysteries alive under a thick veil so it could continue to live on but in secret.

The Dark Days and the Secret Chain of Initiates

THE DARK DAYS

Around the third century, Christianity, until then a simple religious group, began to constitute a substantially greater political power. In the year 356, Constance II, successor to Constantine, forbade the celebration of traditional rituals and of all kinds of prophesying. He ordered the closing of temples; the confiscation of the personal belongings of people called "pagans" (peasants); and proscribed worship of the traditional divinities. The prophecy began to happen.

In the fourth century CE, despite the efforts of the Emperor Julian to restore religious tolerance and equality of worship, it was not possible to restore what had been broken. The light of Alexandria began to disappear. Emperor Julian was assassinated on June 26, 363, and I can say that his death put an end to the ancient world. After this, political and religious powers tried to eliminate by every possible means the respectable old traditions. The simple possession of books, and more so of religious treatises and written rituals, became punishable by death. Even today there are many examples of religious groups working in the same way. Some followers fearfully burnt their libraries. This loss was absolutely disastrous for the Western world. Fortunately, some of them could not resign themselves to it and hid some of their documents. This was also true for some followers of the Hermetic Tradition. Some tried to hide their books in tombs, while others put them in jars buried in caves.

Some of these hiding places have been found in modern times close to the ancient city of Thebes. The hiding place in which were found most manuscripts close to the Hermetic gnosis is now famous: Nag Hammadi. Another hiding place was discovered in Thebes and contained principally magical and alchemical papyri.

The philosophical Neoplatonic and Hermetic schools continued to be specifically attacked and persecuted. In 380 CE, Emperor Theodose ordained the complete destruction of all ancient traditions as well as their practice, even in private life. In 529, the Neoplatonic academy of Athens was closed by the authorities, and in 550 the last sanctuary of Isis, the temple of Philae, was forced to close its doors. All creative endeavors were censored (books, art, etc.), religious or philosophical meetings were prohibited, and several initiates, both women and men, were incarcerated, tortured, and killed.

This confusion between the spiritual and the temporal gave birth to excesses and the desire for absolute power. So the logical consequence was the loss of religious and philosophical freedom and a totalitarian power appeared, which continued for more than a thousand years. The Roman Catholic empire reigned supreme.

Secrecy, an integral part of the initiatic process, then became a necessity, allowing the protection of the initiatic tradition. It was necessary to keep the teachings alive and to transmit them to trusty followers. As stated in *The Lost Symbol*, the initiated began to form brotherhoods and fraternities, designed to share and pass along the Ancient Mysteries in safety as the authorities strove to extinguish the light.

And so the darkness increased during the next centuries, lasting the whole of the Middle Ages. Any form of wisdom other than that of the rulership was considered dangerous, and so was hunted down and eliminated. Of course, it was the same for all forms of traditional initiations, divination, or theurgy. Fortunately, the inheritance had been veiled and it survived through the centuries. This secret tradition perpetuating the mysteries did not have specific name. It included the followers of the initiatic school transmitting the traditional knowledge and was sometimes called the *Aurea Catena* ("golden chain") of initiates.

This "golden chain" became the heart of Hermeticism. It is this chain that allows contemporary Freemasonry to continue to receive the powerful beneficent influence of its founders. This invisible and indivisible familial link between the initiates had constituted, for the first centuries, a powerful chain, which Freemasons later physically made a symbol of this concept and wear as an emblem of their brotherhood. You will find it on every officer of a Masonic lodge in the collar that he wears around his neck. You also find it on the walls all around some Masonic temples, delimiting the sacred place. This cord oftentimes has special knots called "lakes of love." Freemasons also use the symbol of the chain when they sometimes create a "chain" at the end of a ceremony, holding each other by the hands. The French Freemasons call it a "union chain." It symbolizes this indefectible fraternity and the link of the adepts that travels through the ages until today.

The symbol of the gold chain may have been first mentioned in the eighth song of Homer's *Iliad*. Zeus, presenting himself as the most powerful of the gods, says: "Gods, try me and find out for your selves. Hang for me a golden chain from heaven, and lay hold of it all of you, gods and goddesses together—tug as you will, you will not drag Jove the supreme counselor from heaven to earth; but were I to pull at it myself I should draw you up with earth and sea into the bargain, then would I bind the chain about some pinnacle of Olympus and leave you all dangling in the mid firmament. So far am I above all others either of gods or men."[14]

This text will be the subject of several interpretations and become "the chain which links the initiates of the same Hermetic revelation as the various worlds or the different states of matter in alchemy. It is only the symbolic representation of the whole Hermetic Art and the functions of the Magus."[15] Jean-Baptiste Porta,[16] in his book on natural magick, wrote: "[The gold chain] is a cord stretched from the first cause to the infinite things, by a reciprocal and uninterrupted link: so that the upper virtue shines from this point, and if we touch a part of it, we will be affected and will move all things." Here this symbol linking the initiates goes much further and veils a philosophical doctrine in which man is the central point of creation and receives the impulses of divine wisdom. This gold cord constitutes the link that divine providence uses to weave the rug of human destiny, creating continuity between macrocosm and microcosm, between gods and men. But above all, it continues to represent the link of unfailing brotherhood that joins those who chose to transmit the light of initiation, keeping undamaged the flame

---

14. Homer, the *Iliad*, Book 8, trans. by Samuel Butler.

15. Françoise Bonardel, *L'hermétisme*.

16. Jean-Baptiste Porta, of Naples, is famous for his book about physiognomy written in 1586. At the age of fifteen, he wrote three books about Natural Magick, printed in 1563.

of wisdom and knowledge across the centuries of obstruction. This transmission took the form of a secret society of mysteries, which I will describe when I speak about symbolic principles and rituals.

However, even though the followers were hidden, this does not mean they did not have influence in the following centuries. On the contrary, their presence was constant and they often influenced ideas and symbolic art of their time, going as far as political and religious oppression allowed. Recruiting new candidates with caution, they perpetuated the sacred rituals, keeping as the most precious treasures the doctrines and Hermetic practices, allowing humanity to again discover its true nature and origin, making man capable of undertaking what was called, in the words of the hymn to all gods by Proclus, the "sacred way of return."

SYMBOLS OF THE MYSTERIES

Dan Brown's *The Lost Symbol* mentions that, surprisingly, keys were used throughout the centuries as markers indicating the presence of the Tradition: keys such as allegory, symbols, and myth. You saw the importance of myths and the main role they play in the allegorical transmission of esoteric and mystical doctrine. They also play an important part in the ritual use of symbols. But other markers were used by the initiates like footprints to show their presence. It's in art and architecture that these symbols are undoubtedly even more visible and therefore paradoxically even less recognized as such. It is well known that to hide a secret in a very efficient way it is necessary to put it in the most visible place. We find it in the story of the gods trying to hide the secret of the humanity, deciding to put it where one would lastly go to search: hidden in the depths of the human being.

It was the same here, and arts were one of the ways chosen by the Tradition. Naturally, to be real and vital symbols, it is necessary that they are consistent and coherent, and they have to relate to the same doctrine that can be interpreted from them. It is absolutely appropriate for Freemasonry that architecture was a means of transmission. I have already mentioned some of the symbols that were used to point out and even to demonstrate their power and meaning in the spiritual and invisible plan. This is the case of the pyramid, the triangle, the four directions, and some particular numbers.

In *The Lost Symbol*, where Freemasonry is central to the novel's theme, it is natural that we find several references to numbers considered to be symbolic. Among these numbers, the number 8 is very important to understanding the novel. It's a prime example showing how a novelist can intuitively perceive the importance of a symbol even though the number 8 is not emphasized in Freemasonry. This number is used several times in the novel, and Eight Franklin Square is presented as a clue.

The Western Tradition came from Chaldea, and the Masonic founder myth showed us that the first human construction was the Tower of Babel. It was the predecessor of the pyramid, the temple tower of the ancient Assyrians and Babylonians, having the form of a terraced pyramid called the ziggurat. The etymology of this word's roots is in the Assyrian words *ziqquratu* ("height, pinnacle") and *zaqaru* ("to be high"). This origin is very interesting at many levels. The design shows a representation of an eight-pointed star. You can find it above the symbol of Ishtar and in some coins of King Mausolus (fourth century BCE).

The eight-pointed star was found on a seal in the ruins of the ancient city of Ur (2000 BCE). Some pieces of black marble were found, showing this star very closely resembling the interlaced star of eight points. Excavations from Ur reveal early use of the eight-pointed star, often in the form of an eight-petal rosette used in gold jewelry. The Sumerians used an arrangement of lines as a symbol for both *star* and *god*. The linear eight-pointed star represented the goddess Inanna, Sumerian queen of the heavens, and Ishtar (Astarte), the Babylonian goddess known as "the Lightbringer." An eight-pointed star enclosed within a circle was the symbol for the Sun god.

Freemasonry's early roots in the Hermetic Tradition are shown in a very rare representation found on some ritual Masonic glasses called "cannon," from their use in the ritual Masonic banquet.[17] On these cannons, an eight-pointed star appears at the top of a ziggurat. On both sides you can see the Moon and the Sun in triangles. Historians have doubts regarding this representation, but

Figure 16: Representation of the eight-pointed star and the ziggurat from the Aurum Solis tradition

---

17. These glasses have a massive stem to give the possibility to hurt the table and create a loud noise called "battery." This sound acts as an element of the ritual.

the identification is very clear if you connect it to the Hermetic tradition. Albert Pike understood this and wrote in *Morals and Dogma*: "We learn this from Celsus, in Origen, who says that the symbolic image of this passage among the stars, used in the Mythraic Mysteries, was a ladder reaching from earth to Heaven, divided into seven steps or stages, to each of which was a gate, and at the summit an eighth one, that of the fixed stars. The symbol was the same as that of the seven stages of Borsippa, the Pyramid of vitrified brick, near Babylon, built of seven stages, and each of a different color."

Of course, this civilization (followed by the Egyptians) is well known for the use of astronomy and astrology connected to architectural principles. The eight lines are symbolic of the four corners of space (north, south, east, and west) and time (two solstices and two equinoxes). So the double square is a perfect illustration and connection with this early representation of the eight directions.

In Greece, this representation was connected to the eight divinities of the winds. It was the same in Rome with the utilization of the double square.

The latter is also a symbol that can be found in Greece and later in Italy. A relationship is created between the pyramid (possibly a stair-pyramid), the number 8, and the first mythical buildings rising to the sky, built by the most ancient Freemasons. But this surprising connection does not stop there, because I am going to prove that it was a constant indication of the presence of one of the most ancient traditions: Hermeticism, which permeates Freemasonry.

Figure 17: Main symbol of the Ogdoadic Tradition today called "Aurum Solis"

The myth of Hermopolis shows the creation made by four couples of divinities. Egypt gives us several examples of this division of the number 8 into two by four. This number represents a balanced group. The architects of ancient Egypt knew the use of the four cardinal points. Inner organs withdrawn for the embalming process were protected by four "Horus' sons," themselves protected by four goddesses. Sarcophagi texts explain that Shu created eight infinite beings to help him to support the body of Nut. The Egyptian tradition also gives us the star of eight points. But considering this number 4, it is going to be linked to 8 by the natural doubling of the square, moving by a rotation of 45 degrees. This symbol often appears in the history of the

Western Tradition and it is interesting to see how it combines with and follows from the eight-pointed star.

Another important symbolic aspect of the number 8 is an interlaced star. This very ancient star can be seen in famous Roman mosaics such as that of Demeter in Villa Roman del Casale near Piazza Armenia, Sicily, in 320 BCE. This symbol is also found in the Coptic Tradition, which directly follows the ancient Egyptians.

Hebrew esotericism is an important part of the Western Tradition and has often been associated with Freemasonry throughout its history. In one of the most famous Qabalist books, the *Sepher Yetzirah,* the numbers are associated with the ten spheres of the Tree of life called Sephiroth, and to the planets. So Malkuth corresponds to Tellus (Planet Earth), Yesod to the Moon, Hod to Mercury, Netzach to Venus, Tiphareth to the Sun, Geburah to Mars, Chesed to Jupiter, Binah to Saturn, Chokmah to the sphere of Fixed Stars, and Keter to the Spiral Nebula.

If we consider this succession of spheres from the bottom (closest to Earth) Moon, the representation comes from Chaldean astrology, which puts the Sun in the center, the first planet being the Moon, and the highest of the seven traditional planets is Saturn. Beyond that, the eighth sphere is the Ogdoad, the zodiacal sphere.

In one of the Hermetic manuscripts discovered in Nag Hammadi, Egypt, it is said that the revelation of Hermes must be kept in a secret place protected by eight guards. Further along in this old text, we read: "Rather, by stages he advances and enters into the way of immortality. And thus he enters into the understanding of the eighth that reveals the ninth."[18] Considering now the succession of Sephiroth in a descending movement, which in the Qabalah is the descent of the divine power, the eighth sphere is that of Mercury, Hermes. Esoteric tradition attributed a magical square to each of the planets and so to every Sephirah. The eighth sphere is Mercury and corresponds to the kamea 8 x 8, and so to the "square order 8." Dan Brown's novel is right to focus on this number.

The number 8 is the manifestation of the Ogdoad of the ancient Hermetists is in the same time the number of Hermes in the Qabalah. It is also interesting to say that the eighth sphere in the ascending path is the zodiacal one that moves on the fixed stars sphere. Albert Pike, the reformer of the Scottish Rite Southern Jurisdiction (United States), explained these ideas in a paragraph of his most important book, *Morals and Dogma:*

---

18. *The Discourse on the Eighth and Ninth,* trans. by James Brashler, Peter A. Dirkse, and Douglas M. Parrott.

The number 8, or the octary, is composed of the sacred numbers 3 and 5. Of the heavens, of the seven planets, and of the sphere of the fixed stars, or of the eternal unity and the mysterious number 7, is composed the Ogdoade, the number 8, the first cube of equal numbers, regarded as sacred in the arithmetical philosophy.

The Gnostic Ogdoade had eight stars, which represented:

the eight Cabiri of Samothrace,

the eight Egyptian and Phoenician principles,

the eight gods of Xenocrates,

the eight angles of the cubic stone.

The number eight symbolizes perfection: and its figure, 8 or ∞, indicates the perpetual and regular course of the Universe.

One can find this symbolism of the seven planets and the twelve zodiacal signs in the Mythraic Tradition. Two Mithraeums show it very well, one in Doura Eutropos, Syria, and the other one in Ostia, Italy. Again Albert Pike describes this number symbolism, saying:

[T]he Mithraic ladder was really a pyramid with seven stages, each provided with a narrow door or aperture, through each of which doors the aspirant passed, to reach the summit, and then descended through similar doors on the opposite side of the pyramid; the ascent and descent of the Soul being thus represented.

Each Mithraic cave and all the most ancient temples were intended to symbolize the Universe, which itself was habitually called the Temple and was the habitation of Deity. Every temple was the world in miniature; and so the whole world was one grand temple. The most ancient temples were roofless. . . . All temples were surrounded by pillars, recording the number of the constellations, the signs of the zodiac, or the cycles of the planets; and each one was a microcosm or symbol of the Universe, having for its roof or ceiling the starred vault of Heaven.

All temples were originally open at the top, having for their roof the sky. Twelve pillars described the belt of the zodiac.[19]

---

19. Albert Pike, *Morals and Dogma*.

The starry arch that you see in the Egyptian, Isiac, and Mithraic temples, and in some Christian churches, represents this Ogdoadic sphere as the border of the spiritual world between the visible planets and the divine space where can be found the One, the Grand Architect of the Universe of Freemasonry. This representation of the zodiac can be found in many places throughout history. One of the most famous is in the temple of Denderah, Egypt. The representation of zodiacs is significant for two reasons: (1) it indicates a specific moment useful to understand the purpose of the builders; and (2) it can have an effect on the place itself, like a real talisman increasing the power of the planetary group.

It is an importing element found in various Washington buildings. Today, one might think that a zodiac is a simple representation of the celestial world, but it was different in the past. Stars wer considered to be divine powers and the manifestation of their special function was very real. A representation of the zodiac in a sacred space is therefore an invocation of divine power. It is a way to keep alive the divinities' memory and influence in a world that lost its belief in and understanding of its relationship with them. But during this period, during which the darkness of obscurantism reigned over the known world, the sacred tradition was perpetuated and was soon to reemerge in the Renaissance, in Italy.

From Renaissance to the New World
Florence, Rebirth of the Light

The Tradition was veiled during the Middle Ages but it did not totally disappear. Most people were no longer aware of the ancient wisdom or other beliefs. Christianity imposed its unilateral vision of the world, abolishing all the scientific and medical knowledge that had existed previously. Under Christianity's literal interpretation of Biblical texts, other theories or practices contrary to the official texts or dogmas were not tolerated. It was the same on the intellectual level because only monks and theologians were authorized to study other subjects. There was no role for rational thought, for the mind always had to be in the service of faith and its only use was to prove the truth of the revealed writings. Independent thinking was dangerous because it could lead to awareness of contradictions to the literal interpretation of scripture.

But not everyone had forgotten the ancient traditions. Many in rural areas still practiced magick, used traditional medicines and herbal remedies, and followed customs linked to the old celebrations. The church was aware of this and opted to include what could not be erased, as was the case with the date of December 25, the celebration of Sol Invictus, birth of Mithra, which became Christmas. The death sentence was often the answer of the church to men and especially women who continued to obscure the old ways.

But the gold chain of the initiates transmitting secret knowledge and rituals that had been given to them in the sixth century had not disappeared. The light of the ancient philosophy of mysteries was always alive. It is very plausible that the Grand Master in the fifteenth century was a Greek scholar, Giorgios Gemistos Pletho. This remarkable man had gathered a group of followers in the city of Mistra who secretly practiced the ancient traditional rituals. Hermetic and Neoplatonic teachings were preserved and transmitted in the traditional way. Publicly Christian, Pletho as a scholar and theologian was regularly consulted on important points.

At that time, the Christian church was divided in two groups, the Western Church (Catholic) and Eastern Church (Orthodox). Both groups were looking for a common position in order to find a solution to their conflicts. Come of Medicis, chief of Florence,[20] in 1439 called together a council to resolve the conflict. Among the Greeks invited was eighty-five-year-old Pletho. Knowing Christian tradition as well as Greek, he was capable of breaking through the theological subtleties in which the Christian theologians had locked themselves. But his real goal had nothing to do with that of the council. As leader of this Neoplatonic school, he sought to secure the resurgence and continuity of the ancient Hermetic and Ogdoadic Traditions. Deeply Platonic, he transmitted a vision renewed by Hellenism, purified by Neoplatonism, and able to avoid moral and spiritual decline.

During his stay in Florence, Pletho was regularly received by Come of Medicis. He managed many philosophical debates outside the council. At the instigation of Come, he opened a school, dividing the students into Exoteric (those who were linked to Christian doctrine and could not accept the totality of the teachings) and Esoteric (those who were initiated to the teaching of emanations and to complete Hermetic knowledge).

---

20. A famous Italian city in the Tuscany area.

This school included practices, rituals, initiations, and philosophical teaching. Plato's Academy, closed for centuries, could come back to life.

Pletho's school continued its activities secretly until some years later, and in 1459, Marsilio Ficino, son of the personal doctor of Come, founded the first new Platonic Academy. The headquarters was the Villa Careggi, near Florence. For many years, the intellectual elite and the best artists met, lived, and worked there. It was a real nondenominational monastery opened to all talented men without discrimination of religion. Texts missing or hidden until then were translated and published. The *Corpus* of Hermes, the *Chaldaic Oracles*, Plato's writings, and several other sacred writings were once again revealed.

The academicians dedicated themselves to the search for truth and studied in an atmosphere of complete freedom. Their only obligation was to respect the freedom of others. To be accepted, the "Brethren in Plato," members of the academy, must above all be good, honest, and have the desire to cultivate the best in humanity. As Ficino wrote: "Friendship is the Union of will and desires. The academicians' brothers must have the same purpose. If this goal is wealth, honors and pure science, there cannot be friendship, because these purposes cause on the contrary jealousy, vainglory, desire and hate. True friendship is possible only between brothers who search for the good together."[21]

You can imagine this sentence as a moral statement of Freemasonry and its real origin.

The brothers worked nonstop to awaken the Hermetic Tradition from the Neoplatonic philosophers and, through them, all of Ptolemaic Egypt. They gave new life to the gold chain into which they all had just been introduced. Besides Marsilio Ficino, the founder of the academy, Pico della Mirandola, Fortuna, Giovani Cavalcanti, Alessandro de Rinaldo Braccesi, and, of course, Come of Medicis himself, were the first and the most renowned of the academicians. Campanella, Giordano Bruno, Dante, and others were also connected to this fraternity.

These ancient sacred mysteries were composed of aspects that I can summarize in two parts:

1. The symbolic and philosophical part

2. The theurgic and religious part

These two parts further involved moral, ritual, mystical, and epicurean dimensions. This school remained complete for almost three centuries, but was progressively divided

---

21. Marsile Ficin, *Opera Omnia*, vol. 1.

into these two parts. The first part would give birth to Freemasonry and the second to Hermetic theurgic orders.[22] It was quite common for the initiates and chiefs of these schools to stay connected. Their shared history and use of philosophy and rituals are important to the study of this book.

During the centuries that began with the Renaissance (in the fifteenth century), they continued to restore the forgotten values of freedom, awareness, and development of science. Giordano Bruno was the last to be burnt by the Catholic Church for his ideas, but this work discreetly continued. The Christian Qabalah sometimes clothed the initiates' studies, but their writings show us that there was no barrier between the ancient and biblical myths. Among the initiates were artists, architects, writers, etc. Desiring to manifest their tradition, their creations revealed, through codes and symbols, the presence of this heritage. We can see this in drawings, paintings, sculptures, and architecture. The Freemasonry created by these initiates incorporated such codes, accurately showing its true origin. It was these Renaissance initiates who started to build the New World, which America would bring into reality some centuries later.

The Symbolic Architecture

It is impossible to study here all the symbolic aspects of the Hermetic Tradition manifested during the Renaissance that continue to have an effect today, so I will examine only the symbols pertinent to this study of the Masonic Tradition that you can find again and again in the symbolic architecture of Washington DC.

The number 8 is related to a very important architectural form, the octagon. Religious and symbolic buildings have incorporated this octagonal pattern throughout history. It is not possible to identify the first buildings to be constructed according this octagonal layout, but they were immediately connected to the symbolism of this number.

In Athens, the Tower of the Winds, also called a *horologion* ("timepiece"), is an octagonal Pentelic marble clock tower; it stands over twelve meters high and eight meters square on the Roman agora in Athens. It was built by Andronicos, from Kyrrhos (in Macedonia) around 50 BCE or even earlier, and before the rest of the forum. At the top of each of the eight sides, there is a relief representation of a wind, symbolized by a male figure with the appropriate attributes and its name inscribed on the stone. All align ex-

---

22. The Order of Aurum Solis is undoubtedly one of the very few survivors (http://www.aurumsolis.info) of this second way.

actly to the compass, and above each figure the names of the eight winds were written in large Greek letters.

The earliest baptisteries were copied from the ancient *thermæ*, or baths, with a font in the center, allowing room for the baptism candidates, as well as for spectators. The font, like the building, was octagonal. In Italy there are several examples of octagonal baptisteries. The ones in Milan and Ravenna are from the fifth century and have the same symbolic shape. Christians connected very early specific symbolism to the number 8 as the number of regeneration, just as baptism signaled redemption in Christ. Jesus rose from the dead on the eighth day of the Passion and the world began on the eighth day after Creation. The symbolism used by Christianity is very close to the seven planets followed by the eighth sphere. The number 8 is a real state of consciousness symbolized by a veil opening onto an upper world.

If we look carefully at the octagonal layout of the baptistery, we can see that it is connected to a Templar Cross Patee (four spear-headed arms symbolizing solar light),

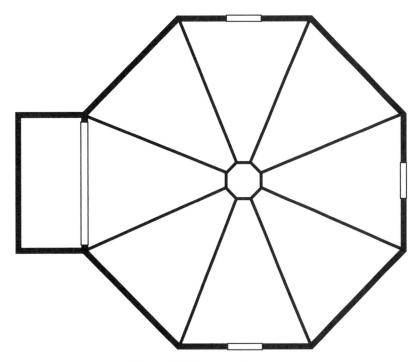

Figure 18: Florence's Baptistery

which can be easily formed within the confines of the octagon. This special cross is also connected to the Rose-Cross Tradition. Historians said that this octagonal shape came from the construction of the Dome of the Rock in Jerusalem[23] at the top of the rock where Solomon's Temple was built. This place remains a model for all Templar masons. In the Middle Ages, Christians and Muslims believed that the Dome of the Rock was the Temple of Solomon. The Templars incorporated this octagonal shape in building their churches, as for example in Tomar, Portugal and its octagonal chapel called the *chorola*. This shape became the standard for Templar buildings. A typical design is an octagon within a circle, eight arches within a round circle. Firstly, its eight walls formed a superior edifice of structural stability; secondly, it called to mind the overall shape of the Templar Cross Patee; and finally, the octagon, especially when combined within the circle, formed a sacred geometry that reminds us of the ancient Hermetic text allowing the passage from the Eighth to the Ninth (the circle). The octagonal shapes usually represent the link between God (the circle is a symbol of eternity) and Earth (the square). This symbol can also be found in Christianity as the eight-pointed star that guided the magi toward Bethlehem, mythical birthplace of Christ. A splendid mosaic of Ravenna, Italy shows it very well.

Many writings showed this mythical relationship between Templars and Freemasonry, and especially the Scottish Rite. Many degrees speak of this filiation and involve this brotherhood. Myths and rituals follow from it, as you will see in the practical part of this. This octagonal shape persisted throughout the Middle Ages because of this important symbolic number.

Florence was the center where these Ancient Mysteries were reactivated. Various buildings of the city reveal this symbolic architecture. Undoubtedly the most significant is the cathedral of the city, Il Duomo. This religious place is composed of two buildings: the first is the cathedral itself and its famous octagonal dome; the second is the baptistery close to the cathedral. The Baptistery of San Giovanni was built with marble from a temple of Mars and remains from an Etruscan city of this area, Fesiole. The baptistery has a wonderful octagonal shape built according to the tradition. It is one of the oldest astronomical places in the city of Florence and is a *gnomon*, which demonstrates the apparent motion of the Sun. Through a hole in the dome, solar radiation lights the signs of the zodiac engraved on marble, thus tracing the path of the Sun during the year. At

23. The Dome of the Rock is the oldest Islamic monument, built from 688 to 691 CE.

the summer solstice, the Sun lights its representation in the center of the zodiac. Late in the thirteenth century, following a reconstruction of the floor, the marble was moved to the eastern part of the baptistery where today it is no longer possible to assess its accuracy. The body of the astrologer reposes beneath the pavement of the baptistery, where the spot is marked by a slab with the signs of the zodiac.

It is interesting to point out that the representation on the floor puts the Sun in the center of the zodiac (and not Earth). So this representation is heliocentric, the theory so violently fought by the Church, which remained faithful to the geocentric text of the Bible. The Sun is surrounded with a cryptic sentence: "*In giro torte sol ciclos et rotor igne.*" It is a mixture of old Italian and Latin that translates as, "I am the Sun, I am this wheel moved by fire, which twisting moves the spheres." The sentence emphasizes the importance given to the solar star.

In adition to its octagonal architecture, this baptistery contains other representations painted on the walls, which were not much studied until recently. I cannot describe them, but it is interesting to see the important group of double squares interlaced, which as we discussed are associated with the number 8. This whole place was built in order to illustrate the symbolic and mystical power of the number 8.

Florence emphasizes this close relation to Hermeticism through the number 8. The circular dome of the cathedral (one of the biggest in the world) was built on an octagonal base. The Medicis' mausoleum was built with the same layout.

During the Renaissance, in Germany, Albrecht Dürer was a prolific artist. Among other professions, he was a philosopher, an alchemist, and a student of the mystery traditions—the epitomy of the Renaissance man. Dürer, and the Renaissance in general, play a very significant role in *The Lost Symbol*. Dürer's art incorporated much mystery tradition symbolism, the likes of which have not been adequately explained. Dan Brown used the famous painting by Dürer called *Melancholia* as a plot point in the novel. But it is very interesting to note that Dürer made many drawings of the Mantegna Tarot, the only tarot on which he ever worked.

As clearly recorded by the historians of tarot (Heinrich Brockhaus, for example), it was during the council of Mantua, held between June 1459 and January 1460, that Bessarion,[24] Nicholas de Cusa, and Pope Pious II secretly conceived of the idea of the

---

24. In 1431, Bessarion was received as a monk into the circle of the initiates of Mistra. He studied with Pletho and was initiated into the secret Ogdoadic and Hermetic doctrines.

Tarot of Mantegna.[25] This deck was different from the more widely known system that was synthesized into the Tarot of Marseilles. The Tarot of Mantegna (named for the artist Andrea Mantegna) includes fifty pictures, organized in five groups of ten. The fifth group, the Most Divine, includes the seven planetary gods in the Chaldean order (including the fixed stars). Of course, the eighth is the sphere of the fixed stars followed by the ninth, the *Primum Mobile,* and the tenth is the *Prima Causa* ("First Cause"), which shows a perfect representation of the Hermetic system.

It is possible now to understand why Dürer so well represents this tradition and how he can be connected to a system containing many esoteric keys that are blatantly Neoplatonic and Hermetic in origin.

---

25. This Mantegna Tarot is a part of my forthcoming book, *The Divine Arcana of the Aurum Solis: Using Tarot Talismans for Ritual and Initiation.* The Mantegna Tarot deck can also be found at www. llewellyn.com.

chapter four
SPIRIT OF FREEMASONRY

Building a New World

The City

Along with many other books, *The Lost Symbol* shows Washington DC as a special place, built with a real purpose as the capital of a new independent country. From this grand vision and this powerful desire, wise men rose to give life to this idea. But unlike the beginnings of humanity, these men had personal backgrounds and came with their own knowledge and cultural heritage.

It is difficult to imagine someone abandoning his or her own culture and finding common ground large enough to accept different beliefs while at the same time proposing something to share. It was a big challenge, but the founders had the will to create more than a simple assemblage of independent parts. Such an important creation as independence required extremely strong founders and corresponding symbolic acts. Such was the case with the Declaration of Independence, and the search for and founding of a federal capital.

The personality of the architects and city planners is important to any project and its development. It is often their vision that gives dynamism and a special ambition. In this case, it was architect Pierre Charles L'Enfant, chosen by George Washington. Even though he was fired after one year, his influence and the work he had done provided a definitive plan for the city. Principles, maps, and overall organization had charted the future of the city. In fact, L'Enfant had given birth to a movement and a desire that was more powerful than himself: building a capital in the New World as expression of an ideal, the visible manifestation of the nation's desire to be raised to a universal reference.

Well-versed in classical culture, L'Enfant gave substance to a philosophical and humanist vision. Like some of those who worked on the conception of Washington DC, L'Enfant was not a Freemason. Nor was Thomas Jefferson. It is interesting to wonder how these noninitiates were able to work according to principles close to those of Masonry and how they succeeded in keeping the Masonic way of thinking. There are several reasons for this, but one of the first was the morals and intellectual principles they used for their work. The scholars, artists, and Freemasons of this epoch were influenced by the Renaissance and the "philosophy of the lights" that followed from it.

Before the revolutionary storm destroyed the French monarchy, the United States and France developed a new nation-model through American and French cultural interactions. I can name John Adams, Benjamin Franklin, James Madison, and Thomas Jefferson for their influence. The presence of Benjamin Franklin in a lodge (notably in the Lodge of Nine Sisters in Paris) next to French intellectuals such as Voltaire, as well as contacts between Thomas Jefferson and Condorcet, were very important in this exchange of ideas.

Let us remember that Masonry came from England, then at war with the fledgling United States. It did not mean that the rituals and lessons of the brotherhood had to be rejected, but undoubtedly Masonry in America ceased being strictly British and adopted the original and truly ideal American philosophy that has gained worldwide influence.

Masonry became really American when regular Grand Lodges were created in each state. This shows that the founders of Washington DC, Freemasons or not, used the same philosophy and consciously and unconsciously received the influence of this intellectual and initiatic inheritance, which finds its body in the earth and the stone of the federal capital.

The first Freemasons, connecting their doctrine to the ancient master-builders, used what was familiar to them. This was the case with the Roman Vitruvius, a famous architect with a huge influence. Freemasons read his text on architecture, and even non-Masons like L'Enfant and Thomas Jefferson used this book as a main reference.

While it was necessary for the Founding Fathers to put aside old ideas about monarchies and military empires in establishing the democratic principles underlying the new nation's government, they were able to turn to the ancient symbolic principles of

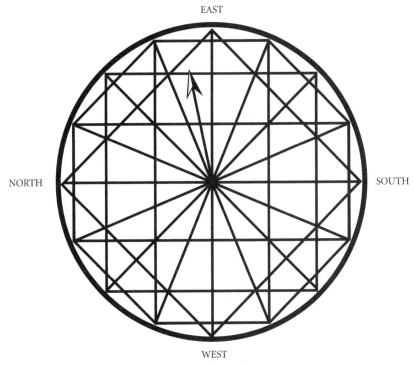

Figure 19: Vitruvius's gnomon traditionally used to organize a new city

Masonry in the placement and building of the new capital. In their development of the District of Columbia and orientation of the city, they turned to the hidden principles used by the architects in respect to the occult tradition. But an important city conceived according to the principles of classical architecture must be developed around its center. This is what was called in the past the *forum*. It was around this place that the "temples of the Gods, protectors of the city, also those of Zeus (Jupiter), Hera (Juno), and Athena (Minerva), should be on some eminence which commands a view of the greater part of the city. The temple of Hermes (Mercury) should be also in the forum."[1]

The Mall is the central place, the forum, surrounded by the buildings sacred to the nation and the manifestation of its power. The Temple of the Gods, the protectors of the city, the Capitol is at the place recommended by the traditional rules. Its site on the east of the Mall (forum) is also used to emphasize its symbolic purpose as the major temple

---

1. Marcus Vitruvius Pollio, *The Architecture*, Book 1, Chapter 7:1.

of the city. As required, Hermes' temple is very close, and the Library of Congress is the best identification possible for it considering the architectural keys.

A strange process was at work in this city. It seems that everything was progressively built according to a hidden grid and an original purpose. This real synchronicity demonstrates an intention greater than its creators. Following the text quoted above, there are two other important buildings identified with this hidden grid. Vitruvius wrote "the temple of Ares (Mars) should be out of the city, in the neighboring country." The Pentagon fits this description quite accurately.

Rooted in a traditional and symbolic grid connected to the ancient divinities, the federal capital became a powerful center of the new nation. It is difficult to understand and explain the hidden forces that would create over time the power hub that is Washington DC. This power is the same as that coming from a sacred place, creating a real icon for this purpose. This was the case for the city and for the buildings, as you will see now.

The Architecture

THE CORNERSTONES

Every important building has a special ceremony at the beginning of its construction. Of course this is the case for a building with a symbolic or sacred purpose. These ceremonies are not ordinary and their origins can be found early in the Western Tradition.

The installation of the cornerstone joins the space on which the building is built to the intention of the builders. Putting a stone in the ground was always considered a magical act and those who understand the use of geomantic and geobiologic architectural processes know that both the place and the moment are decisive elements. We saw that in the activation of the sacred space of the District of Columbia and the center of the Capitol Building. I can say that placing this cornerstone is the materialization of the building's beginning, just as a human being receives the planetary influences of his or her moment of birth. This action will influence the construction and completion of all parts of the building. This same process also works on larger areas such as the Mall, regardless of the architects themselves. Invisible energies have a function and an action linking the intention of the master-builders and the place where the building is built.

An interesting but invisible pattern is manifested by the various cornerstones buried and dedicated according to the same rituals and with the same importance in the most important buildings of the capital. Undoubtedly rituals were performed according to Masonic ritual. It is important to realize that these rituals were (and are) not religious or congregational, but symbolic and Masonic. It is a very unique example in history that a capital was systematically consecrated by Masonic rituals in order to create a powerful and universal marker in the new American egregore.

Before going further, it is necessary to recall an important element explained in the first chapter of this book. I compared the cornerstone, the hidden stone of philosophers and alchemists, to the soul of the man hidden in the mortal body. This soul/stone points out the divine presence, which gives immortality to the microcosm, giving the man the capability to manifest his divine destiny. It's the same for a building; every construction has a hidden stone that gives it a soul that interacts with its destiny. Some buildings have a real life that can manifest part of their consecrators' intention. It is the ritual performed, and the inscriptions, messages, and memorabilia deposited in the cornerstone, that are all decisive elements.

The origin of this Masonic tradition is extremely ancient and symbolic. In Mesopotamia, as well as in Egypt, the priests included different elements like statues, jewels, precious metals, documents, and even food in the cornerstones. The inclusions in Egypt were very similar to the Masonic way. The cornerstone of the White House has a brass plate announcing the date and names of the participants, and invocation of a blessing. It was the same for the cornerstone of the Capitol. There's a story about the Jefferson Pier Stone (not exactly a cornerstone) that tells how Jefferson and his wife were present at the foundation ceremony and Mrs. Jefferson put her thimble under the pier as a symbolic gift.

The placing of a cornerstone was just one part of an eight-part set of rituals composed in Egypt. In ancient buildings, the foundation stone was placed at the northeast (some Masonic rituals choose northwest) corner of the structure, which was considered an auspicious position. In the Capitol, it is possible that the cornerstone was buried in the southeast corner of the north wing.

Freemasons today emphasize the nonmagical and nonreligious character of this ceremony. The meaning of these declarations is not that the ritual is not effective or sacred; rather it is to say that the Master of the Lodge conducting this ceremony is not a religious man performing a special sacrament in the sense of the monotheistic religions.

Nevertheless, he is performing a sacred act, a ritual that has real power to change something in an intended way.

Associating different biblical references (corn, wine) with the hidden Egyptian and Hermetic origins, Masonry composed this interesting ritual that has been used since the eighteenth century. These elements are the standard used for the original ceremonies performed at the laying of the foundation of different buildings in Washington DC. Contemporary ceremonies are not much different as can readily be seen all around the country and world.

The ceremonies performed at the founding of the federal capital show deeper consequences than these symbolic elements. Despite the fact the new nation was composed of many different religious congregations, the Founding Fathers found a way to consecrate the shape of the city using sacred and symbolic acts without involving religious power. Masonry was the perfect solution, since it shows that the sacred can be disconnected from religion without a loss of purpose. In some ways, Freemasons acted like priests, and the use of a sacred ritual without sacramental aspects founded a republican standard in which everyone was able to find a place. Even the prayer shows an open mind, calling upon the "All-bounteous Author of Nature" and not a precisely named god. Masonry began to appear with a patriotic significance in a way very close to the Hermetic philosophy. Since this time, Masonic ceremonies have continued to be used in the great buildings of different states.

THE TEMPLE OF THE GODS: THE CAPITOL

The Capitol Building, is one of the major symbols of the American nation, home of the new form of government created by the Founding Fathers. Its architecture is the perfect expression of the presence of tradition in the modern world. It is a manifestation of this original will—majestic, powerful, and symbolic without appearing pompous.

In its situation to the east of the Mall, the Capitol can be seen as the temple of the protector gods of the city, something Dan Brown commented on in *The Lost Symbol*.

The Capitol Building is perfectly oriented to the four directions. The best place to see this is standing at the center of the rotunda (where the action of *The Lost Symbol* begins). Four arches open in the four directions. Surrounding this symbolic heart, and in utilizing the powerful number 8, are eight large paintings representing eight symbolic steps of American history. Just above this wonderful rotunda, we see Constantino

Brumidi's *The Apotheosis of Washington* showing the first president raised to heaven and sitting in the usual place of the supreme god, here between the representations of Liberty (right) and Victory (left). Interestingly, there are also seven representations of ancient divinities on the outer circle: Athena, Poseidon, Hermes, Hephaestus, Demeter, and Ares.

According to traditional symbolism, the gods as designated protectors of the city would be located at the rotunda's highest point. "The heights of those of Zeus (Jupiter) and the celestial Gods are to be as high as they may conveniently be."[2] When we look up to this symbolic sky, instead of Zeus (Jupiter) we see George Washington. These representations of the divine are a real invocation of their powers. In the manner of a talisman, which concentrates and attracts the power of the signs and symbols, the dome has the power to invoke the divinities protecting the city.

But the power of this place is not limited. The energy must radiate, and the reality of this symbol can be seen because the Capitol is the place in Washington with the maximum number of streets radiating from it. The statute of Freedom above the dome, facing east and the sunrise, emphasizes again the personality of this power given by the Founding Fathers.

The temple of Hermes equates to the Library of Congress. Vitruvius pointed out in his book that the temple of Hermes had to be close to the forum and the temple of the protector gods. From this point of view, the Library of Congress has a symbolic place and is a very important structure for the Masonic and Hermetic traditions. It is fascinating to see so many symbols present in a single building. All seems in perfect coherence. If I identified the Capitol as the central place of the American nation, it is possible to say that the Library of Congress is the central place for the illumination of humanity.

I had spoken earlier about the number 8, its symbolic value, and the representations associated with it. We will see how powerful is the link between this building and the influence of the number 8. In the Great Hall, the design on the marble floor is very interesting in regard to the symbolic standard of the tradition. In the center there is the Sun in its ancient form of a large eight-rayed orb, which aligns with the four cardinal directions and the direction of the main axes of the building. Surrounding this bright Sun is a square and the twelve zodiacal signs. Note the very close similarity to Florence's Baptistery, which was the definitive structure illustrating the esoteric meaning of the

---

2. Marcus Vitruvius Pollio, *The Architecture*, Book 4, Chapter 9:1.

number 8. The Sun on the floor, the rays, the zodiac, the double squares present on the floor in the corridors, these all synthesize the traditional teaching.

The inspiration of the architects and artists involved in the construction of the main building can be directly found in the classical Greek and Roman period. As expected, several Hermetic symbols can be found in this "Hermetic Temple." The main reading room is octagonal in shape. This form is the pure and discrete expression of the Hermetic Tradition, and its culmination. The architecture of this monumental room is a close copy of Florence's Baptistery. When the photos of both places are put side by side, the inspiration for the main reading room becomes clear. The columns of the first level and the pillars of the second level are exactly the same.

Above the room, the ceiling imagery is not as religious as in the Baptistery. Here, the purpose is a powerful and symbolic representation, called by the Hermetists *Religio Mentis*, which glorifies at every step the faithful union of the mind and spirituality, the material and the spiritual. This building is the perfect representation of the Hermetic vision "as above, so below," the union of the earth and heaven, using harmony and beauty to rise to the ideal world.

Above the main reading room, the upper lantern, with its eight windows, creates eight shining stars illuminating a zodiac surrounding a female figure sybolizing human understanding. The situation, the symbol of the veil, and the zodiac remind us of the Hermetic representation of Isis. It is not a surprise to see her in this place.

It is interesting to note that the Library of Congress was named for Thomas Jefferson, who designed an octagonal house at his private retreat and plantation house, Poplar Forest.

Now we can understand better why Dan Brown wrote in *The Lost Symbol* that Washington DC was laid out and constructed using astrological and cosmological signs and symbols, by men who paid close attention to the earth and the heavens above.

THE TEMPLE OF DEMETER: SCOTTISH RITE BUILDINGS

Undoubtedly the House of the Temple plays a central role in *The Lost Symbol*. But there are some errors in the story. For example, it seems that some initiations, including those in the first three degrees, were performed in this temple. This isn't correct because these initiations are always performed in a Blue Lodge, a Masonic temple yone can visit in many places in the United States.

The House of the Temple is the headquarters of the Scottish Rite Southern Jurisdiction and the place of the administrative meetings of the Council. According to Vitruvius, "The temple of Demeter (Ceres) should be in a solitary spot out of the city." The followers of Eleusis in Greece were among the most famous initiatic mystery schools of antiquity. Their connection with the initiations in Masonry is clear, and the Scottish Rite Center can be seen as this initiatic place.

In this building there is an auditorium where the Scottish Rite gives "classes." During two days, candidates are gathered and participate in the different initiations from the 4th to the 32nd degrees. Some of these degrees are performed in full ritual. During these ceremonies, the initiates sit on bleachers in the auditorium. On the stage, the initiatic ritual is played by officers/actors with a candidate who represents all those present in the auditorium. Sometimes all present stand up and pronounce sacred words and oaths. The power of evocation of the initiations is huge. This representation of the sacred mysteries is deeply moving and the performance can really touch the soul of the initiates.

Some persons may be surprised by this way of initiating many candidates at the same time, thinking that every initiation must be individual, as is generally the case. But this ancient group ritual was the method used for centuries in the famous Mysteries of Eleusis and has been kept alive by the American Scottish Rite. During this group ritual, the initiates gathered to receive the "Grand Mysteries." After swearing to keep these rituals secret, the initiate was able to enter the main sacred temple, the Telesterion. The details of these initiations were, in fact, generally kept secret. However, the writings of converted Christians and the help of archaeology give us enough elements to have a good idea of the process. It is interesting to note that the Telesterion was a large room with bleachers. Mysteries transmitting initiatic teachings on the origin and destiny of the soul were performed by priests in the center of the sacred space with the candidates surrounding the stage. Sometimes during the ceremony, they had to get up, move, pronounce sentences, etc. Sacred gestures were shown and holy words communicated. Lighting and sound technology added power to the celebration of these rituals.

It is always fascinating to see respectable traditions that remain active for millennia and can be found today under a new body with a quite similar purpose. Masonry sometimes works in a miraculous and surprising way.

Exoteric and Esoteric

Exoteric (outside) and esoteric (inside) are two words often used to speak about the Western Tradition. For many years, their use has been common. Everyone interested in spiritual studies used them in many ways. But their definitions are not always very clear and this uncertainty created a lack of confidence in those interested in the ancient traditions. For years, scholars influenced by rationalist philosophy and scientific perspective had rejected all studies relating to magick, occultism, and esotericism. This was also generally the case for Masonry as well. There are some exceptions in the Masonic Tradition, as Albert Pike's work is absolutely accurate and fundamental for the revival of the Western Tradition.

The phrase "esoteric teachings" means "teachings from the inside" or "knowledge veiled to the public." In the mystery school of Pythagoras, students were divided into noninitiates and initiates. From this separation came the idea of an *inner circle* and an *outer circle*. It is possible that this distinction was borrowed by Pythagoras from the Egyptian priests.

The word *esoteric* was only popularized in the nineteenth century in the works of the French occultist Eliphas Levi. But the use of these two words remains at this time a simple convention that means *in* or *out*, *initiate* or *not*. In the last century, scholars really began the academic study of this important part of Western heritage. The French scholar Antoine Faivre defined this work in a way accepted today by the large majority of researchers. Faivre used the theory of correspondences, which states that all things are linked in the cosmos. There are no gaps, just links or currents that may be obvious or hidden. These hidden relationships are shown by markers like color, shape, etc. For example, a yellow flower will be connected by its color correspondence to the Sun. As he further explains, the means to study these currents consist of five characteristics:

1. The conviction that nature is a *living entity*: there is a real spirit or being of nature. The consequence is the possibility to interact consciously with it.

2. The need for *mediating elements* (symbols) acting like information icons to access spiritual knowledge.

3. An awareness of *personal transmutation* when arriving at this knowledge: *apotheosis*.

4. The *initiatic process*: initiations can be a real and active part of this inner development.

5. *Concordance* between religious traditions: the different religions are all relative aspects of the same reality.

Esotericism is somewhere between religion and materialism. There are different schools in the Western Tradition such as Christian esoterists (Theosophists), Hermetists, Rosicrucians, Pagans, Wiccans, etc. Even if their beliefs and practices are sometimes quite similar, they are not the same. Each school as its own specific teachings and methods like the Qabalah, astrology, alchemy, magick, theurgy, etc. While these different aspects of esotericism are not scientific in the modern meaning of this word, they are parts of the basic curriculum of the Western esoteric tradition. Any magick or symbolic ritual contains elements and symbols from alchemy, astrology, etc. The Scottish Rite Degrees reorganized by Albert Pike show the interconnection between these traditional fields.

Esotericism generally shares another aspect: the determination not to reveal inner secrets to someone unprepared. What can be called the *secret sciences* can give special abilities, which may be dangerous if used with negative intentions. The same applies to fire, as it can either help or hurt. Esoteric knowledge can help us progress toward the divine and at the same time these hidden human abilities can be used for an egotistical or selfish purpose.

To analyze whether Masonry is an esoteric brotherhood, we can compare the Masonic texts and rituals to the definition provided above. Masonry can immediately match five points out of six. Even if the point regarding the correspondences is not explicit, it does not contradict the Masonic teachings or texts. All the other elements are present in this tradition and sometimes more fully developed in the initiatic rituals. Rituals use symbols that have specific meanings and sometimes have a dramatic effect on the initiate.

Considering the open mind promoted by Masonry, we see that its structure is not restricted to any specific faith. Moreover, its teachings come directly from the Hermetic Tradition and the constant use of the initiatic process is one of the main manifestations of this original connection. As Albert Pike has shown, Masonry is the largest visible group on the planet capable of presenting a coherent and constant Western Tradition. Of course, Masonry is not the only one, and doesn't develop some specific aspects like theurgy. But the teachings, philosophy, and ideals are a unique example of this harmonious union between these different traditions. There is no philosophical school in the world that continues to give access to the ancient process originating from esotericism. As in the Platonic and Neo-platonic schools, Masonry emphasizes the moral aspects, the development of virtue. This is the main aspect of the inner development of the human being. Many Masonic rituals develop this traditional idea, but their purpose is not related to increasing the inner abilities.

For the last century, explicit and open references to the esoteric dimension of Masonry began to disappear. At the same time, many Freemasons don't consider this dimension to be an important element that needs special care. Masonry was (and continues to be) focused on brotherhood and philanthropic purposes. Every Freemason is encouraged to increase his awareness about humanity and realize that there is just one human global family. The goal is not to explain, but to give birth in consciousness, as in the subconscious, to the recognition that everyone is a part of humanity and responsible for his or her brother and sister humans. However, this consciousness comes with a realistic vision of the human being that "man is a wolf to [his fellow] man."

For the Freemason, this observation is not pessimistic; on the contrary, it is a realistic view of the world, but not a definitive one. The Hermetic teachings are hidden in the heart of Masonry. The material dimension of the human being is surrounded by the illusion of the material world. The soul is jailed in the cave of the body. The passions, desires, and impulses act as the actual guards who jailed the soul and keep it imprisoned. These are not sins, but desire(s) that act as the master of the ship (our being). To refuse to see this situation is like staying, like the Platonic prisoners, at the bottom of the cave, unaware of their situation, and yet to be persuaded to be free of their illusions.

But the Masonic teachings also show the presence of this immortal soul jailed by the passions, and that show something must happen to change the situation. The process must be reversed. The soul must be put in charge and instead jail or contain the passions and desires. But it is important not to misunderstand the words used. "Jail the passions" doesn't mean to kill the passions. As the Hermetists and philosophers wrote, passion is very useful! It can be a pure dynamism that helps in one's daily life, as in making the most important decisions. What must be jailed or controlled are the unbalanced desires, the uncontrolled passions that destroy inner liberty. The right balance between no desire and too much desire must be found. This is the true middle path. The quest for beauty is the same thing. When we realize that we are half angel and half human, really half-gods, we will understand the power we have for good or bad. We will be able to make real choices between these two aspects. Masonry shows the philanthropic way, raising humanity close to divinity. This is not an esoteric dimension and purpose. The main Masonic activities are social and humanitarian, as shown on the websites of the Grand Lodges. But remember that one of the most important parts of the Platonic philosophy was to change Greek society and politics. Masonry did and does the same thing, building temples for the virtues and acting directly in society. The text of the Declaration of Independence is a perfect example of this incarnation of the Masonic and universal virtues. It was not a philosophy disconnected from social realities. It was a philosophy in action.

It is important not to forget the heart that animates the body. The implicit affirmation of all these actions is the existence of a visible world in which men are fragile, along with another world that is spiritual and hidden. This affirmation is not religious, but philosophic, and esoteric.

But during the time when Freemasons emphasized this very important dimension of their heritage, the esoteric part was in disgrace. As usual in this situation, other groups, religious and initiatic, began to develop this aspect. Some were able to use the esoteric Western Tradition with authority, according to their origin. This is the case for the theurgic orders. But others, often with good intentions, used the ancient writings without understanding their esoteric dimensions. Some groups, like the New Age movement, Rosicrucian orders, and other self-development organizations, focused their work on inner abilities and alternative spirituality without roots and heritage. Sometimes the result was very positive, but many times it was merely confusing.

During the past centuries, people interested in this inner dimension, the spiritual perspective and alternative spirituality, began to believe that a tradition like Masonry was unable to teach and give solid support to the esoteric dimension. I can say now that it was generally true and this respectable tradition began to lose the esoteric way. The philanthropic purpose was (and remains) noble but incomplete without the esoteric element. There is a paradox here. Saying that Masonry began to neglect esotericism doesn't mean Masonry lost this part of its heritage. But as the definition and the true essence of esotericism was distorted and not well understood, Masonic leaders, themselves unaware of the true meaning of it, began to question it.

Through the efforts of some initiatic orders and scholars, esotericism today has a better presentation. Scholars can "explain" the outer aspects of esotericism, but to go further requires real and personal experience. Masonry today is always able to reveal the traditional inner teachings. As you will see in the practical part of the book, this tradition really does have something to say and to give on the esoteric level. Actually, this field is linked to very advanced aspects of science like the neurosciences, or as Dan Brown wrote about, the noetic sciences. Modern Masonry has a lot to gain in this reactivation of the serious and traditional teachings and the practice of esotericism. This is something deep, important, and able to open the secret and sacred gates to a spiritual level totally harmonious with the philanthropic ideals.

Freemasonry vs. Religion: A Modern Challenge

In a few words, *The Lost Symbol* summarizes the Masonic approach to religion: it has no religion. This summation is interesting and important in understanding the modern challenge of Masonry. It is relatively easy to discover what contemporary religions think Masonry is. Monotheistic religions (perhaps with the exception of Judaism) are opposed to Masonry. Catholicism and a large part of Christianity, as well as Islam, are against the Masonic view of religion and morality. That doesn't mean there are no Christian or Muslim Freemasons, but it does mean that the religious establishment is against Masonic principles. Christianity declared that Freemasons are heretics because they are thinking, acting, and teaching differently than the church's dogmas and scriptural truths.

Religion is rooted in a special belief that humans are composed of a physical body and an invisible part generally called the soul. In the same way, religions teach the existence of immaterial worlds and divinities larger than us. Masonry was born in the English Protestant Reformation as a universal brotherhood, now present in many places on Earth. Its portals are open to every man without consideration of his religion. At the beginning of Masonry, this point was not a problem, for there were only a few categories of people: Protestants, Catholics, and later, Jews. There were no religions other than those with a Biblical background. This was the original context of the birth of Masonry, and in its original texts, this fraternity didn't ask for a specific faith.

Anderson's Constitutions[3] ask for obedience to moral law, meaning one should not be a stupid atheist nor an irreligious libertine. Freemasons in every country were asked

---

3. James Anderson (1679–1739) was a minister in the Church of Scotland and a Freemason. He was commissioned by the Grand Lodge to write a history of the Freemasons, published in 1723 as the "Constitutions of the Free-Masons" (see Chapter One).

to be of the religion of that country, whatever it was. In this case, the "true" religion was the one on which all men agree, in order to be men of honor and honesty.

These declarations were presented as a statement for Masonry. There were obligations and preconditions to be met before being initiated. For the founding Freemasons, the challenge was to find the elements common to each man without religious identities, while keeping the best of the spiritual dimension. It was a challenge in a time when religion was everywhere and had real earthly powers. What might be the main obligation to accept someone whom you can trust? Is it possible to be like God and see into his soul? Of course not, and it would be very presumptuous to think so. Is it possible to judge him by his religion? According to what Anderson wrote, no.

So three aspects were important and remain so today: (1) the prerequisite, (2) the statement, and followed by (3) the consequence.

The prerequisite states there is a moral law. Atheists and the irreligious (those without morality) cannot be part of the Craft. Someone wanting to be part of the Craft must have an inner belief in the existence of a spiritual world and a divine power. But these two elements are not defined. If Anderson had explained these aspects, the prerequisite would call for a statement of faith and would therefore be confessional. However, he was looking for a large consensus without losing the best part of the religious dimension. So yes, Freemasons must believe in or recognize the spiritual dimension as an inner part of the human being.

The statement is a religion on which all men agree, keeping for themselves its definition. If one can't find a unique definition for all, the only thing asked is to be good men and true, or men of honor and honesty; nothing more is asked. All is said, complete, and perfect.

Finally, the consequence. If the prerequisite and the statement became a living reality for the Freemason, Masonry would become the center of union. This center is the place where different people with different understanding will be able to build a true friendship, revealing a true possibility for all human beings: brotherhood.

It is important to remember that Anderson wrote in the earliest years of Masonry, asking for a private expression of religion. The consequence is an open mind, and the possibility for Masonry to be present everywhere at all times. There is no geographical, cultural, or historical limit to its presence in the world because this brotherhood gives a center: the lodge, the Craft, able to receive humans who perceived this inner and common world, while trying to be better. This is the foundation of Masonry.

These questions were exceptional at the point of history when they were created. At the same time, we can be amazed by the reintroduction of the Hermetic way, suddenly interpreted in a public text for a "new" initiatic fraternity.

Somehow, Hermetism can be seen as a religious philosophy. This is a religion (spirituality in action) because Hermetists believe in the existence of a spiritual world and an immortal and divine soul, able to ascend to the divine, and present in all manifestations of nature. Here is the power that created, organized, and continues to animate the universe. But this divine power is far from us and the name given by Masonry is the best illustration of it: the Great Architect of the Universe. But we must be careful with this name because today we tend to think with a monotheistic *a priori*. For this divine power, present everywhere in the universe, the question of gender is nonsense. It is also impossible to know whether or not this divine power is personal. Maybe it is also impossible to say if the impulse of creation was or is the result of intention. As human beings, these questions are beyond our understanding. But undoubtedly this idea of a supreme being is impossible to represent. This fact was felt in the monotheistic religions, but not always with the same success. In philosophical terms, the supreme being is immanent. That means the Great Architect of the Universe is inside its creation and not outside. After its creation, nature was not abandoned by its divine creator.

But these Hermetists and Freemasons don't reject *a priori* the existence of a supreme being that can have a will. Although it is quite impossible to say something definitive on this subject, a philosophical prudence tells us to not to reject this possibility. It's why I can say that all nature is in God and at the same time that a supreme being created the universe, which is a theory called "Deism."

The Deists believed that reason and observation of the natural world are the necessary elements to understand the essence of the divine. Faith and organized religion are not necessary for that. Hermetists called this the "religion of the mind." In fact, faith is not rejected, but appears second, after reason. This is why religion and philosophy are connected. Because of the divine and the supreme being, religion can be an inner and essential feeling, but always under the control of reason (philosophy), which was given to humanity for this purpose.

Freemasons, and Deists as well, have no real dogmas. Anyone is able to choose what seems good for him according to his own inner beliefs. Eclecticism is the result of the benevolent consideration of any expression of human faith. Generally, Hermetists, Freemasons, and Deists are very prudent regarding organized religions. They appear often as more political and secular powers than an enlightened organization. They tend to assert that the "Supreme Architect" has a plan for the universe.

But the existence of miracles or supernatural intervention is a different question. Generally, Deists don't believe that God intervenes in the affairs of human life or is able to suspend the natural laws of the universe. Laws are universal and constant, even though all the laws are not yet understood by humans. Theurgy is the expression of the possibility to interact with these hidden and unexplained laws.

It is important to know what happened in the confrontation between the monotheistic religions, and particularly between Catholicism and Masonry. Freemasons chose to be loyal to their beliefs and moral statements. They expressed their ideals of tolerance and freedom in the presence of God, opening their portals to every good man wanting to work in peace for the betterment of humanity. Philanthropy, while not a religious prerequisite, became one of the wonderful realizations of Masonry. At the same time, Masonry found a way to maintain the presence of the sacred separate from religion, and sacraments as a consequence of perceiving divine providence and revering symbols and places. They were not sacred because a clergy declared God's presence but because the Freemasons, as human beings, revered these values and their representations as paramount.

These short examples show us the reaction of a church that still has political power today. There are many modern examples of this power applied against freedom and tolerance. The Taliban and all forms of religious fundamentalism are the modern aspect of the Inquisition and a contemporary echo of the burning of thousands of women and men in witch-hunts in Europe at the end of the Middle Ages. Freemasons as well as the Founding Fathers were never opposed to a belief in God, nor a religious and spiritual life. It is for us a manifestation of an inner and true feeling for creation and God. But this sacred part of the heart remains under the control of reason and always the love of humanity. Of course, it is possible to have a good understanding of a question and to be right. But the affirmation of respect for others and the relativism of any expression of an inner understanding avoid a Freemason attacking another man to impose his certainty. Proof of the falseness and the danger of unmitigated belief is the manifestation of intolerance and violence. This tendency has no age and remains active today.

Just as the Founding Fathers did, Freemasons must view all fundamentalism with attentive consideration that implicates rules and laws. They denied at every occasion the possibility for a political religious power to rule the new nation they were building. They knew the risks of division and civil conflict. They'd seen the power of religion in many countries, and on their own land too. This is why they wrote the Bill of Rights and the Constitution of the United States in this special way, respecting a mighty god and his benevolence and divine providence. But the Freemasons refused to build in Washington DC the national church planned by L'Enfant.

These ideas were also shared by the Founding Fathers who were not Freemasons, such as John Adams, Thomas Jefferson, and Thomas Paine. Generally, they were close to the Deist interpretation or free thinkers like Thomas Paine.

In this quest for freedom, every human is considered as equal under God. The consequence is for men to be able to build a new system closer to the natural order. It is sometimes necessary to cut out the old structures in order to begin a new age. Setting religion apart and emphasizing the power of the mind opened new possibilities. Thus, it was possible to act as free legislators confident in divine providence, which gave them freedom to think and accomplish. This allowed them to imagine a new political system in which the king was absent, and was replaced by the people. The law would be written by free minds. While a definition of the presidential function was difficult to find, the Founding Fathers succeeded in using the Masonic model of the Master of the Lodge elected by the initiates.

Following these respectable founders, Congress chose to add an amendment to the United States Constitution, stating that "Congress shall make no law respecting an establishment of religion." Together with the free exercise clause, this amendment prohibits the establishment of a national religion by Congress, the preference of one religion over another, or the support of a religious idea with no identifiable secular purpose. Freemasons can be very proud of this validation of their principles in the new nation, finding a way to retain the private expression of one's beliefs and while avoiding any link of religion to political power.

Figure 20: The sacred book, present on every central altar of the Masonic Temples

Sacred Book and Lost Word

Sacred Book

Most spiritual traditions have holy or sacred books. Centuries before the birth of monotheistic traditions called "the religions of the book" (Judaism, Christianity, and Islam) the Egyptian god Thoth gave his teachings to humanity.

In the biblical tradition, God reveals his word to humanity through the prophets in a process similar to what is called "channeling" today. God speaks directly to the prophet in an inner or outer way. Sentences or texts are dictated and the prophet copies God's voice. Men and women are chosen according to criteria different for every religion. According to

Christian beliefs, God's message is only to be received and is not to be interpreted. This is not a philosophical or literary process; God's word is definitive.

For centuries, parts of the Bible were written by this process and this belief. The ancient followers accepted all the written words as the divine truth and the manifestation of God's will. The Bible became the absolute reference for everything (even "scientific" tpoics). The book was sacred because it was considered as the place where God's words could be found. Freemasons came from this spiritual family and the Sacred Book (called the *Volume of the Sacred Law*, or *VSL*) became the powerful symbol of a window open to the divine world. *The Lost Symbol* describes the Bible as a vehicle of transmission for the mysteries of the ages, and the Freemasons recognized this fact.

It is interesting to note that the Bible was not used in the earliest rituals of Masonry. But progressively the Bible was accepted and called "a Great Light of Freemasonry." The Bible is used as a symbol of God's will. But we must be aware of what seems a real paradox. Freemasons consider the Bible as a sacred book. At the same time, they claim that moral values are the highest reference of the Craft. However, as Thomas Paine wrote, "The Bible is a history of wickedness that has served to corrupt and brutalize mankind: and for my part, I sincerely detest it as I detest everything that is cruel." Of course, Paine was not someone who could be called a religious man, but he pointed out something important and possibly disturbing.

Many of the Founding Fathers and Freemasons said that in order to be realistic, everyone must accept the idea that all the sacred texts might not be the sole expression of God. Albert Pike wrote that the prophets used ancient stories or myths as allegories to reveal a hidden reality. It is easier today to see incoherencies, errors, and behaviors that cannot be the expression of God's love. Undoubtedly, there are some human parts in the texts.

This is also the idea developed in Dan Brown's novel and is the subject of many books about biblical codes and cyphers. Many initiates, believers, and other seekers have noted these contradictions and singularities in the Bible. If one is not totally convinced of the holy essence of the text, the only rational way out is to accept the idea of a symbolic text, a supernatural and holy code, which constitutes the structure of the text. The Qabalah showed the way. All the esoterists, occultists, and initiates followed. *The Lost Symbol* uses the same concept. The structure of the Hebrew language allowed this exercise according to precise rules defined by Hebrew and Christian Qabalists. Furthermore, some passages of the Bible said that the truth is hidden, veiled, and not accessible to the profane. In fact, it is totally possible to accept the idea that some parts of the text are symbolic and may be coded. The final theory in Dan Brown's novel is this continuity of an ancient tradition by way of the sacred book called the Bible.

Of course there were contacts between initiates and some openminded Christians. It seems probable that teachings from the Ancient Mysteries were incorporated into the book (or stolen and adapted by the writers), so it is possible to analyze the text in order to find these permanent and immortal divine truths. But this research into a sacred text, even on an esoteric, mystic, and spiritual level, must not become an excuse to accept any declaration as true. The terrible acts, kidnappings, and many acts of violence regularly accepted by God in the sacred text must not be seen as justification for similar acts.

Of course, we can view some of the Bible stories symbolically, but we must be very prudent about considering them as literal, and allowing their use as standards. If the sacred book contain a true divine revelation, your mind—created by God—must be used to find it and select the human portions as Thomas Jefferson did. This is clearly different from the idea of a Neoplatonic god's expression of beauty, wisdom, and strength. But the solution is not what Jefferson did in renouncing to any form of the spiritual or "supernatural" in human beings or in the world. It is clear that everyone has hidden abilities and the universe has more hidden power than it is possible to imagine. This is the esoteric dimension of all living beings. The solution is to find a good balance between excesses. In one direction, it would be an excess of the supernatural, destroying reason and accepting as complete and definitive truths scientific errors (creationism, for example) or dangerous literality. In the other direction, it would be the excess of rationalism, destroying any possibilities of investigating "paranormal" or any spiritual dimension. Freemasonry, keeping in its subconscious the Hermetic tradition, found a way to balance these temptations. The shift from no book to the Holy Bible (the holy book), to the sacred book, and from the sacred book to the sacred books, opened this door to a better understanding.

This is why sacred books can be seen as a window of a house. God is inside the house and maybe every window allows us to feel God and maybe to see his actions in a different way. Of course, God can change the presentation according to the orientation of the windows and the time of the work. As a result, it is impossible to say that one book is superior to another; rather all can be useful in understanding who did what and why. The best method would be to read and study all the sacred books in order to see what they have in common and what came from our limited perspective and fallible interpretation. To believe that only one window is able to show the truth is to limit God. Just imagining that people outside the house can fight and kill others because of looking into different windows is both amazing and frightening.

There is a wonderful illustration of this Masonic solution in the House of the Temple in Washington DC. In that temple, on the large marble altar, any visitor can see various sacred books of the different religions, and not just one. Every initiate is able to provide the book he considers as sacred. This possibility to share something sacred without religious judgment is a wonderful challenge to humanity to find unity in a place of divisiveness.

Lost Word

The climax of *The Lost Symbol* is all about the sacred book and recovering the lost word. Dan Brown felt the importance of this subject as it related to Freemasonry, even likening the reclamation of the lost word to a search for an invisible gate. Even in Freemasonry, the "lost word" continues to be a main concept, but with rare, deep developments.

A sacred book is very often considered as a symbolic text composed of occult sayings. The logic is to imagine a deep meaning to a text given by a divinity. Somehow it seems obvious for esoterists that the hidden meaning of the Bible was lost. The divisions are an illustration of this loss of the divine character. The idolatry of the text demonstrates the loss of the sacred meaning.

Everyone can understand that a sacred text might be a manifestation of the divine that can help humanity to progress, and maybe more. In fact, the book is the materialization of the living word. The Bible emphasizes the power of this word. The creation of the world by the use of the word is the light: "Then God said, 'Let there be light!' And light began to shine." This word (and light) is a real creative power. Later in the text, this power is given to Adam, who gives a special word to every animal. Adam, the universal man in the Qabalah, received the ability of the word and the power to give life in using it. Adam was able to work as an auxiliary of God, as a demiurge. After some temptations and mistakes, his father/creator banishes him from Eden without any power. According to the Bible's myth, we can see here the clear origin of the lost word. It is not a big Masonic secret. Every Christian knows this text. But the connection is sometimes not so obvious.

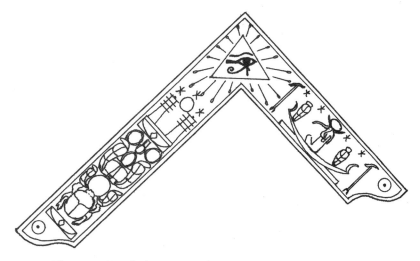

Figure 21: Jewel of a Master of a Lodge using Egyptian symbols

Freemasons are optimistic. According to their founding myth related in Anderson's Constitution, it seems that the first humans didn't completely lose their memory. Something remained in the human subconscious and their unique language was still capable of creating demiurgic miracles. Maybe their incomplete memory was not enough to control these abilities. The story of the Tower of Babel illustrates the moment when God pushed his children away from the divine world. The lost word seems a story of separation, or rejection . . . But as modern science shows, human memory is deeper than expected. As Freemasons have said, some people, wise men and initiates, continued to possess this knowledge and tried to preserve it. Of course, it was necessary to keep this knowledge secret. Humanity has been banished twice from heaven, and you can imagine that initiates keeping this in mind did not want to receive another punishment. At the same time, they kept this secret away from people who were not able to control this power.

The tradition coming from the Bible myth is universal. It can be found in other cultures, like the Egyptian. I spoke about the trick used by Isis to rob the word from Ra. It was the use of its power that allowed Isis to give a new birth to Osiris. This power can be found also in the Ogdoadic Tradition story of the creation. You remember the cause of Hiram's death described in the first chapter of this book. It is obvious that a mythic murder like this one has nothing to do with the theft of a password

116 SPIRIT OF FREEMASONRY

(or even a better salary). It would be simplistic to imagine a coarse explanation like this one for the most important Masonic myth. In fact, and following the origin of the word, the goal of the ruffians was to steal a real demiurgic instrument. The analysis of this act can be explained as a moral allegory, but at the same time can reveal a part of the great stake of every initiate. The consequence in Hiram's myth was the definitive loss of the word and the introduction of the substitute word.

Freemasons were aware of this loss and began to accept the idea that its quest would be their most important task. Dan Brown is correct when he uses this notion for the plot of *The Lost Symbol.* But maybe he is wrong when he imagines that Freemasonry still has this secret. With this new myth of the substitute word, Freemasons began a new "quest for the Grail," which can be called "quest for the lost word." However, the quest for the Grail has an advantage over the other quest: the knights knew what they were looking for. Freemasonry lost the nature of the word, its use, and its localization. Even more, the goal began to become the quest itself. How and why find a lost word if you don't know its use? It is very strange to try to find it if you already have one that is enough to work: the substituted one. But Freemasonry continued to be faithful to its heritage. Its rituals and myths kept the footprint of this origin. The "quest for the lost word" kept alive the idea of a truth perhaps divine and now hidden.

The consequence can be seen on three levels: esoteric, exoteric, and Masonic. Let's begin with the esoteric level. For centuries, some occult researchers, sometimes initiates, understood the true nature of the quest. Their readings of sacred texts, such as the Bible, showed that the word was known at the beginning of humanity. The word(s) was the original language of humanity, allowing connection with our deepest archetypal memory, able to give us original truth and the power to use the divine language confiscated by the creator. Esoterists believed that clues could be found in the symbols of various religious and spiritual traditions, but also in the roots of current human languages. They compared the languages, studied words' roots, and created interesting esoteric theories. Examples of this quest can be found in the works of St. Yves d'Alveydre or the abbot Johannes Trithemius.

On the exoteric level, people were unaware of these issues, and perception of this lack was present. The limitation created by the multiplicity of languages was seen as a problem for the progress of humanity. Moreover, the difficulty in understanding the true meaning of the languages created a lack of understanding and conflict. The solution was to create a new language avoiding grammatical difficulties in order to provide the best way to communicate. It was the creation of international auxiliary languages. Somehow this is a quest for the lost word as a lost common language, but maybe the real one will be a spontaneous emanation of a global consciousness.

On the Masonic level, Freemasonry finds its own way in this quest—not in the past, nor in the future, but in doing nothing. Freemasonry kept intact the memory of an ancient knowledge veiled by wise men that apparently had their reasons to do so. Every quest must have a purpose, even an old one. As Masonic texts explain in a symbolic way, the original word was the expression of the divine truth.[4]

But we must not confuse a definition with a purpose. Freemasons felt that the word was a major key. To find the solution to this enigma, we must remember the origin of the myths and discover whether there are some connections. As James Anderson said, Egypt was the great land of mysteries and of stone-masons.

The Egyptian Tradition is able to show us the purpose and some uses of the lost word(s). One of the most relevant texts is *Book of the Dead, or Coming Forth by Day*. The use of questions and answers, the redundancy of sacred words, secret words, passwords, handgrips, etc. can be seen as a leitmotif of Masonic rituals. It's difficult to imagine and explain a real and coherent origin in a mythic tradition. In the Egyptian sacred book, this initiatic process is present, but with a precise purpose. These dialogues are good examples of this process: "The god Anubis said: 'Do you know the name of this door?' The scribe Ani said: '*Driven away of Shu* is the name of this door.' Anubis continued: 'Do you know the name of the upper leaf and of the lower leaf thereof?' The scribe Ani said: '*Lord of right and truth, standing upon his two feet* is the name of the upper leaf, and *Lord of might and power, dispenser of cattle* is the name of the lower leaf.' Anubis said: 'You can pass, you who know the names.'"[5]

Everyone who has read a Masonic text or experienced an initiation can be amazed by these tales. This is really an initiatic process. Its purpose is the description of an invisible and mystical portal. Dan Brown was right: an invisible gate was really at the center of the quest.

Later in *Book of the Dead*, the dead person is tested by forty gods, asking him different sacred words, and a password connected with architecture: "'I will not let you enter,' said

---

4. "Before the world began, the Word was there. The Word was with God, and the Word was God." John 1:1–5.

5. *Book of the Dead*, 125:18–27.

the bolt of the door, 'unless thou tell my name.' '*Weight of the place of right and truth* is thy name. I will not let thee pass in by me,' saith the right post of the door, 'unless thou tell my name.'" Later (in Chapter 144), we read that the dead had crossed seven doors with the knowledge of the secret names of the outer and inner guards.

The similarity of these texts is revealing and we are beginning to understand the purpose of the lost word. This is a matter of life or death. The lost word(s) was able to help us to cross into death, to overcome these supreme tests in which our hearts will be weighed and checked as the cornerstone of the masterwork, which is the self. The passwords are vital, and the knowledge given by the sacred book is essential. This book's title is also translated as *The Book of Coming into the Light*. As Freemasonry says: "We are in darkness seeking for the light." The intitiate is or will be in the darkness of death (3rd Degree) looking for the light. He must be able to use the sacred words in order to be raised like Hiram/Osiris.

The quest for the lost word is essential! Freemasonry shows the way, a novelist like Dan Brown intuited the solution, and the tradition gives the esoteric key: being able to use the sacred words found again to overcome death, to come back to heaven, and to reach the highest transformation called apotheosis.

Apotheosis

The Washington Monument was intended to be a monumental statue to George Washington. By the virtue of a beautiful synchronism, this project evolved into the building of an obelisk, rising toward heaven from Earth. But I must now explain why Dan Brown linked the obelisk, the circumpunct, and the notion of apotheosis.

As mentioned here and there in *The Lost Symbol*, the obelisk seems not to be a Masonic symbol. However, the ancient gnomon can reveal more than we might expect. In the Christian painting tradition, there is an important subject: the two Saint Johns or the Holy Saint John. Generally, Saint John the Apostle and Saint John the Baptist are on each side

Figure 22: Circumpunct

of the Virgin Mary with her baby. Freemasonry chose these two saints as protectors (patron saints). Further, Freemasons "created" a symbol composed of a circle with a central point and two vertical lines touching each side. This representation can be seen in the Blue Lodge. The two vertical lines represent the summer and winter solstices, the shortest and longest nights of the year, respectively. These nights, since antiquity, have been important in the pre-Christian Mysteries. They are also connected to the two solstice points on the zodiac, Cancer and Capricorn.

These astrological indications are interesting, but it is possible to go further with the symbolism of the numbers 4 and 8. The obelisk, at center of a circle, indicates the four directions. By rotation of the square, a double square is obtained, birth of the symbol of the 8 the limit between the material world and the spiritual world.

The shape of the obelisk shows its function of dispersing negative forces, piercing the dark sky in order to attract the higher energies in this symbol of the light. There is no better function that could be given by divine providence to the federal capital. A monument was given to this new nation that was able to destroy negativity and to invigorate the exact center of the buildings used to house its government. As in antiquity, the obelisk was built in the center of large open place, as were the temples of the solar god Ra, raised on a sacred cornerstone in a city that would also be called the "City of the Sun."

The obelisk, emblem of resurrection, would be connected to the birth of the new nation, the new age, and the new man. All these elements are coherent together and reveal the key of our being, transformation, and destiny.

Like Freemasonry, the Hermetic Tradition[6] uses the symbol of the triangle and the square to represent the soul and the body, respectively. This is well represented in the Craft by the cube and the pyramid above it. The same symbolic principles are found in the obelisk with the trunk (body) and the capstone (soul). There is a place in Washington DC to perfectly understand this ancient mystery: the Mall. But the special position on it can be found in the *Corpus Hermeticum*: "Thus then, my son, stand in a place uncovered to the sky [. . .] at sunrise be face to the East wind."[7]

Imagine you are at the west of the Mall, in front of the Lincoln Memorial, facing east. In front of you, the Sun will rise above Capitol Hill and continue its daily movement, rising to its highest point at the vertical of the obelisk. The reflecting pool, between you and the obelisk, shows its reversed reflection. The stage is ready and the symbolic mysteries can speak again.

---

6. Explanations of these symbols can be found in the book by Melita Denning and Osborne Phillips, *The Foundations of High Magick*, first volume of *The Magickal Philosophy* (Woodbury, MN: Llewellyn Publications).

7. *Corpus Hermeticum*, Book 13:16.

In the beginning was the principle of all things, the Great Architect of the Universe, the creator. The most ancient representation is the Sun, high in the sky giving its power, its light to Earth, and allowing all creatures there to live. It is the origin of all things, the center of the universe. To represent this character, the symbol chosen by the first initiates was the circle. The eye, also representative of Ra, reminds us that the strongest and best source of light is the Sun. With its help, we can see clearly around us.

But all these very interesting symbols are yet Exoteric. In order to figure out this message, it is necessary to go deeper in the hidden world, and listen to the teachings of the Esoteric and Hermetic Traditions.

Plotinus, chief of the Neoplatonic Tradition, explains that God is always present in all beings, inside us, even if it is not possible to feel it or know it. The soul is immortal, without beginning, without end. Eternity and immortality are represented by an unbroken circle, turning around a central point that is the source of all emanations.

The circumpunct (#1) is the Neoplatonic representation of the soul in the spiritual world and in relation to the One, beauty, right, and truth.

But there came a time when the immortal soul, keeping this original light, began its descent in nature. Going through the different veils of creation, through the eight spheres, each planet, your soul entered into your body. If you are west of the reflecting pool, face east: this situation of the soul incarnated can be seen in the reversed image of the obelisk (see the figure below). The triangle, representation of the divine soul, is at the bottom, close to you, the central point in your direction. This is the indication of the descent accomplished in the matter. The square (really a rectangle) is above. This is really a reflection, an unreal representation of the reality, the symbol of the material world.

This is your situation as a human being. Your soul is often under the domination of your body and your passions (#2). But it is possible to begin the work on your inner "stone" in order to recreate a harmonious union of this composite (#3). Purifying your microcosm, the hidden memory of the divine world begins to work subconsciously. At the beginning it is not precise and it is very difficult to be aware of it. In *The Lost Symbol*, Dan Brown mentioned the engraving by Dürer titled *Melancholia*. This is your situation when your inner work increases this strange feeling of regret, of nostalgia. Your soul sighs trying to understand the cause of this strange feeling. Then another emotion appears that will progressively increase: desire. Maybe your spiritual and initiatic inner work allows you to understand your situation and your destin*y: coming back to your origin, your homeland.* This is a conversion, a real turnaround.

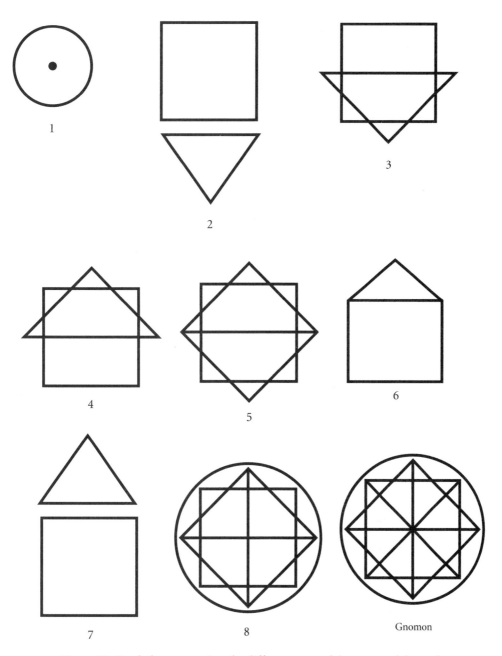

Figure 23: Symbols representing the different steps of the ascent of the soul

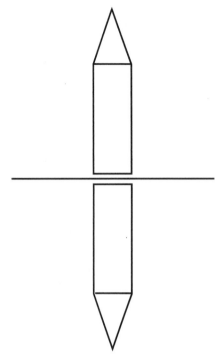

Figure 24: The obelisk and its reflection

This understanding is simple in this beautiful place of Washington DC. You just have to look up and forget the reflection. The real obelisk is in front of you, vertical, now showing the right direction. The direction of the triangle, symbol of the soul, has been reversed. It is pointed now to the sky (#4), creating the symbolic representation of the double square (#5). Each element must be animated by the soul united to its previous position under the aspect of the two triangles constituting the second square. This association of the triangle, apex of the obelisk in the reflecting pool oriented below, and the other one at the top oriented above, recalls the Hermetic declaration: "As above, so below."

This second square shows the two moments of the soul capable of giving the inner and divine animation of your being. You must imagine that you are now standing up straight as this axis at the center of the circumpunct. Your body, surrounded by the elements and activated by the human soul, can look up again and use the energy of its desire to ascend into the light. This axis shows you the mystical way. The ascent of this ray of light is an invocation of your inner divinity. For the first time, consciously, you will be crowned by the soul (#6). But you must ascend to the first principle. This step is a strange paradox because you are not already dead. You are a living human, trying to allow your soul to come back to your homeland. As you can see at the top of the obelisk, the soul is oriented to the sky. But that means that you are going to the center of your soul too. The connection between you and the highest level is inside you. This can be represented by the ascension of the soul above the body (#7) but at the same time by the mystical inner union (#8).

This is an important part of the divine mysteries. The thousand pages of the Bible can give you only one or two sentences, while the most accurate sources and explanations can be found in a text called "The Key" in the *Corpus Hermeticum*. According to these sacred writings, the direction of your quest is given by the feeling of good and beauty. Around you, on the Washington Mall, in the beauty of the place, the harmony and the goodwill of the Founding Fathers are still here. The aspiration to ascend to the divine can be manifested.

As Dan Brown analyzed correctly, the word *apotheosis* is a main concept in the Hermetic texts. The great mystery of this divinization, this apotheosis, is shown as a union with the divine principle, but not a fusion. The apex, the capstone, shows the Sun, concentrating the power of the soul, creating this enlightenment that is the higher expression of this essential part of one's being. Thoth-Hermes says: "And the soul's vice is ignorance." This is the expression of the Hermetic (and Masonic) philosophy. Faith is not enough. We must use our rationality, all our mental abilities to enlighten the virtue of the soul, which is knowledge.

The understanding of the Western Tradition is often lost, sometimes confused, or reduced to the Eastern spiritual interpretation. The contact of the soul, the contemplation of the divine unity, is at this moment a real and intimate union without fusion and disappearance. We are like singers around the chief choir's representation of the One.

This is the time of your divine transformation. In this contemplation of beauty, truth, and good, your own divinity is revealed and manifested. We are becoming gods. But don't be mistaken. You are not becoming a god, the One, but gods (plural!). Somehow the Biblical monotheism overlooked this reality, and even Dan Brown noted in *The Lost Symbol* that God was not one but many.

As the initiates of this tradition said, the manifestation of this inner experience is generally incomplete because of the physical body. You are still connected to your living body, so this representation of your apotheosis is an allegory. It will be a reality later, when you become a "Completed Master" as stated in Masonic terminology. The classical tradition, well understood by the architects of the federal capital, represented this allegorical apotheosis as the physical incarnation of divine beauty, a divine metamorphosis. The physical body becomes a divine body, an expression of spiritual beauty. Classical art represents the body as a god in the middle of the other gods on Olympus, and sometimes as Zeus the Great. "God [the One] knows the man, and God wants be

Figure 25: Dome of the U.S. Capitol

known. This is the only salvation for a man: God's Gnosis [knowingness]. This is the Way Up to Mount Olympus. By this way only the soul becomes good."

You remember the Capitol (in front of you at the east, beside the obelisk) as the temple of the gods, the protectors of the city. This is the place to show the masterpiece of these mysteries, and as for the Washington Monument, the stage is also ready. *The Apotheosis of Washington* clearly depicts George Washington being "transformed into a God."[8]

You can see the same allegorical subject in the mysterious statue depicting again the Founding Father in Zeus' exact posture. Nothing comes from the biblical tradition in this sacred place. The immortal divinities surround the representation of the One,

---

8. *Corpus Hermeticum, Book.*

a bright sky without representation. Immediately below, the Olympians are seated all around the enlightened apex. Like Zeus, George Washington is enthroned in the middle of them. The gods are invoked in a coherent way and their presence is welcomed in the purity of the tradition. The new nation can be protected and is shown the way to stay free, expressing the highest spiritual level a human can reach. Because a "human being is a living divine," you can keep your perception of the sacred and your reason for the realization of your own divinity together in a balanced way, for the good of humanity.

chapter five
THE MASONIC STRUCTURE
& THE ROSE-CROSS

The Structure of Freemasonry

In *The Lost Symbol*, Dan Brown emphasizes the mysterious and highest 33rd Degree of Scottish Rite Masonry. As the villain Mala'akh said many times, there are circles within circles, brotherhoods within brotherhoods. It takes only a few seconds on the Internet to learn how Dan Brown is correct in his writing. The Masonic "plot" seems to be everywhere. The main accusations deal with political, religious, racist, or even diabolic associations. They are as old as the existence of Freemasonry and are similar for other initiatic groups. In the nineteenth century, an Anti-Masonic Party attempted to destroy Freemasonry in the United States. But since the beginning of the nation, the Craft has been well represented everywhere, its philanthropic actions are well known, and these accusations didn't succeed. It isn't necessary to debate the falseness of these accusations of conspiracy, but it is interesting to explain how Freemasonry is organized and how it works.

First of all, it is worth noting that information about Freemasonry is available in books, on the Internet, and directly through the Freemasons themselves. Even more, it is always possible to visit Masonic temples in the United States and around the world. It's a wonderful way to receive explanations of the structure, goals, and symbolism of this famous brotherhood.

Dan Brown's novel presents the different degrees of Freemasonry as a pyramid-like hierarchy, controlled by the Supreme Council, the governing body of the Scottish Rite in America. The accompanying artistic illustration shows you the complete structure of Freemasonry.

*Figure 27: Square and Compass
in the 1st Degree*

*Figure 28: Square and Compass
in the 2nd Degree*

*Figure 29: Square and Compass
in the 3rd Degree*

The foundation of the whole system is based on the first three degrees: 1st Entered Apprentice, 2nd Fellowcraft, and 3rd Master Mason. This is the original structure and for many years nothing more existed. Consequently, the 3rd Degree completes the Masonic structure. All you need to know in Freemasonry can be found in these three degrees. It is important to know that, because the huge chart could suggest a different idea.

What I called a Masonic lodge or a Blue Lodge is composed of members of these three degrees. You may become aware of a local lodge from a road sign showing the square and the compass, and the meeting days, or simply a Masonic flag on the building itself letting you know that a traditional organization of the Craft is meeting there. Then, a common question arises: how to join them?

From time to time, you can see a sticker on cars stating "2B1 ask 1" or "To be one, ask one." This advice means that the best approch is to ask someone already a Freemason. If you don't know someone, you can simply go to the website of your state (or country) and send an e-mail or make a phone call. The Western Tradition says, "Knock, and the gate will be opened for you." So really, this first step in Freemasonry is simple.

After a few interviews, you may become initiated in a lodge and begin your Masonic journey. You will participate in ritual meetings, banquets, and instructional meetings. Some months later you may be initiated to the second step, Fellowcraft, and later to the third one, Master. The work and your apprenticeship are not finished after your 3rd Degree initiation. But Freemasonry considered that, as Master, you have most of the tools necessary to learn, practice, and improve your knowledge of the Craft. This is the main and the most traditional progression in Freemasonry, practiced in the same way every-where on the planet. It is never required to go further, and many Freemasons continue to practice in the lodge just as Masters.

All the lodges of a state or a country are administratively governed by a Grand Lodge with a common statement and bylaws. They are working under the protection of the Grand Lodge, keeping alive the high standard of the brotherhood. It is important to remember that a Grand Master (as a Master of the Lodge) is elected for one year and then is a Master Mason.

Considering this structure and its functioning, it is easy to see that a Masonic "con-spiracy" would be visible to everyone. The villain of *The Lost Symbol*, Mala'akh, began with these three degrees and, as expected, found nothing more.

In this case, the solution is to imagine another occult government, another secret circle inside the outer circle. If you look at the representation of Masonic structure, you can see several steps above the Blue Lodges. In this upper structure, you must consider three parts: (1) the Scottish Rite steps (on the left); (2) the York Rite steps (on the right); and (3) the Allied Organizations (in the center).

These names (Scottish and York) are missing in the Blue Lodges. In fact, there are several further rituals, sometimes different, in the Blue Lodge too. The two most impor-tant are called the Emulation Rite and the York Rite. There are other rites, less numer-ous (though interesting): Scottish Rite and others with local characteristics, Canadian Rite, French Rite, Memphis-Misraim, etc. In fact, this multiplicity can be considered an illusion. Most of the time the differences are minor and rarely involve the basics: sym-bols, myths, initiation, etc. Every Freemason practicing one of these rites can immedi-ately understand the other ones. The diversity is just an illusion.

However, things are quite different in the superstructure.

Since the beginning of Freemasonry, the Masters were interested in the development and the deepening of some parts of their tradition. They gathered outside of the Blue Lodges and worked, learned, and developed other rituals to explain some secondary as-pects. Some of these groups were more focused on esotericism, others on symbolism or mythology. From these original groups of researchers came new initiatic steps, comple-mentary to the first degrees. After several centuries, the most significant of them were organized in complete and coherent systems. The two most important are the Scottish Rite[1] and the York Rite.[2] Some others, like Egyptian degrees, were developed here and there. Some have disappeared over time.

The Lost Symbol focuses on the most representative of this system, the Scottish Rite in 30 degrees. Don't be confused by this number. Remember that the first three degrees in the Blue Lodge are for everyone, so the next step is the 4th (Secret Master, 1st on the left scale), the highest being the 33rd (Sovereign Grand Inspector General, 30th on the left scale). The complete name of what is called the Scottish Rite is in fact "the Supreme Council, Ancient and Accepted Scottish Rite, Southern Jurisdiction, USA" (commonly known as the "Mother Supreme Council of the World"). It was the first Supreme Council of Scottish Rite Freemasonry.

The Scottish Rite charters Subordinate Bodies in cities (called Valleys) or states, territories, or countries (called Orients). A Valley can have up to four Scottish Rite bodies, and each body confers a set of degrees. In the Southern Jurisdiction (the one described by Dan Brown), these are the Lodge of Perfection (from 4° to 14°), Chapter of Rose Croix (from 15° to 18°), Council of Kadosh (from 19° to 30°), and the Consistory (from 31° to 32°). The Supreme Council confers the 33rd Degree of Sovereign Grand Inspector General. So instead of talking about just the structures of the Blue Lodges, I am now talking in this scale of the Scottish Rite of Lodges of Perfection, Chapters, Councils, and Consistories.

In the United States, these degrees are separated in two jurisdictions: Northern and Southern. So there is not, as *The Lost Symbol* implicitly states, a unique Supreme Council governing the whole planet, but instead several, and, in this case, two in the United States. The one with its headquarters in the House of the Temple in Washington DC is the Southern jurisdiction, overseeing the Scottish Rite in thirty-five states (the other states fall within the Northern Jurisdiction, which is an independent body).

Just as you did for the first steps in Freemasonry, you can ask to begin your progression in the high degrees of the Scottish Rite. However, you cannot ask to receive the 33rd Degree, but must be proposed for this final step in recognition of your engagement, dedication, and work for the ideals of the Scottish Rite.

---

1. http://www.scottishrite.org/

2. The other branch is known as the York Rite, consisting of Royal Arch Masons, Royal and Select Masters, and the Knights Templar (http://www.yorkrite.org/).

Dan Brown's *The Lost Symbol* shows a challenging set of initiations, and an occult government manipulating people and initiates. This is a part of the "conspiracy theory" surrounding Freemasonry. There are accusations of diabolic purposes. Some fundamentalists believe that Scottish Rite Freemasons worship the devil in bloody rituals. But it is difficult to imagine that the funny hats of the Consistory can be a cover for some purpose more worrying or shameful.

It is, of course, quite impossible to disprove such hostile fantasies to someone already convinced of them. The character of Mala'akh in the novel shows such suspicious behavior. But facts are facts and you must not forget the novelistic features of *The Lost Symbol*. This advice is more important considering Dan Brown's bold declaration in the front of the novel that the geography, organizations, architecture, and rituals used in his novel are real and nonfictional. Maybe it would be better not to place the words "real" and "rituals" side by side. Maybe it would be better to say that such rituals were published by detractors of Freemasonry. The reality is that for many centuries detractors have published false rituals in order to discredit Freemasonry. Leo Taxil in Europe is one very good example of this, and a few minutes on the Internet will show you different satanic-Masonic rituals. So, yes, there are rituals in which the candidate kills lambs and others in which the candidate is obliged to drink blood. *But these rituals are imaginary!* They are inventions intended to discredit the fraternity. Don't be misled by fantasy presented as "fact."

But, if this is the case, it is difficult to understand why it is useful or desirable to keep such an initiatic hierarchy. Of course, as Mala'akh declared many times, all would be revealed in the 33rd Degree—but in order to figure out what is really going on, I must provide more information about the goal and activities of this Supreme Initiatic Hierarchy.

There are two main actions: one visible, another invisible. The first one can be seen very easily. It is the main activity of the members. Philanthropy is the first manifestation of the Scottish Rite in society. Through different programs (such as RiteCare Childhood Language Programs, Youth Programs, Scholarships, Internship Program, Disaster Relief) the organization and its members secure donations and help people in all these areas. These actions are for the benefit of everyone, regardless of color, gender, religion, etc. This is a real, powerful, and visible social action resulting from the brotherhood's individual and inner work on philanthropic values. This is a key to understanding the heart of the Scottish Rite and Freemasonry. The second aspect is educational. Freemasons are encouraged to increase their knowledge of the Craft, and many elements are available for that. Most of this work and learning is also available to non-Freemasons and they are welcomed to participate.

But I spoke about another dimension, one that is invisible to the outer world.

A stone building is more than a quantity of stones. Even when the word *lodge* is used to speak about the building, it is also used to speak about the group of initiates who gather there. The lodge is the basic cell of Freemasonry. This group of brethren, initiated in the same way and sharing the same ideals, will reveal a real psychological dimension as well as a spiritual one.

The lodge can become a community of spirits sharing the same goal. Every initiate is in the group to become better, to work on his own realization as human being, overcoming the unbalanced passions that so often lead him in wrong ways. In this temple, a space entirely devoted to this purpose, each member is able to focus on this essential goal: to keep away for a while what is selfish or much too personal. Far from any social judgment, the lodge is the perfect place where human brotherhood can be practiced in order to do the same in society. The work in the lodge is the expression of a utopia in progress. Every initiate can experience it, feel the difficulties, and make some improvements. All these common efforts have both an inward and an outward result. By using this method, the initiates can access this special experience and knowledge of a better humanity. They can understand the remaining efforts necessary to share these precious values with other people. This knowledge can help us work for the common good.

But as in a real family, such fraternity doesn't deny individual character. It does not demand every follower to blindly abandon his own essence. Nevertheless, there is more to the lodge than the mere sum of its parts. Like the stone building, the lodge becomes a kind of independent psychological creature, progressively developing its own special character and becoming more and more effective. This identity is larger than each brother and sometimes gives the feeling of being in another space. The name and the history of the lodge are important factors in the constitution of this invisible counterpart. Its longevity is another factor that contributes to this invisible essence. The more an initiate is involved in the life of the lodge, the more he will feel this strange presence. It seems that the will, the desire activated by the founders, progressively gave birth to this. Even more, this presence, sometimes called the egregore of the lodge, somehow helps the new initiates. It is the same for a lodge in trouble. Some help can appear by "chance." I spoke about a psychological entity rising from the group and producing a result larger than itself. Noetic science can lend some elements to theorize these manifestations. Even the theory of synchronicity can contribute to our understanding of how this results from the actions and thoughts of the brethren.

In the Western Tradition, different initiates have considered this idea in another way. In saying that there is more to the group than the sum of its parts, I didn't speak about the existence of an invisible and independent entity. But it's possible to claim the existence of an archetype of a Masonic lodge. The ritual work performed over many years can give birth to something called a "thought-form," to use a Theosophical expression created by Helena P. Blavatsky. As an archetype, the thought-form can be the result of a conjunction of wills, thoughts, and ritual acts. Over the years, this archetype can become somehow autonomous. If you want to imagine this phenomenon, think about the preparation of a pancake. Different elements are put together and mixed. But sometimes in the preparation lumps appear. They are representations of the archetypes, the thought-forms. Of course, they appear because of what you did and what you put in. Of course, in the case of a lodge, these archetypes are a good thing, contrary to the lumps in the pancake batter. Even more, an archetype can be consciously invoked by the inner work performed by the officers during the ritual. As I explained in another chapter, each initiate builds an inner temple. He works in his heart prior to working on the visible plan. So the ritual you can see is the result of spiritual and inner action. This is the origin of its power and efficiency. This is a real invisible action. The visible lodge becomes the manifestation of the spiritual lodge existing in the ideal world.

There is really something "magical," which is better named "theurgic." The beauty of such traditional theory is its intrinsic character. If this spiritual archetype exists, it can be a powerful help for every initiate as well as for the ideals of Freemasonry. If it is not the case, nothing changes regarding the inner work and the social philanthropic actions. Nothing is to lose, but something can be won and it will be fine to act as if it was the case.

For centuries the initiates preserved this important idea of a spiritual level. This is a good indication of the founding Masters' understanding. Of course, what is right for a lodge is right for a Grand Lodge. I can say also that there is more to a Grand Lodge than the sum of each lodge. This Masonic organization, this meeting of all the lodges in its jurisdiction, gives a special character and may be a particular egregore. While a Grand Lodge is firstly an administrative institution, its purpose and goal is larger. Every Grand Master has an insight and gives the best he has to be the worthy heir of an old family. Every action, every proposition he will undertake becomes part of this familial story.

The presence of respectable authorities as the founding fathers is still there and is a part of this egregore. It is impossible to act lightly this duty is felt. This is an occult part of Freemasonry, and may be underestimated. Freemasonry has the full weight of its tradition, this synergetic progression capable of keeping the ideals alive, no matter the period of time. And when leaders understand that, the result is powerful and beautiful. What you are doing today echoes in all of eternity! This is the exactly the meaning of this occult action of the Craft.

I am often amazed by the power of the invisible plane. Authentic traditions seem guided by some divine providence, which organizes the occult life of the orders according to definite spiritual laws.

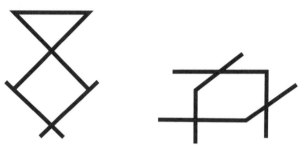

Figure 30: Mason marks found on old stones of the White House, Washington DC

This was also the case with the formation and development of the United States. A very old tradition, which is still used in Hermetic orders today, is called the "magical chain." One central sacred stone is consecrated and put in a symbolic place. Later, other stones are brought into contact with this central stone and then given to initiates of the order. After this transmission, they are able to work in spiritual and vibratory contact with the mystical center. In 1948, during the presidency of Freemason Harry Truman, the White House was restored. It was impossible to find the cornerstone, but several stones were discovered, complete with Masonic markings. President Truman decided to distribute each marked stone to one of America's Grand Lodges. The spiritual chain was formed!

And so, you (the reader) may still be wondering about the secret 33rd Degree. Dan Brown suggested in his novel that this 33rd Degree would be the place where all is revealed to the initiate, the moment of the manifestation of the divine powers the initiate has been working to receive. This degree has been associated by its founders with a rich symbolism. As the novel accurately states, this number (33) can be connected to many symbols in the Western Tradition. From the symbolic age of Jesus Christ at his death, to the number of discs in the human spinal column, to the height of the capstone of the Washington Monument, this number seems omnipresent. The founding Freemasons noticed this far-reaching and symbolically important number and used it as the upper level of the scale of advancement within the order. From this perspective, I could say that the Supreme Council of the Scottish Rite has in its grasp an enormous and invisible power: the ability to find ways to keep alive this high standard of morality and to continually develop it, in order to help with the construction of a more evolved humanity.

Mysteries of the Rose-Cross

In *The Lost Symbol*, Dan Brown is focused on certain aspects of Freemasonry, but he also mentions other groups that are connected to Freemasonry. These are called Allied Organizations. The chart on the structure of Freemasonry provided earlier in this chapter diagrams the most important Allied Organizations; these may be found in the middle of that diagram, under the arch. Most of these groups are composed of Freemason groups such as the Shriners, Grotto, etc. Others are feminine adjuncts of Freemasonry groups, such as the Order of the Eastern Star and the Daughters of the Nile. The third listing is composed of the sons or daughters of Freemasons. It is important

Figure 31: Symbolic representation of the Pelican and the Rose-Cross

to understand that, even though these organizations are connected with Freemasons or restricted to Freemasons and their families, they are not a part of Freemasonry. The reasons these adjunct groups are not a part of Freemasonry may be simply stated: (1) Freemasonry only accepts adult males, and (2) Freemasonry is composed of initiatic degrees validated by the tradition.

In reality, these Allied Organizations are groups that are devoted to the Masonic ideals. They are focused on different social philanthropic activities. Despite its name, the Shrine (Ancient Arabic Order of the Nobles of the Mystic Shrine) is in no way connected to Islam. The Shriners International is a fraternity managed by Master Freemasons that supports the Shriners Hospitals for Children. This is an international health-care system of twenty-two hospitals dedicated to improving the lives of children by providing special needs pediatric care, innovative research, and outstanding teaching programs. Of course, any child who needs help will receive treatment at the Shriners Hospitals and no child is ever turned away. There is no requirement for any child to be related to a Freemason in any way in order for him or her to be eligible for care; any child in need will receive care there. All services are provided at no financial obligation to families. The Daughters of the Nile group is the feminine equivalent of the Shriners.

As Dan Brown remarks in his book, these philanthropic organizations are very remote from the concept of any secret organizations connected to the Egyptian pyramids. However, there are other circles connected to Freemasonry that are perhaps less well known, which Dan Brown seems to be unfamiliar with. These groups, which are commonly found all over the United States, fall into the category titled Allied Masonic Organizations, or Masonic Appendant Bodies. Membership in any of these organizations requires the applicant to be a Master Mason, while others require a membership in the Royal Arch (right of representation). These degrees or initiations are detached degrees, some of which, many years ago, were conferred under Craft warrants and formed part of the then loosely governed Freemasonry of that period. (See the glossary at the end of this book for the definition of any special terms used here.)

Many of these detached degrees became dormant, although in others they were conferred as side degrees. In time, the most worthy of these degrees were grouped together in an organized body under the title of Allied Masonic Degrees. These organizations not only work to foster the ideals of Freemasonry (such as the hospital work already mentioned), but another purpose of these organizations is to improve the opportunities for study and research. Of course, these groups are not a different Masonic path, unique unto themselves; they are adjuncts and, just as the name states, allied organizations.

Among the large number of allied structures found in the United States, one of them is a society called the *Societas Rosicruciana*. In his novel, Dan Brown employs the symbol of the rose cross as an explanation of the mystery of the cube of stone. In a few lines, he summarizes the traditional legend of the rose cross, mixing errors with truths. As you will see in Chapter Seven of this book, the 18th Degree of the Scottish Rite is called the Knight Rose Cross. This degree is actually connected to symbolic elements of the famous fraternity of the Rose-Cross. However, several initiations in Freemasonry also use this name or the symbol of the rose cross. Of course, none of these degrees pretend to be the heir to the ancient Rose-Cross that emerged in the eighteenth century. As Dan Brown noted, several philosophers and scientists from this time (such as Paracelsus, Bacon, Fludd, Descartes, Pascal, Spinoza, Newton, Leibniz, John Dee, Elias Ashmole, Robert Fludd, etc.) claimed to be members of the Rose-Cross or were associated with this mysterious order in some way.

However, Dan Brown is wrong when he asserts that the Order of the Rose-Cross is the same as the Ancient and Mystical Order Rosae Crucis. As you will soon see, the second name refers to the AMORC, which is the name of a modern organization founded in 1915; this founding is subsequent to the already extant Orders of the Rose-Cross that still exist. In order to clear up some of the confusion created by *The Lost Symbol*, I will offer some precise elements about this important Western Tradition (the orders of the Rose-Cross) in order to help you to decipher the rose cross symbols used in that novel.

The first chronological markers are easy to understand and summarize.

The years 1614, 1615, 1616: The publication of the fundamental writings of the Rose-Cross by John Valentin Andreae and his "circle" of friends. There was no Rose-Cross organization prior to this.

1777: The organization of a German order connected to Freemasonry called the "Golden and Rosy Cross." This initiatic group was active for approximately nine years.

1867: The organization, in England, of the *Societas Rosicruciana in Anglia* (S.R.I.A.)[3] derived from the *Societas Rosicruciana in Scotland* (S.R.I.S.) following the admission of William James Hughan.

1888: The organization, in France, of the *Ordre Kabbalistique de la Rose-Croix* (Qabalistic Order of the Rose-Cross)[4] by Stanislas de Guaita.

Only the two last organizations still exist. Any other such organizations you may find in your research are modern inventions, after the beginning of nineteenth century.

In order to understand the origin of these mysterious Rose-Cross organizations, it is necessary to look at the history of this developing movement. Between 1614 and 1616, three strange books were anonymously published in Germany. The authors were the pastor Johann Valentin Andreae and his circle of friends. They published the *Fama Fraternitatis Rosae Crucis*, the *Confessio Fraternitatis*, and *The Chymical Wedding of Christian Rosenkreutz*.

According to modern historians, there is no indication of any occult group called the Rose-Cross or *Rosae Crucis* prior to these publications. As for any esoteric traditions or religions of the same name, the founding myths of the group formed by Johann Valentin Andrae claim their works originated in antiquity and these myths continue to persist today. To clarify the situation, I will offer some facts. It is perfectly true that the symbols of the cross and the rose are ancient. Both symbols have demonstrably been used in poetry, religion, and esotericism since ancient times. However, the modern development of the pictures of the rose on a cross is new and not part of any ancient lineage. There are also several writers who have claimed that some such fraternities did exist prior to Andreae, but these writers held that they existed in secret, and their symbol was a rose on a cross.

Although it is never possible to absolutely prove or dismiss such assertions, it is certainly very easy to accept the existence of hidden/secret circles transmitting an initiation that was linked to the Ancient Mysteries. This was decidedly the case for the Hermetic and Neoplatonic Traditions I described earlier in this text. Christian Qabalists were directly involved in the perpetuation of this inheritance. Of course, they were Christians, which generally meant they were Catholics (as nearly everyone was at that time) with a few being ecclesiastics. However, it is very easy to see that their interpretation of the

---

3. *Societas Rosicruciana in Anglia*: http://www.sria.info/

4. *Qabalistic Order of the Rose-Cross*: http://www.okrc.org/

dogma was not very canonical. Heinrich Cornelius Agrippa von Nettesheim (1486–1535) and Dr. Heinrich Khunrath (1560–1605) are two very good examples of the existence of this esoteric tradition. As you can see in the magical books written by Agrippa, the ancient pre-Christian traditions are everywhere. There are no differences between the ancient divinities and the Hebrew divine names (as described in their works). It would be fair to say that all the writings of these authors, such as Khunrath and others, are closer to Christianity and the Hebrew Qabalah, but that they all have the same goal: to unveil the mysteries; thus, to penetrate the veil.

There are several examples of evidence of the existence of a real esoteric brotherhood prior to the publication of the Rose-Cross manifestos. Various special symbols were carefully chosen by the initiates of these Qabalistic circles. For example the Qabalistic Order of the Rose-Cross used some esoteric representations from Kunrath's book called *Amphitheatrum Sapientiae Aeternae (Amphitheater of Eternal Wisdom)*, first published in 1595. One of the most famous illustrations portrays a rose of light with a central body in the position of a cross. This very complex and beautiful engraving was identified as a Qabalistic and occult symbol of the Rose-Cross Tradition. The analysis of this mandala shows a circular representation of the Qabalistic Tree of Life and can be seen as the first and most complete union between the Hebrew and the Christian Qabalah, in the shape of a hidden rose cross.

Nothing of this deep symbolism is present in the publications from Andreae. The origin of the texts he published and his purpose appear to be of a different nature. As I said, Andreae was a German pastor. He published those manifestos one century after the Reformation movement that was initiated by Martin Luther (1483–1546). Another of his books presents a city-state named Christianopolis. Undoubtedly, his purpose was to use antique esoteric "clothing" in order to present his ideas on religion, philosophy, politics, and society to the world. It is traditional to use allegories in such discreet publications and this was also true in the past. The alchemical symbols linked to some powerful founding myths gave birth to many a creation that outstripped its creator(s). In this way, Christian Rosenkreuz (in English, his name translates as "Christian Rose Cross") became the mythic father of the fraternity, a mythical hero, illuminated and immortal as a Master of the Tradition.

As a young German noble, Rosenkreuz was sent to a monastery for education. However, he left it to begin a pilgrimage to Jerusalem and the Middle East, looking for masters who would be able to give him the esoteric wisdom he was looking for. He found them and was welcomed as the one they were waiting for. After three years, he left with a sacred book called *M*. This may be a reference to the *Book of the World, Liber Mundi*. After spending time in Egypt in order to receive the esoteric teachings available in that part of the world, he came back to Europe and founded the Fraternity of the Rose-Cross. Under his direction, a temple called the House of the Holy Spirit was built.

This new monastery was the place where he developed and transmitted his knowledge to seven other members. After taking an oath of fidelity, silence, and work, they lived in different countries to work as members of the Rose-Cross, helping the poor without payment. Their seal was the acronym "R+C." They promised to come back once every year. Nobody knows when the master died, but 120 years after his death, his body was discovered by a brother of the order, in a state of perfect preservation. He was buried in a chamber that had been previously erected by him as a storehouse of knowledge. On the sarcophagus in the center of the crypt was written, among other inscriptions, the Christian declaration "*Jesus mihi omnia, nequaquam vacuum, libertas evangelii, dei intacta gloria, legis jugum*" ("Jesus is everything to me, nowhere a vacuum, the freedom of the gospels, the inviolate glory of God, the yoke of the law").

Following this first myth, the *Confessio Fraternitatis* appeared as a more socially oriented text and *The Chymical Wedding of Christian Rosenkreutz* appeared as an allegory describing a very interesting spiritual journey. Despite the constant use of alchemical and esoteric symbols, this myth is rooted in the Christian tradition with very little emphasis on the ancient Hermetic inheritance. The Hermetic and Neoplatonic Traditions are not present in this work. It is almost as if the author was not interested in these traditions, or at least not aware of this important knowledge. This ignorance of such important traditions (perhaps unintentionally) gave credit to scholars who set about explaining the political and religious character of these writings. Some studies go so far as to assert that these publications were jokes. Yet the mythical idea was firmly established and continued to exist after the death of Andreae as a new expression of Christian esoteric teachings.

After this period, the Rose-Cross Tradition found two main means of expression: (1) inside of or directly linked with Freemasonry (Christian character), and (2) linked to esoteric groups (Hermetic character).

Rose-Cross, the Masonic Lineage

Around 1755 in Germany, various groups called the Golden Cross and the Rosy Cross appeared. At that time, these groups were not part of Freemasonry. These groups were not organized together and continued to be isolated from each other for some years after their creation. However, close contacts were initiated between them and Freemasons interested in esotericism. In 1757, some Golden Cross and Rosy Cross groups took on a more Masonic structure. At this juncture, the relationship between Freemasonry and Rose Cross was only the result of specific individuals who decided to explore and cross-pollinate. However, in 1777, one of these circles became a unified group and took the name of the Golden and Rosy Cross of the Old System. Its structure was Masonic and it was composed of nine high degrees. It required its members to take a strict oath regarding rites and initiations, and it maintained a rigid hierarchical structure. This initiatic group recruited many Freemasons who were interested in the esoteric sciences, such as alchemy, the Qabalah, and Christian esotericism. The group initiated members of different political affiliations; since they worked in harmony with each other, the group became quite so-

cially influential. Despite the fact that it grew in size very quickly, the order disappeared approximately nine years after its birth.

At about this same time in France, a Freemason named Tschoudy devised a new set of degrees, which he named Knights of the Rose Cross. These degrees were progressively integrated into other Masonic systems, as you can see in the Scottish Rite today.

The next important step in the evolution of this line was the constitution in Scotland of the first *Societas Rosicruciana*, known as the *Societas Rosicruciana in Scotia* (S.R.I.S.). This group was directly influenced by the Rose Cross publications in Germany. It is difficult to say whether there was a direct link between the two, but they claimed that there was. In 1867, the famous *Societas Rosicruciana in Anglia* (Society of Rosicrucians in England, or S.R.I.A.) was constituted from the S.R.I.S. and the discovery of certain

Figure 32: One of the representations of the Rose Cross

manuscripts in the archives of the Grand Lodge. This order continues to exist today and is the center of all *Societas Rosicruciana(s)* that have been set up in every country around the world, including those in the United States. Its statements of philosophy are identical everywhere in every group that is set up using this model, and this is valid evidence of the presence and influence of this line of the tradition.

The *Societas Rosicruciana in Anglia* is an independent Christian society. Admission is limited to Master Masons who are subscribing members of a lodge under the Grand Lodge of England or a jurisdiction in amity with this Grand Lodge, and who accept and believe in the fundamental principles of the Trinitarian Christian faith. Even if the affiliation is restricted to the Freemasons, the very restrictive confessional clause is absolutely not in the spirit of what was built by the founders of Freemasonry at its inception. All Masons remember the power of a belief in a supreme being without defining him. This is one of the critical and fundamental elements of Freemasonry; it is a warranty for world peace in our time.

The above is why this society of the Rose Cross is linked to Freemasonry, but must not be confused with the Rose Cross degrees present within Freemasonry. I am differentiating here between two disparate entities: one inside Freemasonry (R.C. Degrees) and the other outside of that body (the S.R.I.A.).

With this in mind, it is interesting to note that the S.R.I.A. has a very useful set of degrees that utilize the structure of the Qabalistic Tree. Three orders compose the progression (up the Tree): 1st order: Zelator, Theoricus, Practicus, and Philosophus. 2nd order: Adeptus Minor, Adeptus Major, and Adeptus Exemptus. 3rd order: Magister and Magus. The society is focused on the practice of the rituals, their Qabalistic studies, and the writing of various research papers. These groups are very close to what are called now "research lodges." Despite the obligation related to faith, the famous magical society called the Hermetic Order of the Golden Dawn emerged from the S.R.I.A. The three founders, William Robert Woodman, William Wynn Westcott, and Samuel Liddell Mac-Gregor Mathers, were Freemasons and members of the *Societas Rosicruciana in Anglia*. The complete system was a magical offshoot of the S.R.I.A. system, which attempted to integrate other esoteric elements such as the Enochian magic of John Dee, the writings of Agrippa, and, perhaps, some other documents that came from the old German Rose-Cross movement. Its hierarchy was built along the same structural lines as Freemasonry. However, as soon as these organizations began initiating women and non-Masons, they immediately lost recognition by the Masons, since women cannot be initiated into Freemasonry.

The original S.R.I.A. gave birth to two groups in the United States: the *Societas Rosicruciana in America*, and the *Societas Rosicruciana in Civitatibus Foederatis* (Rosicrucian Society of the United States). The first group is mostly inactive today. The second group, created in 1880, is still active according to the original tradition of this branch.

Rose-Cross, the Hermetic Lineage

France is well known to be the place where the first symbolic Western nonreligious texts were written during medieval times. The *Romance of the Rose* and the *Grail Quest* are important texts revealing a real esoteric tradition emphasized by the troubadours in the south of France. Some of the founding Hebrew Qabalistic schools were developed during those years. This esoteric inheritance was linked to the Christian Qabalah of the Renaissance. It was for this reason that the south of France was always a special home of the Hermetic tradition. Many famous religions had their birth here, including those coming out of eastern Gnosticism and the gnostic beliefs of the Cathars. In these regions, religious freedom was the most powerful element, and the Catholic Church organized a crusade to exterminate all these "dangerous" belief systems. The south of France was also the birthplace of various high Masonic degrees that were designed to integrate Hermetic and Esoteric teachings. This region of France continued to be the center of the main Western initiatic societies, and it maintained this place in the collective imagination, which is, of course, larger than the actual country. For example, you might recall the examples of the mystery of Rennes le Château, the Priory of Sion, *Holy Blood, Holy Grail,*[5] and *The Da Vinci Code,* all of which center around mysteries that had the south of France as their geographic and mystical home. The Hermetists and occultists were always present and it was there (in the region of Toulouse) that this Rose-Cross lineage appeared. This was the result of three influences: the troubadour tradition, the work of the mystical and symbolical German Rose-Cross group, and the efforts of the Mediterranean Hermetic traditions. This last group's influence led to an emphasis on alchemy, astrology, and theurgy. This Rose-Cross group was independent from Freemasonry, even though its members were very often Freemasons. They created little groups whose study and work were focused on the Qabalistic and Hermetic inheritance. In 1850, the Viscount Louis-Charles-Edouard de Lapasse, who was both a physician and esoterist, became the master of this secret school.

---

5. Michael Baigent, Richard Leigh, and Henry Lincoln, *Holy Blood, Holy Grail.* (city: publisher, year).

A few years later, in 1884, the Marquis Stanislas de Guaita met the brothers Peladan, who were linked to this order. De Guaita was initiated by Firmin Boissin, the Grand Master at that time. From Boissin, he received the transmission of this Hermetic Rose-Cross Tradition, its teachings, and a mission. His duty and goal were to organize a nonreligious order focused on serious theoretical teachings and powerful theurgic rituals. Because of the oaths of secrecy, the only part that remained visible to the public was the aspect composed of their studies.

In 1888, in order to honor his obligations, he founded the *Ordre Kabbalistique de la Rose-Croix* (Qabalistic Order of the Rose-Cross). This date was not chosen by chance. You may remember that the Golden and Rosy Cross of the Old System was reorganized in 1777. According to its teachings, the new order was to be recreated exactly 111 years from that date. (With a beautiful synchronicity, the Washington Monument was officially opened in the same year: 1888.)

Among the most famous members of the O.K.R.C. (Q.O.R.C.) were: Papus (Gérard Encausse), Paul Adam, Jollivet-Castelot, Marc Haven (Dr. Lalande), Paul Sedir (Yvon Le Loup), Pierre Augustin Chaboseau, Erik Satie, Emma Calve, Camille Flammarion, and many other prominent figures of this time. The chiefs of the order were very regularly in contact with English initiates of the S.R.I.A. and the Golden Dawn.

This order continued to be the inspirational source of several Western spiritual schools. The tradition was transmitted on the visible plane as an honorific consecration in some French Masonic orders. However, at the same time, the real lineage was preserved in secret by Grand Patriarchs of the order, thus keeping intact the original and theurgic rituals, even today.

Strangely, Dan Brown came very close to uncovering these traditions in *The Lost Symbol* on two different occasions, but he never made a precise identification. Nevertheless, his intuition was extended into several other important areas, through his use of the Rose-Cross symbols. I will look at this aspect in the next section.

From the Rose-Cross to the Pyramid

In *The Lost Symbol,* a doubly symbolic connection becomes evident between the symbols of the cross, the rose, and our mundane selves. There is also a symbolic relationship between the cube and the cross. The cube is a symbol of the material world, of the "hidden stone" found at the center of one's being. Thus, the symbolic relationship is obvious between the physical body and the stone. As Dan Brown explains, an opened cube in a two-dimensional representation is a cross. Of course, this symbol is not merely a Christian one. Very often the symbol of the cross is interpreted as a man standing erect, with his arms extended at both sides on the horizontal plane. This early form of adoration is represented by the vertical axis of the cross, which is the site of the ascending and descending movement of the divine powers. The

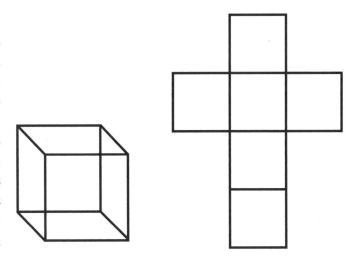

Figure 33: The cube and its development in the cross

horizontal bar of the cross represents materiality, our humanity balancing the spiritual energy of the vertical axis. The intersecting point of these two lines was later linked to the solar plexus, the Sun, and the heat at the center of our being. For this reason, this point was associated with the symbolic rose. In this way, the rose cross was born.

Even if this symbol is very often used by different modern Rose-Cross Orders, or in Freemasonry, it is not as old as claimed. The truth is different. The rose was associated with the cross every time in the opposite position as we saw on the figure of Kunrath, the cross being in the center of the rose. The illustration by Kunrath and Luther's coat of arms show this original position. This is an interesting point of view, to consider that you can be at the center of your rose. They are several connections between the rose, the development of its petals, light, perfume, etc. and

Figure 34: Valentin Andreae Arms

your aura. If you are at the center, the connections are obvious. The hidden stone is really in the center of your body of light. With the mysterious cube inside you, the rose cross can be a clear illustration of an invisible reality. This symbolic representation will be used in a practical ritual in Chapter Seven.

There is also another hidden symbol that Dan Brown never mentions. In *The Lost Symbol*, you may recall the description of the cube and the unfinished pyramid, which is the capstone of this cube. Apparently, (given his omission of mentioning any connection), we are to assume there is no connection between this important Masonic shape and the rose cross. In fact, there is strong connection, but it is less known than the first one I spoke of. If we consider some of the ancient symbols, we find that there is not one rose but four, one for each element. This is the case in the "first day" of *The Chymical Wedding of Christian Rosenkreutz*. After receiving an angelic message in a dream, Christian Rosenkreutz prepared himself in order to begin his spiritual journey. He put on a white linen coat and girded his loins with a blood-red ribbon bound

Figure 35: Qabalistic Order of the Rose-Cross

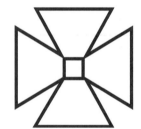

Figure 36: The unfinished pyramid and its development in the cross

crossways over his shoulder. Then he stuck four red roses in his hat. There is some interesting symbolism that associates the red cross and the four roses. But before considering its meaning, I should point out a clear and obvious link between these elements and Valentin Andreae's coat of arms. Out of respect for this symbolism and its origin, the Qabalistic Order of the Rose-Cross chose a seal composed of four roses, a cross, and a pentagram. This cross is different from the red cross, which was the result of the esoteric development of the cube. We must keep in mind the Hermetic character of this lineage of the Rose-Cross.

As a consequence, the development of its central symbol is different and complementary. There is also a two-dimensional symbol. If I recreate the three-dimensional symbol of this cross, the result is not a cube, but an unfinished pyramid! These results are amazing. From one lineage of the tradition, we can obtain a cube, and from the other one we obtain a pyramid. If we add together the results of our investigation of these two lineages, by joining these two main symbols the manifestation of the tradition is complete: we have the cube and the unfinished pyramid. The human being (represented by the pentagram) can receive illumination at the secret meeting point of the circumpunct, his solar center: apotheosis.

Noetic Science & Hidden Abilities

The Interview

Dan Brown's *The Lost Symbol* describes an interesting connection between the Ancient Mysteries and the modern field of noetic science. As the author noted, both the mysteries and this new science have brought under consideration the untapped potential of the human mind as mentioned in several Masonic texts. Of course this is not an "official" science; it really sounds more like magick than science. The interesting thing is to see the emergence of a new scientific expression that might have enormous ramifications across every discipline: physics, history, philosophy, religion, etc.

This idea is very powerful and can open our future to a radically different perspective. As every initiate of the past has repeatedly said, if we are really the masters of our own universe, we will be able to participate in it. These investigations may be a real key to a markedly different future for all of us. It may allow us to analyze reality differently than we have in the past, which may further allow us to demonstrate the reality of many ancient theories.

In order to continue with these considerations, in order to determine which parts of Dan Brown's novel are real and which are fiction, I met with Dr. Jaden Francis Ward, a scientist who is well versed in noetic science, and who is also well aware of the mysteries, since he is himself an initiate in two initiatic orders of the Hermetic Tradition. The following chapter is the transcribed interview that took place.

Q: Can you introduce yourself?

In short, I am a scientist with an interest in spirituality. After obtaining a Ph.D. in neuroscience, I started to work as a researcher in brain science. I study brain imaging using electro-encephalographic recordings (EEG) and functional magnetic resonance imagery (FMRI). These brain imaging techniques have revolutionized the theories of the mind—neuroscience is sometimes called the "new alchemy" because of the wide range of the unknown this new field of science deals with. I am also a Master Mason, and an initiate of the *Ordo Aurum Solis*.

Q: Dan Brown's novel *The Lost Symbol* speaks about noetic science. Can you explain exactly what is this new field?

Noetic science is a neologism that was inspired by the original definition of *noetic*, a branch of metaphysical philosophy. The word *noetic* comes from the Greek word *noetikos* ("mental"), itself a combinations of the words *noein* ("to think") and *noûs* (for which there is no exact equivalent in English). The original noetic was only concerned with the philosophical study of mind and intuition (a philosophy of mind).

My own definition of noetic science may help the reader to understand the context: noetic science is grossly the combination of new models in neuroscience and quantum physics, with a refined definition of parapsychology. Despite the fact that the former are well accepted in the scientific community, the latter is not—parapsychology is not scientific (yet). This is said without judging the quality of research performed in noetic science, or the integrity of scientists involved in this field—but just to stress that noetic science is still considered as a fringe science. In other words, contrary to what may be understood from the book of Dan Brown, noetic science is not accepted as a new academic field of research in what some would describe as "mainstream science." You will not find Chairs in noetic science, neither in universities, nor in scientific academies. The scientific community tends to react conservatively to new ideas infringing on its established paradigms—for good reasons; we could not speak of science at all if its paradigms were changing every now and then. I am nevertheless often shocked to see eminent scientists defend, publicly or privately, preconceived, narrow-minded, and outdated materialist opinions. With the leaders of the scientific community having such a perception of reality, I cannot imagine how science could one day integrate noetic science. However, this does not mean that noetic science is not of interest, and I believe that such researches are necessary—and hopefully, I am not the only scientist with this opinion!

Nowadays, the most emblematic group involved in noetic science is probably the Institute of Noetic Sciences (IONS), which was created in 1973. IONS defines noetic science in its own terms, as the explorations into the nature and potentials of consciousness using multiple ways of knowing—including intuition, feeling, reason, and the senses. Noetic science explores the "inner cosmos" of the mind (consciousness, soul, spirit) and how it relates to the "outer cosmos" of the physical world. In other words, the concept does not only include consciousness, but also all aspects of spirituality. Cassandra Vieten, director of research at the Institute of Noetic Sciences, recently defined noetic science as a multidisciplinary field that brings objective scientific tools and techniques together with subjective inner knowing to study the full range of human experience. A very spiritually oriented definition!

Another definition comes from the popular science writer George Zarkadakis. In 2001, he presented some radical novel ideas about a scientific approach of noetics during an academic conference in Sweden. His ideas can be found in the paper he presented, called "Noetics: A proposal for a theoretical approach to consciousness." In this paper, he defined noetic science, mainly based on the recent progress in neuroscience about consciousness. He defended the idea that the mechanism of consciousness may be described by a finite set of quantifiable laws, which may be called "noetic laws." These laws could be verified as the fundamental causes of mental phenomena.

The definition of Zarkadakis goes in the direction of the Australian philosopher David Chalmers. Chalmers states that all forms of physicalism (what laypersons usually call "materialism") have dominated modern philosophy, and science fails to account for the existence of consciousness. Chalmers defended this opinion in a famous book, *The Conscious Mind* (1996), which is still hotly debated in academic circles.

As a scientist, I know that spirituality is far from being well understood. Science just came out of the positivist period, when astrology, parapsychology, and spiritualism were severely attacked by public scientific figures. Consequently, spirituality kept an aura of taboo in many laboratories, and in the minds of most scientists I met. As I explained above, noetic science is labeled as a fringe science. What is accepted, instead, is the field of neurotheology. Neurotheology tries to approach religious experiences with the means of modern neuroscience and brain imagery; and contrary to noetic science, professors of neurotheology exist in universities. Despite the philosophical concept of neurotheology being mentioned before, in a book written by Aldous Huxley (in his novel *Island*), real scientific investigations in this field were later on shaped by the studies of Dr. Michael Persinger in the 1980s. Persinger tried to provoke religious experiences with a magnetic stimulation of the temporal lobes of the brain of his subjects (the magnetic stimulation induces an electrical stimulation inside the brain). When the field of neurotheology was developed, it followed a dominating materialist interpretation—where consciousnesses, and especially spiritual experiences, would be delusions generated by material mechanisms inside the brain. Persinger even claimed that spiritual visions were the outcome of epileptic seizures, and a few scientists tried in vain to demonstrate that the practice of meditation could induce epilepsy! However, an emblematic scientist of this field, Dr. Mario Beauregard, defends a nonmaterialist approach of neurotheology (I would direct the interested reader to his book *The Spiritual Brain*). This field of science is however still making its first steps, and we are far from having a thorough knowledge of the human spiritual experience.

Why are the latest researches in neurotheology of interest for us? Because it can bring a clear answer to the question of the status of spirituality. In psychiatry, a patient with an interest in spirituality and who reports a mystic experience may be labeled with a "mystical delirium." But in traditional societies, he would become a spiritual leader. The fine distinction between wisdom and madness is not easy in our modern world, but neurotheology could help us see through our preconceived ideas. For instance, it was believed for years by some psychiatrists that the well-known phenomenon of out-of-the-body experience (OBE, sometimes referred as astral travel) was a hallucination created by a diseased psyche, most probably due to schizophrenia. OBE was however shown by Professor Olaf Blanke to have no causal relationship with schizophrenia or any other brain disorder. Similarly, it was shown by Dr. Sara W. Lazar that meditation reinforces the brain's cortical thickness. In her own words: "Meditation might offset age-related cortical thinning."

What was shown by neurotheology researches (especially those of Beauregard) is that meditation and spiritual experiences are to be distinguished from relaxation and hallucinations. In other words, spirituality is a valid human experience, not a symptom of madness (spirituality is not a delusion). What science has not shown yet is an interaction between mind and matter—in other words, one cannot prove if spirituality is only psychological, or has instead some effects such as those claimed by classical parapsychology (moving objects with the sole power of your mind, etc.). In my opinion, science is lacking the epistemological tools to study such effects, because it remains stuck in a strict causal-materialist model of reality (despite it having already evolved away from the traps of positivism).

Modern epistemology excludes the concept of teleology. In this model, what happens in the world has to be induced by a cause (causal explanation). In simple words, the world is seen as an assemblage of Lego blocks (the atoms), which interact through physical forces. This generally accepted view was not considered as dogma in antiquity. It was once believed that the visible effects in reality could instead happen not because of, but for, a purpose (teleology). In addition, models of physics other than the Lego block atoms exist: string theory, ondulatory representation of matter, etc. These models could be used to explain spiritual phenomenology—with the condition that we reform scientific epistemology. As a matter of fact, what modern science tries to prove is a system of causal effects applied to Lego blocks. If instead we try to prove effects based on their meaning, then the experimental conditions should be reversed. To prove causality, one needs to restrain the number of possible causes (to keep only the cause under study). But if one wants instead to study teleology, it will be necessary to explore an array of causes matched against one constrained outcome (the experimental thinking should be upside down, and this would be a conceptual revolution). This unusual experimental concept is not philosophically accepted in scientific circles—actually I never met a scientist who dared to question the concept of causal experimentation. Until such a new paradigm is accepted, I believe that experimental proofs will always fail to ascertain the existence of spirituality.

As a conclusion on this point, let us cite the beginning of the book of Beauregard: "The fact is materialism is stalled. It neither has any useful hypotheses for the human mind or spiritual experiences nor comes close to developing any. Just beyond lies a great realm that cannot even be entered via materialism, let alone explored."[1]

Q: Do you really believe that we have inner and hidden abilities or powers?

Yes, I am convinced that we have inner abilities—but with the limit that I do not believe in "Hollywoodian spiritual powers." I am convinced that the world is more than an assemblage of Lego blocks—I am definitively not a materialist. In my opinion, nothing "supernatural" exists in the classical definition of this term; the material and spiritual aspects of reality are intricate, and are organized in complex schemes (embedded, like fractal dimensions) rather than pyramidal, top-down simplistic systems. My vision of reality is closer to Proclus' hylemorphism. Hylemorphisms are metaphysical views of reality according to which every natural body consists of two intrinsic principles, one potential (namely, primary matter) and one actual (namely, substantial form). This idea was first developed by Aristotle, and later Neoplatonist philosophers (especially Plotinus and Proclus) discussed different models of reality where they tried to define the interaction of the spiritual and material aspects of nature.

In the model described by Proclus, reality is maintained through the dynamic interaction of the material and spiritual aspects of reality (in other words, nature is not a passive receptacle). With this kind of model of reality, inner powers or abilities are natural—in opposition with Hollywoodian supernatural powers. Indeed, if nature is interacting with the spiritual planes, then there is no reason for an "invisible barrier" separating nature from the spiritual planes: there is a continuum between material and spiritual aspects of reality. This means that, in my opinion, such inner abilities are to be found in interactions similar to what C. G. Jung described as synchronicities: they do not contradict the general organization of reality. Synchronicity is an orthogonal force, which does not oppose causality, but complements it. In the theories of Jung, reality is the outcome of the interaction of two forces: the material organizing force (causality) and the spiritual one (synchronicity).

---

1. M. Beauregard and D. O'Leary. *The Spiritual Brain: A Neuroscientist's Case for the Existence of the Soul.* (New York: HarperOne, 2007).

Jung came up with this theory when he observed that the deep psychic content of the dreams of his patients could interact with random events in reality. These random interactions could easily be explained in term of causality—they did not contradict the law of causality. Yet, they had a numinous spiritual signification, which could change the life of a person. As an example, let me describe a typical synchronicity. Let us imagine a young man who is questioning himself about his future. He is walking in his high-school library, wondering about which university he should apply to. While he is lost in his thoughts, he accidentally bumps into another student who lets go of the novel he was holding, which falls down and opens up. As our student picks up the book, he reads on the open page, "Being a lawyer was always his dream." Of course, the sentence refers to the hero of the novel. But our student suddenly understands that he wants to become a lawyer. Without the interaction with this piece of paper, our student will not take the proper decision. Obviously, the presence of the paper is objectively not supernatural. But from the student's subjective point of view, this is a revelation. Something inside of him was, at that moment of time, connecting his mind and the material world. Something that classical epistemology (such as positivism) cannot study, because it would only have an interest in causal relationships.

Now, imagine if you could trigger such events in your life. Imagine if it was possible for you to master the inner mechanisms of synchronicity and use them for your own advantage. This, in my opinion, would be an incredibly useful inner ability, leading to impressive abilities (yet unnoticeable by an external eye).

Q: Do you think the ancient initiates from the schools of mysteries knew that?

Modern science was built upon the premise that causality is the only structural law of reality. Our ancients accepted the concept of teleology, and consequently explored some broader horizons. Furthermore, modern science (with the notable exception of neuroscience) has divorced with philosophy. A kind of administrative "Berlin Wall" has been built to separate experimental disciplines from philosophy. Consequently, academic philosophy became a degraded philology, and science becomes progressively technology. When I read the writings of Neoplatonic philosophers for instance, such as the *Enneads* of Plotinus, or Proclus' commentaries on the *Timaeus* of Plato, I am struck by the depth and complexity of their metaphysical models of reality. Modern philosophy seems sometimes astonishingly poor in comparison. Actually, modern academic philosophy is (unfortunately) pretty much concerned with commenting on previous authors, rather than the development of new theories. When one considers that we only have fragmentary traces of Neoplatonic knowledge (the oral tradition is absent in these texts), the comparison becomes scary: how can these fragments of the past seem so deep in comparison with the full power of our modern academies? Science exists in a dynamic system, where questions are supposed to be asked by philosophy, and answered by experimental trials. Modern science made some tremendous progress regarding experiments, but at the same time regressed regarding philosophy. Consequently, the general image of antique knowledge is profoundly distorted and generally mocked in scientific circles. Nevertheless, the ancient initiates from the schools of mysteries certainly had access to much more than Lego builders (read: materialists) would ever dream to understand.

Q: Do you think they knew ways to use these abilities?

Science obviously leads to technology. The ancients had complex philosophical systems, as well as spiritual training methods. This is only speculation of course, but it seems logical that they knew at least some (if not all) possible applications of these abilities.

Q: The scientific method seems impossible to associate to a mystical or initiatic process. Is noetic science a contradiction in terms?

As I already mentioned, a science intending to study the spiritual aspect of reality cannot be confined in a "causalist-materialist objective" epistemology. Consequently, I am worried that any effort put into a classical investigation of mystical or initiatic processes may be condemned. At the beginning of last century, parapsychology was rejected by mainstream science because it could not integrate the, at that time dominant, positivist epistemology. Why would noetic science be more lucky? Mentalities have evolved, and laypersons are probably less sensitive to positivist theories—this does not mean however that the scientific community is not. Despite the recent discoveries in neurotheology, the dominant philosophy of almost all scientists I have met is still a combination of atheism and materialist monism (in other words, a total negation of the reality of any kind of spirituality). The problem is that most scientists apply epistemology without any second thoughts (with a technician mentality). And how could they accept spirituality as an object of study, when epistemology defines spirituality as a nonevent (spirituality being essentially subjective and acausalist)? In other words, the scientific community will not easily accept any demonstration concerning spirituality, unless epistemology is redefined. And this situation will probably not evolve before long.

Publishing a scientific paper defending spiritual opinions is a professional suicide: scientific careers depend on reputation, and spirituality has a pretty bad reputation. If a young scientist openly professes opinions in favor of spirituality, he might not be able to secure a permanent job. And the situation is not any better for tenured professors: they will lose their reputation, and consequently the possibility to apply for research grants (with the exception of creationism). In this system, those with strong spiritual beliefs are not encouraged to remain in the scientific community (unless they agree to study all but spirituality). Consequently, they usually leave mainstream science or learn to be silent. There is not a frightening plot against spirituality in the scientific community, just the consequence of human fears (fear of new ideas on one side, and fear of losing a job on the other side) with a pretty bureaucratic system of selection. Consequently, in the scientific community, being materialist (or professing to be) became almost a survival skill. If you want a job, you shall respect the *omerta*!

One of my fears is that, in the end, our too-conservative scientific paradigms might give birth to a strong aggressive opponent, which would try to annihilate science once and for all. This is apparently already starting: the U.S., the creationist movement (Christian Science) agrees generally to defend spirituality, but from the perspective of conservative and extremist Christian beliefs rather than attempting unbiased scientific investigations of spirituality. Creationism is growing strong because there is no other sustainable professional option for scientists who refuse materialism. The conservatism of mainstream science gave birth to this behemoth. Do we really need a rebirth of extremist Christians in order to understand our errors? The reaction of public figures of science regarding creationism is too often an aggressive rebuttal—read for instance *The God Delusion*, a book by Richard Dawkins against creationism, but also against any form of religion or spirituality. Such monolithic rebuttals in turn reinforce creationism. Let us hope that the scientific community will find a third, balanced path before it is too late. We need a new science of spirituality; otherwise one of the most precious aspects of human life will be diverted by extremists or charlatans.

Q: Can we imagine soon the birth of a "secret society" of official scientists working in secret to give such orientation?

Actually, science at its inception probably started with an organization very close to a "secret society." Science had to be developed against the dogmas of the medieval Catholic church (ask Galileo Galilei or Giordano Bruno!). For centuries, scientists communicated discreetly through the use of annotations in the margins of books that were communicated from hands to hands through networks of scientific libraries. For instance, in the seventeenth century, Fermat wrote considerably in the margin of the book *Arithmetica*. One of his comments became later famous under the name "grand theorem of Fermat," and was only proved true in 1994! Apparently, Fermat already knew the solution, but lacked space to write in the margin. . . . Many speculations can also be read here and there about the so-called Invisible College, which might have been the origin of the Royal Society in the U.K.—the birth of a scientific academy from a secret society! Taking history into account, this idea seems relevant.

However, in order to achieve our purpose, a society of scientists (in the modern acceptation of this term) would not be enough. Originally, scientists were also philosophers (Descartes and Pascal did contribute as much to philosophy as to science). But science and philosophy divorced, and became techno-science and philology. A secret society of enlightened scientists and philosophers will, in my opinion, certainly be the only solution to this problem. In other words, we need the union of the ideas of Plato and Aristotle. Interestingly, this union already exists in philosophy, in the writings of Neoplatonic philosophers. The experimental application is missing; a Neoplatonic epistemology? As a final remark, keep in mind that as we speculate here on the birth of a secret society, it may actually already exist . . .

Q: Is the gap between science and spirituality impossible to cross?

Actually, modern neuroscience and quantum physics have developed new episte-mological systems during the past few years. Quantum physics has demonstrated noncausal behavior of particles, and the new scheme of neurophenomenology seeks to integrate subjective perceptions into scientific data. This means that, if a new epistemological system was designed, mystical processes could be studied. Neither noetic science nor neurotheology have achieved the construction of such a system. Consequently, the scientific study of mystical processes is not yet fully possible.

However, nothing prevents a new epistemological system from being de-veloped. For instance, noetic scientists such as Dr. Vieten apparently have the intention to integrate teleology in their scientific approach. If noetic science is successful, a new scientific system could be born, allowing science to undergo a true revolution. In order to develop such an epistemology, scientists should however focus on "how" and "why" spiritual interactions are manifested, rather than on "if" they exist. Reintegrating teleology in modern epistemology is easier said than done!

Q: Will this new science be able to speak about the "why" too?

Yes, and this is actually the revolution I have in mind. Science is rickety, as it stands on one leg only: the "how" (causality). If we successfully restored the sec-ond leg—the "why" (teleology)—human knowledge would be changed forever.

Q: Do you think the mind can affect matter as the novel *The Lost Symbol* says? Are the random event generators a solution to verify this theory?

Dan Brown's novel is just that, a novel. It should not be interpreted as a scientific publication. Until now, random event generators (REG) did not provide repro-ducible results (the experimental results vary from one laboratory to another), and it would be dishonest to present this paradigm as a solution to our problem.

Actually, mind affecting matter has yet to be proved, and will certainly not be by REG. This paradigm could at best show that an interaction exists, but does not allow any understanding of how such a process could occur (as I explained above, the problem is not to understand "if," but "how" and "why"). The reader interested in parapsychology can track for instance the recent publications of the journals *Explore* and *Journal of Science and Healing*, where many new results are regularly published. Rather than the outdated REG, I am much more interested in the recent study of Radin and Borges (from IONS), which was published this year, where the physiological constants of subjects are measured while they perform psychic tasks. The subjective state of a subject was, for centuries, impossible to assess, and consequently science had given up hopes to understand subjectivity. Nowadays however, brain imaging, cardiac rhythms, psychological tests, and other measurements allow a pretty good picture of the subjective state. Consequently, the subjective state becomes data that can be exploited by science. Such experimental data can be exploited with phenomenology: an epistemological system where the subjective experience is placed at the center of experience—neurophenomenology is its recent application in neuroscience. Subjective data, in this new epistemology, have the potential to solve one of the two hard problems of psychic studies: subjectivity.

The other problem, teleology, will not be solved unless a new epistemology is developed—which will not be achieved, in my opinion, if a strong interaction between science and philosophy is not restored. REG is not a solution to this problem.[2]

Q: If we can find a scientific way or a technical solution to interact with mind powers and abilities, is it possible to say that we will have the most dangerous weapon?

Yes, and this is a real concern to me. Actually, new discoveries in science remain confined within two entities for ten to twenty years before becoming accessible to the public: the scientific community and the military community. This confinement has several reasons, but is mainly due to the vast quantity of scientific communications (the public cannot read everything) and the lack of competent science reporters (the quality of scientific vulgarization has decreased during the past few years). Consequently, even if the science is here, the public will not be

---

2. D. Radin and A. Borges, "Intuition Through Time: What Does the Seer See?" *The Journal of Science and Healing*, Volume 5, Issue 4, pp. 200–211, July 2009.

informed for a long time. If science was to undergo a spiritual Copernican revolution, the first applications of the new technologies would most probably be military. Let us hope it would not fall into the wrong hands!

Q: Is it possible to disconnect mind abilities from the development of virtue?

First of all, one thing is sure: it is possible to disconnect intelligence from the development of virtue. In other words, a good chess player can be a monster. Actually, serial killers are usually very intelligent persons. In addition, lesion studies in neuroscience have shown that damage to the limbic system can profoundly affect the aptitudes of judgment and empathy, without impairing at all intellectual aptitudes. Similarly, autistic syndromes affect social interaction, but not necessarily the intellectual abilities—Asperger syndrome, for instance, is often associated with a highly developed intelligence.

The question is to know if inner spiritual abilities would be based on a mechanical cerebral skill, like mundane intelligence, or if it requires some higher level of consciousness. The traditional methods used to wake such abilities are usually strongly tied with the development of virtue and the use of alternate states of consciousness. The alternate state of consciousness gives access to abilities, which are controlled thanks to existing virtues. However, if one learns to induce alternate states of consciousness without the development of virtues, the same abilities would be uncontrolled. For instance, like mundane intelligence (set aside the debate about innate and acquired intelligence), meditation is a mental skill. You can be trained with this skill, or even bypass the training using brain-damaging drugs. Of course, this would lead to unbalance, and ultimately to mental alienation. This is maybe the explanation of this classical sentence: wise men and mad men are alike.

Q: Do you see a real connection between Freemasonry and noetic science?

Freemasonry teaches traditional esoteric philosophy and a system to develop virtue. Noetic science seeks to understand some aspects of reality. One could say that noetic science found its inspiration in the traditional esoteric philosophy, but this does not make any real connection between them. Other societies than Freemasonry also show some interest in traditional esoteric philosophy. In addition, noetic science has no interest in moral virtue. Apart from some common interest, I do not see any connection. And if a connection existed, in my opinion it would probably be tenuous.

Q: Any last comments about Dan Brown's novel *The Lost Symbol?*

As usual with this author, there is a lot of controversial material in his book, and some well-documented but somehow distorted ideas. Dan Brown wrote a novel; this book is fiction. Would anyone believe that pigs can build houses after reading the book *The Three Little Pigs*? Certainly not! Why then should anyone believe that the story of Professor Langdon has any more reality? If one keeps in mind that this book is a fiction, then one can enjoy the plot and the nice ambiance of conspiracy and suspense.

This being said, Dan Brown's book contains numerous keys and directions for research. Even if inexact, this book can be a very nice introduction to the mysteries of Freemasonry for laypersons. When reading this book, if a reader becomes interested in learning about Freemasonry, noetic science, and spirituality, then I hope he or she will endeavor to read some additional, more reliable sources—such as this book.

Hidden Abilities & Wisdom

As traditional mysteries taught, special abilities are deeply hidden inside us. In the last interview, we learned that there is more in our brains and invisible bodies than might be expected. Science is developing its investigations and theories. Parapsychology, as well as the new sciences described by Dr. Jaden Francis Ward may be the first to develop in a theoretical way these dimensions of our being. But for centuries, initiates already worked with these inner powers as a real part of our demiurgic inheritance. For them, there was no doubt and no necessity to know exactly the inner process, and nor to prove it. Always looking first to prove what is not physical (and being able to use it) is a scientific and modern approach. For initiates, this step is not necessary, because the success will be a proof of this reality. In this case, why lose time? For students in the initiatic Western Tradition, the first questions regarding these inner powers are how to use them, and why. Are they totally essential for an initiate, even in Freemasonry?

In the case of Freemasonry, these questions seem not to be the main concern of an initiate. But if you want to work on your inner stone (soul) in order to know yourself better, you can't place limits. If a Freemason believes in the existence of a supreme being, it would be strange to refuse the existence of invisible parts in his being, and to reject inner abilities. It is the same regarding his development. To become a better man is also to use what we received as creatures: body and spirit.

At the same time, we recognize that we are very often under the control of unconscious desires and passions. Freedom is often reduced, and in many cases we feel like we can choose based on free will, even if it's not the case. To be able to choose freely, we must reduce outward and inner influences. Thus it is important to use the keys given by the Tradition, such as visualization, the pronunciation of words of power or sacred words, relaxation, and Masonic meditation. As you will see, a traditional ritual combines all these aspects. With these aids, the traditional practices and initiations will be more efficient and able to really have an inner effect on the initiate. In the same way, the initiate will be able to continue the initiatic work, increasing his capacity to understand his inner being, and increasing his own freedom. His choices, work, and philanthropic actions will be more efficient.

However, we must remember the connection between the initiatic way and the development of virtue. It is the same here. An inner work like this one must always be connected to moral considerations. Knowledge (science) without conscience (awareness) is the ruin of the soul. So the development of inner abilities without awareness and virtue would be the ruin of the soul. It is important to keep this in mind as all Masonic rituals do.

In fact, there is often a preconception connected to the inner abilities: interest in or use of them in esoteric rituals, or inner practices will be dangerous or even diabolical. Speaking about abilities will be quite acceptable, but about powers will be too much. Even more, some morally condemn any interest on this subject as a too-dangerous matter. But a risk of car accident is not enough to forbid cars. It is better to teach the use of cars correctly and to develop self-consciousness connected to respect for other drivers. We can imagine a similar consideration given to inner powers bestowed by the Great Architect of the Universe. These divine gifts must be cherished as carefully as the other aspects of one's body. The ability of the mind you are using all day long is a good example of this. It's worth learning how to increase your mental potential in order to express better and better what you have. It is important to not reject your ability to progress and develop. The goal would be to become better and more efficient in order to help mankind. Of course, we must support the idea that anything that is able to harm someone or weaken him physically or mentally must be condemned. Principles and laws are necessary for people who have not enough wisdom to understand their limits. It is necessary to teach and explain the necessity of a virtuous life. Wisdom and virtue must be the main goals to be able to work in goodwill for the betterment of all.

With these principles as our foundation and rule, the question of one's inner abilities becomes minor. It becomes a question of use. It would be strange to forbid any considerations and use. It will be a bad appreciation of the divine gifts and God's wisdom. As you know, the knife is not forbidden to cooks, or the hammer to masons, simply because these tools can kill! We must be focused more on the use of the tools we have as human beings.

In the Neoplatonic Tradition, the development of inner "paranormal" abilities is never understood as a goal in itself. The desire to return to the higher spiritual level is the main aspect of this quest. Freemasonry as an authentic modern philosophical school understood well this inheritance. It's not by chance that moral virtues and philanthropy are major preoccupations of American Freemasonry. Work to be a better man in all aspects, and all else will follow. This inner progression will provide a better understanding of what you are, and what really motivates you. You will feel the importance of a spiritual development connected not to a specific faith, but to a goal shared by every religion: to be closer to the divine in order to be better, more divine. The ancient initiates explained that a spiritual evolution like this one can, at the same time, increase one's inner abilities. Intuitions and a sense of receiving spiritual help, can be some of these manifestations. As the symbols of alchemy demonstrated, any spiritual progression must be associated with an inner purification of the soul. This is the only way to progress in a good balance. So you can begin to work directly on inner abilities when you already have begun the moral work.

But Freemasonry is not only a philosophical and spiritual school. From its origins the Craft received initiatic rituals and esoteric practices. Some are well-known, like the lodge's rituals; others are less familiar, as you will see for the individual rituals. The point is not to reject or destroy these rituals. Every candidate, every Freemason ascends the Masonic degrees through rituals. They are performed by initiates who believe that symbols are important and can have an impact on the candidate. I will develop this very important dimension in the next part of this chapter. Of course, this not theurgy. But it is important that Masonic officers who are dealing with the initiatic process, with powerful rituals, become aware of the processes. If they are well trained, their actions will be clear and more efficient.

It is important to avoid self-pride and always to remember your situation as a fragile and imperfect human. Every scientific discovery reminds us how small we are before the mysteries of the universe. But at the same time, every discovery reminds us how powerful we are in the good as well as in the bad. We must use all the tools given by the Grand Architect of the Universe according to the morality that every man has in common: for the best of humanity.

The Symbols and the Masonic Ritual Process

Freemasonry[3] is a very rich tradition, but its message is in reality simple and universal: be good men! This injunction, so often repeated, lies at the heart of the moral commitment of every Freemason. Honesty, forthrightness, respect for others and the institutions of the state, of trust and faith must become the foundations of your inner being: these are the very values that a Freemason is expected to uphold in the outer world. It is according to these values that Freemasons, and Masonry as an institution, are judged.

Admittedly, they are also fundamental principles of other groups, as well as most religions. However, Freemasonry is devoid of the dogmas that can sometimes alter the fundamental message. And it is unique because it concentrates this moral message in a ritual setting, which gives it a true intensity. Despite the briefness of the initiation ceremony, the Freemason is expected to ponder these principles often so as to gradually integrate them into his daily life.

However, the very simplicity of this message might sound like a real paradox for every new initiate. If the values are that simple, it is difficult to understand why Freemasons need a ritual initiation and need to regularly perform complex rituals.

Trying to understand the nature and usefulness of the symbols contained in Masonic rituals can be sometimes difficult. One of the reasons is that some of the symbols have evolved, so that they may be used and interpreted differently, depending on the time. For example, let us consider the case of the square and compass that rest on

---

3. "The Symbols and the Masonic Ritual Process" was published in French in the book *ABC d'ésotérisme maçonnique* by Jean-Louis De Biasi, (Paris: Grancher Publications, 2008). This excerpt is used here with the permission of Grancher Publications.

the book of the sacred law in the center of the temple. In ancient times, little thought was given to how they are intertwined and what that meant. Those interpretations were added much later, and it is easy to see how multiple meanings can weaken or call into question the value of the rite and the value of the symbols it was trying to transmit.

To be able to understand the role of symbolism in Masonic ritual, one needs to return to the origins of humanity, to a faraway time when man was a defenseless creature in a dangerous environment. Our ancestors were much more exposed to the imposing phenomena of nature. Whenever a natural disaster occurred, whether a storm thundered and shook the sky, or a volcano began to erupt, everyone would wonder about the cause of these manifestations. They would try to figure out what the "intelligent" intention behind them might be. These phenomena were impossible to control, and man was left to wonder why these natural forces would kill human beings. It was natural that they would come to the conclusion that such a terrible demonstration of power came from some divine beings. Trying to explain the unexplainable, our ancestors established a causal relationship between the frightful demonstrations of divine power they observed and the divine beings that must be causing these evils. If a volcano erupted and destroyed lives, it was undoubtedly because it was hungry. And thus the only reasonable thing to do was to offer the volcano god a human sacrifice, so as to maybe prevent further eruptions. If the underground gods obtained what they wanted, perhaps they would spare the remaining members of the tribe.

As humanity evolved into civilization, though, this kind of direct compensation was abandoned, and so symbolic or notational representations were devised as a replacement. Thus the volcano was replaced by the image of fire, the flood by the image of water, the earthquake by that of earth, and so on. What our ancestors were doing was to intellectualize these natural phenomena into a symbolic system.

At that stage of evolution, the original meaning of these new symbols was still relatively clear. For instance, I might offer a libation of water or wine in order to calm down a storm so that my ship could complete its travel without difficulty. Songs might be declaimed at the time of pastoral offerings. It is in this way that the basic ritual gestures that one can find in all human cultures were born. There was still no attempt to analyze the meaning of the symbols used in the rite, although the direct relationship is very easy to see. For example, the wine or other liquid that is poured into the sea is obviously linked to the shipwreck I am trying to avoid. It's the same if I lit a flame to represent a volcano, and so on.

As this development of symbols gradually occurred, it was inevitable that the explicit link between the original phenomena and the natural symbol would become blurred. Thus, the cup that holds the water became associated with water, and it was no longer necessary to physically include water or wine in the rite. The image of the cup truly becomes the symbol of water, a cubic stone that of earth. And so we gradually arrive at a level of pure abstraction, which, while rooted in an objective reality, begins to create a world of pure representations that have symbolic meaning.

The first question that one might ask when confronted with a new symbol (the compass, the trowel, the square, or the apron) is whether it has any meaning. If the symbol has nothing to offer beyond the obvious, we could make it the object of fantasies and intellectual projections. Then any fantasy would be allowed and we could say anything about that symbol. But considering the Masonic rituals, we know that this is not true. However, the ability to feel it and to clearly understand it are quite different things.

These questions are certainly not new: they have been discussed extensively by the philosophers of ancient Greece and Rome, who were themselves initiated into, and worshipers of, the mysteries. Obviously, their analyses would require a detailed explanation. However, it is possible to extract from their theories, the principal idea that will enable us to advance in our own analysis: the spiritualization of natural symbols. This reasoning is based on the following. As I said before, the tempest was linked to the symbol of the cup, so we must rise from the physical world that surrounds us to the world of ideas, from the material planes to the divine planes above. And it means something very important: that just as the body is a manifestation of the spirit, and not the other way around, the symbols must be searched for their true spiritual value, as opposed to their mere material significance.

But searching for the spiritual value of symbols is not easy, and this is where the Masonic rituals come into play. Their regular practice makes an inner conviction to grow, a faith to emerge; in short, something of a higher nature that makes the initiate willing to accept the existence of another reality beyond the material: a spiritual reality. As Freemasons believe in a supreme being and the immortality of the soul, it is impossible to accept the idea that the spirit is reduced to only the body, and that it disappears with death. I am not speaking here about a scientific demonstration, but about an inner conviction, a strong inner feeling. And the Masonic practice gradually makes the initiate realize deeper and deeper that the symbols of the temple are also those of the Inner Temple, analogous to the heart (which stands for the soul) and to the cosmos, behind which you see the divinities and, farther, the Great Architect. What the mystical tradition of the West, from the Platonist and Neoplatonist philosophers to modern theurgists, has always taught is that manifestation, or the first stirrings of the creation of the world, occur in a movement from above to below. The corporeal body is just a visible aspect of a more subtle reality. And as the soul descends into the body, so does an idea descend into a symbol. This downward movement has nothing to do with a fall from heaven or from grace: it is about the envelopment of the soul into a body, just like a body envelops itself into some clothes before going outside. And so a symbol in reality is nothing but the most subtle clothing of an original and unique idea, emanated from the world above. So the natural representation of water and fire, for example, is just the most external clothing of the archetypal unity it represents. This change of perspective leads to a very important truth: that there is a consubstantial and original bond that the symbol establishes between these two dimensions. The symbol becomes the nexus, or meeting point, of the exchanges that take place between the material and divine planes.

So let us now reconsider the principles that I have just stated. According to Platonic philosophy, there is an ideal or spiritual world that contains the root principle, or archetypal ideal, of all that exists around us. As Plato told us in the myth of the cave, we live in an obscure world of darkness and illusions. I am not saying it is a bad world, but it is a deceptive world that could lead us to believe that the greatest pleasures are immediate physical pleasures, and the only satisfactions of the soul are to be found in this world. One of our objectives is to leave the cave and abandon these illusions. To understand what I am saying about the spiritual world, which is the place of ideal forms and first causes, let us take a simple example. There are many varieties of trees in this country, such as maples, oaks, pines, and birches, but if I say the word *tree* in a conversation, you will grasp immediately what I mean without having to resort to a particular representation of the word. This is because you already have in your mind an idealized concept of what "tree" means, even if this idea cannot really be represented in details. This same principle applies to our understanding of human beings. The sacred texts speak about Adam and Eve, or the Qabalah of Adam Kadmon, who is defined as some kind of ideal man. Let us not forget what I have just said: there is a generic ideal that predates every created thing and which generates everything that follows. And so the idea of humanity existed on the higher planes before it came upon this Earth, and what the sacred texts do is help us connect to it via another symbol.

This theory of symbols was very much confirmed by the research of Carl Gustav Jung and his school. It is well known that he was deeply interested in the universality of symbols. Let us take an example that Jung offers in one of his books. During a visit at his hospital, he saw a mental patient in crisis who was looking intently at the Sun and beginning to express great excitement. As Jung questioned him, the patient declared that a "green snake was leaving the Sun!" This sounded like another sentence from a fool, but then a few years after this episode, Jung heard the same account from the mythology of the native peoples of South America. This is what started him to formulate his theory of archetypes, the belief that there are universal symbols or archetypes present in what he called the collective unconscious. This is why, no matter the geographical location, the symbols used in various cultures share a similar appearance: because they are essentially the same and are drawn from the collective unconsciousness of humanity. Admittedly they can differ somewhat in detail, but a more attentive observation can usually bring us to an awareness of their underlying similarity.

Up to this point I have been speaking about symbols as something external to you, something you can see in lodges, temples, or places of worship of various religions, even though you may struggle to interpret them. However, the Western Tradition reminds us that the true object of the work is ourselves. As said in the ancient Western motto, "Know yourself and you will know the universe and the gods," so must you learn how to know yourself to be able to perfect yourself. This is about polishing your own stone. As I said before in this book, you are like the image of a divine statue that has fallen into a seabed and became covered with encrustations. It is up to you to reveal what lies beneath and to restore the beauty and purity of your original form.

The Hermetic Tradition teaches us, "That which is above is as that which is below, to achieve the miracles of the one thing." Thus, you are one with the image of the universe. The Masonic temple and its symbols are a dual representation of the universe (macrocosm) and of the human being (microcosm). The lodge therefore symbolizes each initiate, and all of the visible representations are present in the ideal world, which is internal to each of us. This implies that any action performed on any external symbol will also act on and have an effect on what the symbol represents inside of us. If you gaze at a burning candle, or look at a sacred book resting in a place of honor, then your subconscious will respond by acting upon the corresponding internal force or archetype. Thus, the act of looking intently at a flame will have a real impact on your inner fire-nature.

Imagine a musical instrument, something like a lyre with three strings. If I pluck a string on one side, the string next to it will also start to vibrate. This is exactly what occurs when we look at any true symbol. As for the "string" on the other side, it will also begin to vibrate. The blended sound, which rises from the vibration of these two strings, will have an impact on the first string that I initially plucked. It is the same in our work with symbols; each action we take interacts with every other action at various levels. However, although I have just been speaking here about symbols and the effect of looking at symbols, the work in a Masonic lodge is not a motionless contemplation. Acting through the ritual transmits this tradition through the means of initiations that develop over several degrees. Each particular ritual is a system of symbols, which is put into motion in a particular way.

For example, I could discuss the symbolism of a candle, or I could also light the candle. I may analyze the symbolism of the compass, but I may also open it. Instead of just thinking about the symbolism of the mallet and the chisel, I can also use them to strike a stone and so "feel" the symbols. The rituals thereby amplify the resonance phenomenon that I illustrated with the example of the lyre with three strings. The fundamental principle is that I proceed with resonance from a single note (the symbol) to a symphony of sounds (the ritual). And so the impact on the psyche will be that of a symphony instead of just that of a single note.

In this way, we start to understand how a false note (or false symbol) destroys the quality of the music, and how a continual succession of false notes makes the musical composition completely cacophonous and unable to stir the (higher) emotions, or to have the effect desired by the composer. The ritual is not an entertaining game for grown-ups, but a very serious matter. It has been specifically designed to achieve a precise goal in the deep psyche, and so to transport the initiate towards the highest spiritual planes. It is for this reason that the ritual cannot be something merely improvised; the way the ritual is designed and performed is of the utmost importance.

From the time of the Ancient Mysteries, initiation has taken the form of many different ceremonies to alter an individual's state of consciousness. From a certain point of view, I may say that initiation is a "divine play." On the first level, initiation is a method that introduces symbols through ritual movements in order to act on the subconscious mind of the initiate. The ritual use of symbols causes the person to react psychologically: he begins to pay attention to the archetypes present in his subconscious, and this activates the bond that attaches him to the spiritual and divine planes. And so, if properly carried out, ritual can help us gain consciousness of our divine inner nature; then it is truly self-sufficient.

However, the process cannot stop there, because this method does not work perfectly each time. The candidate is symbolically a "rough stone," and some stones will remain rough throughout their entire Masonic course. Indeed, it seems that some stones are not easy to polish. Is this the fault of Masonry and its ritual? Not entirely.

As I have explained, the rituals are generally performed in a very beautiful external temple. Remember that, in the Platonic Tradition, beauty is equated with goodness and justice. Thus the cultivation of beauty, when associated with the study of philosophy and the practice of virtue, elevates us toward the divine. But we should not assume that the beauty of an external temple automatically connects us with the divine. Indeed, such an illusion would lead us to forget the nature of the true inner temple. Ritual owes its reason for existence to the reality of inner life, as do all of the elements that surround the initiate. It is appropriate that, just as Hiram the student rebuilt his temple, so you will be able to fashion an inner temple from the external temple, in order to give it a true reality in your heart. Those Freemasons who perform a ritual from memory achieve this kind of effect by vivifying their inner nature, because at each moment the temple and the ritual are present within.

From the moment when the symbol becomes alive in the practitioner, it becomes possible for him to give it life in the external world. Thus, we cannot act on the outside world, if we have not first accomplished the necessary work in the inside world. Before lighting a candle outside of you, you must first light the candle inside you, and so if you want to be able to bring light into a temple, it is essential that you begin by illuminating yourself internally. This means that what makes for a real and effective Masonic initiation—that is, one that has the ability to really affect the candidate—demands a real continuity between the inner work and the external work.

The techniques of interiorizing symbols and acting on the symbols with rituals are extremely old and they helped to elaborate some even more ancient initiatic systems, of which Freemasonry was a part. In the ancient world, the orator used to pronounce most of his lectures from memory, and there were special techniques to memorize the work as perfectly as possible. One such technique was to create a mental representation of a chamber where the orator would place the different elements present in the lecture. Such a representation is a physical reality into which it is possible to put specific objects, individuals, or scenes. At the moment when the orator gave his speech, it was sufficient that he revisualize the chamber and mentally hold it in his mind so that the picture corresponded to his original text. Over time, this mental representation gave rise to increasing constructs that became known, during the Renaissance period, as "the theatre of memory." Thus, in the sixteenth century, in a work bearing this same title, Giulio Camillo describes a strong theatrical symbolic system. Camillo said of this place that it is the representation of the soul, of what cannot be seen with the carnal eyes. The number 7 is omnipresent in that work in the number of columns, doors, lines of steps, and so forth. The columns, for example, are associated with the planets, and then with the angels and the Sephiroth from the Qabalistic Tree of Life, and so on. This is, at one and the same time, an image of the world and the spirit.

The initiates of this period began to make an ever stronger connection between this internal representation of the symbol and the nature of the symbol, which I previously described. The inner temple gradually became the place where the initiate stood at the center of the symbols he was working on. Later, the ritual began to take form in this inner temple and was gradually elaborated into a conscious transformation of the self, in which the initiate attempted to reconnect with the upper levels of his consciousness through the exaltation of his soul. The symbols that were used in the rituals were created from what is observed and understood of our daily lives. The ritual was conceived internally, on the spiritual level, using that symbolic knowledge, but in full consciousness and according to the genuine principles of transformation. The operative or theurgic rituals (as they were called) were always worked out in this way. It was according to these very principles that, later, an interpretation of the operative tools of Freemasonry was to be formulated. And it gave life to what I now call Freemasonry. It is clear in the writings of Albert Pike and others that the bond with ancient initiations was conscious and intentional, and that these techniques were used to conceive the modern system of rites and initiations. One may therefore understand why these principles of inner work are fundamental. Without those principles, the initiations and rituals would be nothing more than a mere "stage trick," performed without heart even if the representation is of the highest quality. And this is what "working in the lodge" is truly about.

With the introduction of the inner dimension, the initiate becomes able to place himself on the spiritual level and to really act on his own being. But it needs to be emphasized that this is not an automatic by-product: it only comes about through traditional techniques of visualization (mental representation), pronunciation, concentration, and moving about in the inner temple. More succinctly put, this elevation only occurs when he takes control of all of the aspects of the ritual, firstly on the inner level, and then, secondly, on the external level. So truly nothing is without reason in a ritual. This inner work offers the inspiration to transform the ritual performance in the lodge into such a powerful method that contemporary Freemasons would have nothing to envy in the numerous traditions of the East.

I have just discussed symbols and rituals together, without any more precise analysis. However, one of the characteristics of this initiatic system is that it is built upon levels of various degrees. It was the same in the oratory technique, where the speaker mentally envisioned various parts of a building in which he would walk around. Each part of the building corresponded to a part of the lecture. On the spiritual level, the connection between the material world and the spiritual world is something that is gradually built over time. These degrees of evolving connection are called emanations in the Neoplatonic tradition: they represent advancement on the upward path, bringing us back toward the source of our soul.

Thus, Freemasonry also developed specific and progressive initiations. Each one has its own representations, symbols, passwords, and myths. Each degree offers a particular message, while remaining a part of the whole. Each degree is associated with a specific and personal inner working, which continues to deepen the initiation that has already been received; this is true both for the first three degrees and the "side degrees" (degrees after the 3rd). Each stage brings us closer to the source from whence we came and awakens the memory of our celestial origin.

In ancient times, the initiates of the Mysteries of Eleusis gathered together in a room of the mysteries, which was called in Greek the Telesterion. There the divine rites were played out or ritually performed on stage. Thereafter, they were supposed to apply more specific individual techniques that would enable them to assimilate these rites and to go through each of these stages in their inner body. Participation in a ritual is not adequate in and of itself; one needs to continue the work in the privacy of one's inner temple in order to make this process fully operative. Of course, this is made possible by organizing the teachings of basic techniques and special practices that are specific to each degree. It is the same for the practice of the ritual in the lodge. Training is necessary and possible. (Lodge members eager to do so can contact the author of this book for more information.)

This tradition comes from classical philosophy, as well as from the ancient schools of the mysteries, and is able to transmit a very rich heritage. However, Freemasons must perpetuate and renew it unceasingly in order to reveal all of its facets. With this essential moral step as foundation, the initiatory progression can, as the Platonists and Neoplatonists would say, lead the initiates out of the cave, viewed as a representation of the world and the body. The common grades mark the essential stages of the progression while the individual work completes the evolution and assimilation. The periods of lodge practice, together with individual meditation on the symbols, provide the initiate with a complete system to carry out the true construction of his inner world, something able to elevate him to the highest degrees of consciousness. This is how the participation of Freemasons in both fraternity and the mundane world shall take its true meaning: to help this world become a better place for humanity.

Key to the Symbols: Creative Visualization

Visualization is a natural process, and it is one of the main elements of a good initiatic practice. As explained in the section above, we must give life and vitality to the visible symbols we use, in order to create an effective ritual. This spiritual or symbolic action begins inwardly. The creative power of the mind allows us to immediately begin this training. Knowledge of this process was protected by the theurgic schools during the period of the dark days. Later, a few Masons were initiated in both traditions, keeping alive both the Masonic aspects and the applications of these esoteric practices. Interestingly, visualization is the subject of a strange paradox. This function of one's brain is completely spontaneous, yet its control is a very important aspect of initiatic work. We must learn how to use visualization effectively in our initiatic practices, as well as in daily life.

The ability to visualize comes from the mind's ability to think about things and focus attention on them. This means that visualization is not the result of emptying our mind, as we do in some other meditative practices. It is the result of focusing on a single image. Because the brain does this naturally, we can legitimately say that this ability is a natural one. All day long, our mind is busy thinking about the different things we deal with in our daily life. The imagination processes our perceptions, feelings, and ideas so that we may work, think, and speak. Generally, this process is unconscious. In fact, most of the time this invisible process acts freely, without your control. However, sometimes the unconscious mind gets focused on negative things and acts without conscious intention, which can produce some very negative consequences. Psychosomatic diseases are manifestations of this inner process, which can act very rapidly and destructively on the body. Insomnia and stomach ulcers are two common physical consequences of this destructive process.

By contrast, we can also imagine a constructive and powerful unconscious mind that is readily able to generate energy and optimism. However, the problem is that, in either case, whether the outcome is positive or negative, we have no control over the unconscious imaginative process. Even so, both outcomes show us its power. Through observation of this process and its results, we realize an important lesson: *focus is the key to success*. Thus, creative visualization is an important skill that is the outcome of the ability to focus.

As an initial definition, I might say that creative visualization is the process of consciously focusing the mind on a goal, with the help of the will and desire. However, I must emphasize that this skill must be learned; it requires special training. The control of this ability will be a very important step in the understanding of inner phenomena and the invisible processes of rituals. In any case, visualization is the result of a voluntary action: the intention to focus on a specific goal.

During the period of training, the initiate must constantly control his visualizations. But it is important here not to misunderstand what I mean by the word *visualization*. This concept is easily misunderstood. Most people assume that the term is restricted to a visual mental representation. Therefore, new students often presume that the goal is to create a kind of mental photography, as if they were looking at a printed picture. This is not the case at all, and it would be wrong to begin with that impression. In fact, we already know how to make mental pictures, but we are generally accustomed to reducing our perceptions to a single sense: vision. Of course, not everyone has sight as their predominant sense, but it is generally predominant in today's world. In this regard, it might be helpful to think about the way that a person who was born blind visualizes. His or her visual representations would have to be replaced by a combination of other perceptions, such as smell, taste, touch, etc.

Understanding this principle allows us to begin to recognize how you we can bring our imagination under control. The initial step is identical to the act of thinking of someone or some place that is far distant from you. The subject of your thoughts must be a person or place that is already well known to you. You do this all the time without any effort at all. If you stop reading for a moment and try it, you will see how easy it is.

If you are at the office, or in the living room, think about your bedroom, or think about your wife, husband, friend, child, or pet you love. The result is immediate. You don't have to do anything special. You have been doing this all of your life. This is the beginning of taking control over your visualization, which is the foundation of everything you must accomplish to make progress in the esoteric and initiatic way. This ability is real and you use it all the time. Of course, this is only the first step, and you must not assume that you are already using creative visualization. However, becoming conscious of this ability is the only way to be able to make progress on this path.

Creative visualization is the cornerstone of real esoteric work and its control is essential. In this text, I will give you some basic principles so that you can begin the work. Please be aware that, to make any substantial progress, you will need to begin supervised individual and group work.

The next principle you need to understand is the duration of your focus. You are well aware that, when you focus on a person or place, the duration of time you maintain this focus is generally very short. It is very difficult to maintain the mental representation for an extended period. That is why the first step in developing control over your imagination is to increase the duration of your focus. This means that you must be able to stay focused on one specific idea (one mental representation), and you must hold it in your mind for a while. It doesn't matter if you aren't able to hold a precise representation, in great detail, for an extended period. The goal here is to select one idea and then to hold on to it.

Symbols are very interesting tools for this kind of work. It is generally easier to hold a specific simple symbol in your mind, such as a triangle, a square, or a compass. You don't need to hold a photo of the symbol in your mind, just the idea.

As you practice, you will notice that the representation progressively increases in complexity, with increasing details (whether they are visual or not), and these will cluster together, like bugs around a lightbulb. You may see more details, hear related sounds, smell associated smells, etc. All of these sensations will increase the power of your inner representation, and this will help you to hold it in your mind a little longer. After you have worked on this exercise at several practice sessions, you will start noticing that you are more focused and that your visualizations are much clearer. Moreover, these exercises will improve your other abilities, making them more powerful and effective.

Another key to making progress is to use your curiosity. It is necessary to look very carefully at the details of the mental representation. If you are thinking of someone, you can imagine his or her eyes, hair, clothes, etc. However, if you try to force yourself to do this, you will easily become bored and not wish to continue. If you become curious about the details of the picture, you will see more and enjoy the process more. When you began these exercises, perhaps it was not easy for you to look at the mental picture. But when you engage your curiosity, your progress becomes very different than it was when you first started. Curiosity is a very important ally, and the foundation of good apprenticeship.

Relaxation is another good ally and it is important to be very relaxed whenever you start a practice session. It is quite impossible to continue this kind of training without the ability to relax completely. In that regard, you do not have to adopt any special system; any method you like is fine, as long as you feel comfortable with it. However, it is critical to employ a natural process, one that you are easily engaged in. Relaxation must become a natural ability, one you can invoke whenever you need it. The position of your body is not an important matter. Feel free to choose a position, and then to change it as needed. Test different positions and different places so that you develop a feel for what works best for you. If you set up all your practice sessions at the same time in the same place and then there are disruptions to your routine, relaxing will be difficult. It is important to be able to use these practices everywhere, and at any time the need arises.

For now, don't worry about the duration of this practice. If you are part of a group training, just follow the group. If you are working alone, stay focused on the specific visualization you have chosen for a while. Do this once per day at the beginning. It is better to have a powerful and short concentration session, than a long session that you find it difficult to complete. After a few weeks, it will be fine to define a specific time for your training, and then to relax and train yourself to visualize during those sessions.

The last logical point about understanding visualization is the *subject* you choose to focus on. Even if this practice seems interesting to do because it increases your ability to be more focused in your daily life, you must recognize that these exercises are aimed at a higher goal. Of course, it is interesting to use these exercises to picture your friends and family, and beautiful places you have visited. The immediate success is very reinforcing. Yet, these uses of the practice you are learning are not as exciting as the ability to visualize the spiritual world. In fact, the ability to visualize the inner world, the spiritual plane, is directly connected to all occult and esoteric work. I am not speaking here about something strictly religious or "paranormal." I am talking about the use of an inner ability, such as visualization, and the effect of the correct use of this process on our spiritual body. Every initiate to the mysteries knows about the invisible dimension that many religions describe as a body of light, an aura. Eastern mystics also know about this dimension, and their writings talk about the chakras, etc. All these dimensions of the body are generally dormant. But when an inner work is consciously undertaken, something occurs at this level. The ancient initiates spoke of inspiration, of spiritual awareness. All these ways of describing our spiritual body are correct, and the consequences of understanding these elements are very important for our inner and spiritual development. Of course all these aspects are a part of a traditional Masonic method that comes from the Hermetic inheritance: the Masonic meditation.

As you will see, once you have been practicing these exercises for a while, details that you have not consciously introduced will manifest themselves into your mental representation, and this can include symbolic connections, spontaneous understanding, etc. This phenomenon is the result of regular and conscious training. The esoteric work described in the last paragraph will help you to make significant progress to a step of awareness, which is one of the goals connected to an authentic initiatic way like Freemasonry.

Powers of the Word: Declamation, Evocation, and Invocation

In every Masonic ritual, the word has a central function. There are no silent initiations; there are no ceremonies without words. Freemasonry is rooted in two major traditions, both of which emphasize the power of the word: the Bible, and the Hermetic Tradition. The word is central to the mythology of both traditions. The first few chapters of this book described that mythology in more detail.

The founders of Freemasonry used the word in two ways: (1) they provided extensive texts that explain the mythology surrounding each degree of advancement, certain moral teachings, and various symbolic interpretations; and (2) they used passwords, words that are distinct to each degree, and other sacred words transmitted by the tradition.

The function of the first use of the word is twofold: to teach, and to evoke. These two aspects are complementary. The first aspect is focused on the intellectual dimension; the second one on the imagination and spiritual being of the aspirant.

You may be amazed, when you read some of the ancient Masonic rituals, to discover how large the lessons are, and how short the theatrical part (the action or ritual) actually is. In some ways, things are more balanced today, but these teachings continue to be a major part of the initiations. You must remember that Freemasonry was created at a time when many people were unable to read. Each degree taught mythical lessons combining history, morals, myths, and mysteries in a way that inextricably linked these elements. The founding myths provided in the first chapter of this book offer the reader some idea of the style of presentation of these teachings. Of course, the goal of this transmission and teaching is not to give scientific or historical information but to tell a story in order to build memories that are common to every initiate. The lessons are also an opportunity to learn the tradition, by teaching the students how to reason and understand the knowledge of traditional symbolism.

It is also interesting to realize that some of these lessons were and are more symbolic than purely narrative. The goal of the inclusion of this symbolic material is to use the function called *evocation*. The use of evocation is rooted in the sacred representations of the mysteries that are included in classical drama. The memorization of rituals prior to performing them also employs evocation. This is a mental process limited to our consciousness. It doesn't involve any other dimension. It requires an inner ability to use our capacity for memorization and visualization, to give birth to a myth or story in the initiate's mind.

The art of persuasion is another key to powerful evocation. It is very close to the use of suggestion in hypnosis. For example, when you tell a story to a child at bedtime, and you do so with great conviction, that child will really believe what you are saying. All the characters of the story will be present in the bedroom! Similarly, in a ritual, this kind of persuasion is used when you declaim the myth.

Of course, this process should never be used manipulatively, to corrupt the original intention of the drama. An initiation always respects the freedom of the candidate and he can ask to stop it at any time. This is a fundamental principle of all authentic and respectable initiatic processes: the initiate must be completely free in every aspect of the process and at every moment of his progress along the spiritual path. At this level, this use of evocation has the same function as it has for an actor: to give life to a story in order to allow the public to experience it as a reality.

However, the mental representation, paired with the inner conviction of the initiate, is capable of accomplishing even more. Each ritual is a sort of sacred theatrical play. The myths that are central to these plays are connected to very potent archetypes. The evocation of such universal symbols links the initiate to a center of power (an ancient memory that is external to the play) at the precise moment of evocation. At this point, I am very close to describing what happens during the evocation of a theurgic dimension. Something deeper and stronger is evoked, a memory of the past masters who are always present on the invisible plane and who are also resident in the unconscious memory of all living beings. In this perspective, the words are imbued with a level of intensity that is sometimes astonishing.

The second aspect concerns the passwords and other sacred words. I spoke extensively about this dimension and the use of such words in Chapter Four. You may review that part of the material again if it seems hazy. Otherwise, it won't be necessary to develop those concepts again here.

However, their use in ritual is not a commonplace phenomenon. Any tradition that teaches about sacred words will instruct its students that there is a special process that must be used when these words are part of a ritual, and that there is a specific and special pronunciation that must be used as well. Considering their function, you now understand why these requirements are so necessary. To continue in the consideration of these matters, I must distinguish between the passwords, the common words, and the sacred words.

Most of these Masonic words have their origin in the Hebrew Tradition. At the time of the elaboration of the rituals in use today, the knowledge of the precise roots of these words had been lost. The circumstances of the birth of Freemasonry implies that most of the people involved didn't know the Hebrew language and they therefore lacked the capacity to understand the words they were writing and speaking; they were not able to correct their mistakes. They transmitted what they believed was correct, but it was often wrong or inaccurate. Frequent misspellings, along with various confusions about pronunciation and other matters, were repeated over and over down through the years; this repetition created a strong (but false) belief that they held a precious stone, instead of an ordinary rock. Even the form of some of the sacred letters has sometimes been so misshapen that they are difficult to recognize. Research and study has resulted in some students discovering the real roots, but to correct the errors in the rituals is not a simple matter. Sometimes the tradition itself has a ponderous inertia that resists change.

If you study all the degrees of the Scottish Rite, it is possible to identify sacred words from other traditions that existed prior to the birth of Freemasonry. Albert Pike demonstrated his knowledge of these other traditions many times, and he introduced accurate corrections of the words of power. However, in the first three degrees, this is generally not the case. It is important to remember that Freemasons are using substituted words because they lost the original ones. However, the most important of all these considerations is for the student to have the desire to penetrate the veil, in order to find the root word, whether near or far from the substituted word. The initiate must penetrate the veil to find the real word for both the passwords and the other sacred names. Interestingly, the Hebrew language was used by Hebrew and Christian Qabalists to speak about the spiritual realities. Even the Hermetists in the Renaissance and after chose this system to hide some secrets about their tradition. It is why an understanding of the basic Qabalah is important.

However, it is not necessary to know the Hebrew language and to be able to speak it fluently in order to be an effective initiate. That has never been the point of these lessons. The initiate Iamblicus wrote about sacred names in "barbarian" languages, saying the initiates must retain their pronunciation in order to preserve their power and be in harmony with the superior beings.

These directions (from Iamblicus) reveal the power associated with sacred words and introduce a new concept: *invocation*. All sacred and traditional words contain a hidden meaning. The first initiates chose each word carefully and each word has received power throughout its long life. For the ancient Hermetists and the Hebrews, a sacred word is the material representation of an invisible reality. The letters, their shape and sound, are the appearance, the envelope, and the body of a spiritual being. A word is never a sequence of dead block capitals printed on a piece of paper. A sacred word corresponds to a living being that you can invoke with the use of that word. When an initiate advances far enough in the order and is called to initiate other candidates, the inner work he has done will allow him to really invoke these powers, in order to increase the state of consciousness of the candidate. In this way, they will be elevated, and their spiritual eyes will be opened. For example, if you are working inwardly on the Masonic lights (beauty, strength, and wisdom) with the correct process of Masonic meditation, you create a strong contact with your inner powers and archetypes. When a ritual officer respectfully pronounces sacred words during a ritual, totally aware of their deepest meaning, he will accomplish a real inner invocation that has the capacity to affect the visible and invisible planes. This ritual work is simple, discreet, and can be felt even by someone who knows nothing about the process.

You now should have a better understanding of the difference between evocation and invocation. However, it is important that you don't think of them as being opposite forces.

These two levels can be associated with each other and used together in a Masonic ritual. In fact, every Masonic ritual is a combination of many well-organized aspects, including symbols, gestures, ritual movements, lights, sounds, etc. The word allows us to animate this entire process. The invocation manifests the power of the breath we received at birth. Remember, too, that a ritual is a result of many participants. Their inner and individual work is a key to the expression of that ritual's power.

The Masonic Meditation

Individual and Group Practices

Everyone in the Western world has, at one time or another, read one or more of the voluminous explanations and presentations that expound on the Eastern traditions. Yoga classes are available everywhere; Buddhist temples offer extensive training in meditation, rituals, etc. Even Christian churches have begun to organize meditation classes that are based on their early teachings.

People all over the world are looking for something to help them cope with change. Many people fear that there is something alarming on the horizon, and, as in all periods of crisis and major change, people are looking for a real way to develop their inner abilities, their human potential. At the same time, many people are becoming aware of a need to develop a personal spirituality in order to be able to respond capably to the shifts and changes that they fear. The spirit of freedom, as expressed by the Founding Fathers of America, offers us an example of one such method of coping during periods of crisis. It is a model that teaches how to freely express the individual desire for religious and personal freedom during times of oppression and radical change.

Freemasonry also offers us a model for enduring success during periods of change and disruption. Freemasonry teaches its members the strength of philanthropy, and their response to periods of crisis has always been powerful and effective. The actions of the participants in the Scottish Rite are an obvious demonstration of this power and the spirit it proceeds from. You also see this in the work of the Shriners, which is mentioned by Dan Brown in *The Lost Symbol*. The contribution of these fraternal orders to the history of America was enormous. Today it is easy to see that the efforts of those Freemasons gave a benevolent orientation to our newly forming country, at a critical juncture in the history of the United States.

Yet, despite this great contribution, few things can be found in the historical records about the inner work. Freemasonry almost appears to be a symbolic, initiatic tradition without any inner or spiritual practices. If this were true, it would be the first instance in the history of the Western world of such an honorable tradition that is completely absent of all spiritual teachings. But the idea that Freemasonry is an empty tradition cannot be accepted. Having read the last few chapters, you will surely insist that cannot be the case.

However, there is a problem. It is true that Freemasonry has become disconnected from the spiritual part of its heritage and has continued on with its daily activities as if the spiritual side of Freemasonry never existed. Fortunately for modern adherents, the earlier members of Freemasonry left footprints for us to follow, including various texts that offer us advice from the past. It is possible to use these historical signposts to describe and explain the form and process of the Masonic meditation, and I have done so here in this book. Albert Pike and other initiates worked intensely on both the symbolic and esoteric aspects of the Craft. Yet, the spiritual Masonic practices were often ignored or neglected. I hope to rectify that omission here.

In some ways the Masonic meditation is like yoga. This meditation is completely disconnected from the confessional or religious aspects that are part of other belief systems. I believe that the time has come to explain, develop, and teach the keys to this method to the world, to help those who need a profound way to deal with the radical changes that appear to be looming in our shifting modern world. The keys needed to restore Freemasonry may be found in its ancient Hermetic roots, wherein many of the secrets of Freemasonry were hidden. It is time to associate this brilliant practical tradition (which is rooted in the most ancient Western Mysteries) with contemporary Freemasonry.

However, it is not acceptable to improvise. Each spiritual tradition is unique. Each has its own internal rules and special historical roots. So it is for Freemasonry. The philosophical and initiatic background for Hermetism and the Craft is rooted in ancient civilizations. The use of specific procedures for visualization, the pronunciation of sacred words, evocation, and ritual gestures are all elements of this ancient tradition. Each element must be learned in a specific way. Just as Freemasons cannot improvise initiations or mix one degree with another, the Masonic method must be learned and used in a precise and progressive way. The student must begin by learning how to do individual practices. The lessons learned in the privacy of one's soul will then have consequences for the student's contribution to the group rituals he attends or conducts.

Among the elements of this practice, you find visualization, memorization, relaxation, focusing and concentration, evocation, invocation, and a powerful faith in the existence of the spiritual and invisible planes. Nothing is possible without these elements. If this faith is forgotten, Freemasonry becomes a simple association among men without depth of meaning, anemic and depleted of life. Of course, the complete method must only be revealed and transmitted to an initiate. Powerful tools cannot be revealed to anyone until he has completed the prerequisite inner moral work and received a real initiatic transmission. However, the basics can be given to anyone who wants to use them, so that he or she may immediately begin to practice.

The action of this Masonic meditation is not limited to the lodge or temple. Its effect can be felt in every moment of one's daily life. However, just as there are different elements as one moves up the initiatic scales of Freemasonry, beginning with the 1st Degree and ascending the Masonic tree (Scottish Rite, Royal Arch, etc.), the Masonic meditation reveals different elements at each level of its process. Once you are able to control the basic elements, each new degree will offer special practices and keys to advancement.

This book is not the place to develop all the details of this system. These details will be the subject of another (more advanced) book about the Masonic meditation, which will come later. However, it is important to provide readers with a practice that reveals the applications of the various principles I have outlined up to this point. This will provide an excellent opportunity to practice these principles and to get closer to the fraternity, achieving entry through the only real portal that is always open: oneself.

A Masonic Meditation: The Square

Earlier, I discussed symbolic learning and the necessity for using a specific Masonic meditation. Theoretical studies are always interesting and useful, but it is generally better to have the opportunity to simultaneously put into practice what has been learnt so that these spiritual realities within us can be felt. It is critical not to transform Freemasonry into a satisfying but fruitless intellectual exercise. If you look at the field of art as an example, we that many people learn art theory, but this theoretical approach does not make anyone into a great artist. In order to become a great artist, you must practice over and over again. The same lesson is applicable here. You can learn to be a Freemason; you may even achieve advanced degrees. However, without inner work and spiritual practices, you will never be able to be a Masonic "artist." Even a good architect must know about and experiment with the practical application of his or her art. This lesson applies to every spiritual tradition as well. Group rituals are important, but they are inadequate to achieve the deepest levels of transformation, so that your hidden stone must be found and the temple you must become is built thereon.

The practical ritual I am providing here will enable you to experiment with these elements and learn the fundamentals of this system. However, please keep in mind that this ritual will be performed without direct supervision. It is adequate so that you can begin to understand, feel, and learn the initial steps of the Masonic meditation way, but, if you desire more, you are welcome to attend a seminar, where supervision and individual instruction is possible.

The complete initial meditation is described below. I suggest that you record it and listen to it during whatever time you set aside for practice. You may prefer to print it and read it when you decide to practice. This ritual will utilize the different elements I discussed above: relaxation, visualization, pronunciation, etc.

Before you begin, you must find a quiet place (indoors or outdoors) where you can be alone. Unplug your phone, turn off your cell phone, and let your family and friends know that you need private time. You must also have a chair with a straight back and a table that will serve as an altar. If possible, it is best to be oriented facing east (turn your chair so that it is facing east, with the table directly in front of you). You may cover this table with any cloth you like. In the Masonic lodges, the central altar is covered by an altar cloth made of beautiful fabric. Sometimes this altar cloth is surrounded by a golden edging. On the lodge's altar you may also find the sacred book (also called the book of the sacred law), as well as the square and the compass. Other (optional) items that you may place on the table include a drawing of the Masonic triangle with the Greek letter *G* (Gamma) inside. You may also have three candles on the table and you should place them at the three points of the triangle. Even though it is not obligatory, if you are a Freemason, you may wear your apron, along with any symbols you would generally use in your lodge meetings.

When you are completely ready, sit down on your chair and relax for a while. Remain in this position for a few moments, breathing quietly, with your eyes closed or slightly closed. Be attentive to your breathing; listen to your breath flow in and out. Watch your chest rise and fall. Remain quiet, breathing gently in and out. Breathe in through your nose and not your mouth. Notice the circulation of air through your body as it enters your nostrils, flows into your lungs, expanding them, and remains there for a while. Notice the flow as you exhale. Relax and quietly enjoy watching this flow for a while. Return to this simple observation from time to time during this exercise.

Maintain your state of relaxation and visualize an obelisk (maybe the Washington Monument in Washington DC) in front of you. Visualize yourself at the west of the monument, facing east. Imagine that this is no longer an external representation; you are looking at a real place. This monument really exists. It is not necessary to have an exact mental representation of it. You are standing on the threshold of the inner and spiritual world looking into it. Imagine that you move one step into the landscape of this scene. The landscape that surrounds you is equally vivid.

Stand up physically, and, if you have candles, light them.

Close your eyes, and look more closely at the two shapes that constitute the obelisk. The rectangle of the trunk can be reduced to the general shape of a square, the regular geometric face of a cube. Above the trunk you see the triangle of the pyramid. For now, just look at the trunk and practice recognizing the very simple shapes in this structure. Remain quiet, breathing gently in and out.

The square is the symbol of the physical body. The triangle is the symbol of the soul, which crowns the body. Breathe gently in and out for a while, continuing to hold these two parts of the human being in your mind: the body and the soul. For now, these representations are still external to you; they are shapes you are looking at.

Continue to breathe gently in and out. Release your visualization. Be focused only on your breathing.

After a moment of silence, consciously relax your body. As a child of the earth and the starry sky, you can act as a demiurge and bring order out of chaos. You can activate the essential powers in you, in order to build and organize your own macrocosm, your inner cosmos. As every Freemason knows, the Sun is the center of our system. From the Chaldaic theurgic system, the Sun has always been put at the center. From its light, beauty, and benevolence comes all spiritual and material life.

Imagine the Sun at the center of your solar plexus. The light rays emanating from your center expand outward—all around you.

Breathe gently. Raise your right arm and put the palm of your hand on your solar plexus.

Exclaim:[4] "As the Sun is the center and the origin of all being, may the sublime order of the cosmos organize the universe I am. Under the aegis of the Great Architect of the Universe, may the traditional motto be realized one more time: *Ordo Ab Chaos!*"

Pause.

Say: "The Grand Architect of the Universe selected three sacred letters[5] from among the simple ones and with them he sealed the universe in six directions. May this divine order be realized now!"

Hold both arms straight out in front of you, with your forearms on the horizontal plane and your palms facing the sky. Your back is straight, your shoulders relaxed, and your eyes are looking up at the sky. Holding this position, say: "The Grand Architect of the Universe looked above, and sealed the height with the power of Yod-He-Vav."

Pause.

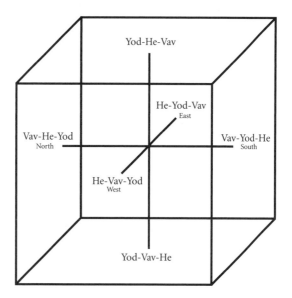

Figure 37: The cube and the pronounciations of the name of God (from the Bible)

Holding your arms in the same position, turn your palms toward the ground. Your back is straight, your shoulders relaxed, your eyes looking at the floor or earth (if you are outside).

Holding this position, say: "The Grand Architect of the Universe looked below, and sealed the depths with the power of Yod-Vav-He."

Pause.

Extend your arms in front of you (on the horizontal plane), to the east. The palms of your hands are nearly vertical, and you are looking to the east. Holding this position,

4. When you exclaim, it is not necessary to speak loudly. To be able to hear one's own voice is enough in this practice.

5. These elements come from the Qabalistic text, the *Sepher Yetzirah*, Book 1, Part 10–11.

say: "The Grand Architect of the Universe looked forward, and sealed the east with the power of He-Yod-Vav."

Pause.

Turn to your right to face south. Your arms are extended in front of you (on the horizontal plane). The palms of your hands are nearly vertical. Holding this position, say: "The Grand Architect of the Universe looked to the right, and sealed the south with the power of Vav-Yod-He."

Pause.

Turn to your right to face west. Your arms are extended in front of you (on the horizontal plane). The palms of your hands are nearly vertical. Holding this position, say: "The Grand Architect of the Universe looked backward, and sealed the west with the power of He-Vav-Yod."

Pause.

Turn to your right to face north. Your arms are extended in front of you (on the horizontal plane). The palms of your hands are nearly vertical. Holding this position, say: "The Grand Architect of the Universe looked to the left, and sealed the north with the power of Vav-He-Yod."

Relax your arms and sit down.

Make sure you are comfortably seated, and that your back is as straight as possible. Place your hands flat on your thighs, breathing quietly for a while.

The six directions of the space have been delimited and sealed. You are at the center of the cornerstone. Visualize around you this perfect stone, its six faces visible in a pulsating light. Take the time to check the six faces in the same order you sealed them, and then come back to the awareness of your breathing.

You are at the center of your inner universe. Visualize the Sun in your solar plexus shining powerfully. Feel this inner balance, which brings you into inner peace.

Think about the dynamic power created by the eight points of the cube around you. They seem to be eight powerful centers of energy.

Feel the position of your body. Your back and your bottom are a living representation of a square. Do the same with your thighs and your legs. The shape of the square corresponds to the ancient Greek letter Gamma (Γ). This letter Gamma is the third letter of the Greek alphabet, as well as the third Hebrew letter (Gimel). Over the next few minutes, think about the presence of this symbol inside the cube, inside you. As you know, this mysterious letter *G* is very often at the heart of the Masonic lodges. Now this hidden square is in your heart, and is manifested by the position of your body. Now exclaim: "The Sun must always be at its zenith to spread the light of Freemasonry all around the planet. By the help of the Great Architect of the Universe, may this enlightenment be accomplished!"

The number 3 is the core number in Freemasonry, its foundation. At this moment, remember that the number 3 corresponds to the place in the alphabet of these two sacred letters (Gamma and Gimel).

Visualize the symbolic shape connected to the top of the obelisk, the pyramid, all around you. This pyramid is formed by triangles put together on the square representing your body. This shape is a symbol of your soul, the place of the divine energy that animates your desire to return to heaven.

When your soul entered your body, you lost part of the power of the word. The place of this cornerstone, the philosopher's stone, was lost. All humans became orphans, forgetting their divine origin and nature. Yet the divine cornerstone has always been inside of us, carefully hidden and veiled. As the Hermetic and alchemical motto says. "*Visita Interiora Terrae Rectificando Invenies Occultum Lapidem*" (Visit the interior of the earth and, by rectifying it, you will reveal the hidden stone).

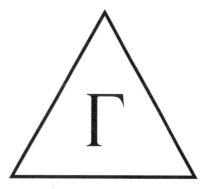

Figure 38: The triangle and the letter G in its Greek shape

You are now in this stone and you have already begun the secret work on the stone, by using this sacred combination of the sacred letters. The Greek letter *G* is also the initial of the divinity Gaia, the planet Earth. Your inner stone manifests this union, this meeting between the heavens and Earth.

In order to continue the quest, you must remember your own sacred word, the name of your philosopher's stone. Once this hidden word is revealed to you, you will be able to transform yourself. For now, as Freemasonry says, you must use a substituted word.

Relax for a while now, thinking about these traditional mysteries. Exclaim: "May the rays of the divine shed their benign influence upon me and enlighten me in the paths of virtue and science! May the power of the mysterious word be manifested in my cornerstone, the most sacred place of my soul, in order to begin my own transformation!"

Extend your right hand in front of you, and visualize yourself engraving the sacred letter G in the Greek shape of a square (Γ), in a letter of flame. Then, in the same way, engrave a triangle of fire around the letter G.

Relax your right arm, resuming the position you had before, with your hand on your thigh. For a few moments, visualize that the place you are in has become extremely bright, spreading beauty, strength, and wisdom throughout all the cosmos.

Relax and breathe quietly without thinking of anything specific. When you feel that the moment is right, stand up, put your right hand on your solar plexus, and declaim the traditional hymn of the Ancient Mysteries written by a master of the Golden Chain, the initiate Proclus (fifth century CE):

O gods, you who hold the rudder of holy wisdom, who light in our human souls the flame of return, bring us back among the immortals, and by the inexpressible initations of the hymns, give us the capacity to escape from our dark caves and to purify ourselves. Grant this to me, O powerful liberators! Grant me, by knowledge of the divine writings, by dispersing the darkness which surrounds me, a pure and holy light. Allow me to perfectly know the incorruptible God, and the man or woman that I am.

May a wicked djinn never overcome me by pains, or indefinitely hold me captive under the rivers of oblivion.

May I never be held captive in the jail of life, for the frightening expiation, with my soul fallen in the icy flows of generation, where I never want to wander too long.

So, O gods, sovereigns of the radiant wisdom, grant me and reveal to one who hastens on the ascending Path of Return, the holy ecstasies and the initiations which are at the heart of the divine words!

Blow out the candles, and remove your apron if you have one. Record your feelings, remarks, experiences, and thoughts about this Masonic meditation in a notebook (which must be reserved for this purpose).

chapter seven

PRACTICE OF THE INDIVIDUAL RITUALS OF THE HIGH DEGREES

Lodge of Perfection

As we saw in the last chapter, each degree develops a specific myth and story. Some are connected, others not. Some are using myths from the Bible. In others, the rituals seems more connected to the Ancient Mysteries, like Mithraism, Eleusian, etc. These higher degrees can be seen as developing and deepening the three first degrees, which are complete in themselves.

These myths are performed in the Masonic lodges, chapters, councils, or consistories as initiatic rituals. This is an important process that allows the candidate to receive a deep experience of the hidden meanings. Of course, these rituals contain lectures, and other more theatrical elements. Participation in these symbolic and maybe sacred ceremonies one helps to go further in one's understanding of the Craft. They are opportunities to progress in the moral and symbolic explanations of the Masonic way.

These rituals are generally used in groups. However, the most important of them have an esoteric structure, which is able to be used privately in order to integrate this spiritual process. Most of the time this framework is hidden. It can be seen in a useful way only with the help of the Hermetic principles I already explained. So don't worry if in some cases you don't recognize the progression. Undoubtedly, you will be able to see it clearly and immediately with the ritual work. The intention of these esoteric individual practices has never been to replace the group's ritual. The purpose is always to create a strong link between the initiate and the egregore of the Scottish Rite with the opportunity to improve this relationship with the heart of the system. With this help, the connection will be stronger for the betterment of the initiate, the Scottish Rite, and humanity.

The Royal Arch of Solomon (13th Degree)

The 13th degree of the Scottish Rite may be linked with the 14th degree that uses the same Qabalistic principles. This degree also has many symbols in common with the Royal Arch high degrees.[1]

THE INDIVIDUAL PRACTICE

Prepare your sacred space for the individual practice just as you did for the Masonic meditation (Chapter Six).

On your altar, place the representation of the Hermetic Tree of Life. You will find this drawing in the appendix.

You will need ten tealight candles. Place one candle on each of the circles. The circles represent the ten spheres (Sephiroth) of the Hermetic Tree of Life. Incense is optional.

Put the symbol of the degree (a triangle with the letter Yod at its center) on the east side of your altar or on the eastern wall. (See the illustration next to this text). If you have an apron or collar of this degree, you may wear them.

When everything is ready, sit down on your chair and relax for a while. Remain in this position for a few moments, breathing quietly, with your eyes closed or slightly closed. Be attentive to your breathing; listen to your breath flow in and out. Watch your chest rise and fall. Remain quiet, breathing gently in and out. Breathe in through your nose and out through your mouth. Continue relaxing for a while.

Maintain your state of relaxation. Make sure you are comfortably seated, and that your back is as straight as possible. Place your hands flat on your thighs. Continue your rhythmic breathing. Light the candle that is closest to the east, in the upper circle. Sit down with your hands on your thighs and meditate. When you feel that the time is right (five minutes maximum), open your eyes and look at the symbolic representations of the Qabalistic Tree. Remaining completely relaxed, simply look at this diagram without focusing on any particular thought.

---

1. The individual practice of the Royal Arch of Solomon was published in French in the book *ABC d'ésotérisme maçonnique* by Jean-Louis De Biasi, (Paris: Grancher Publications, 2008). This excerpt is used here with the permission of Grancher Publications.

Put your right forefinger very close to the easternmost candle (candle number 1 in the chart below). Exclaim the sacred word. (See the list of sacred names in the table below. They are numbered according to the candle they are to be used with. Note that you will not light any more candles at this juncture).

Move your right forefinger close to the candle at the center of the second circle and pronounce the second word. Repeat this sequence for the other eight circles.

Sequence		Sacred names to pronounce (Assiah)
	1	1- Rechit haguilgalim
3	2	2- Maslot
5	4	3- Chabatai
	6	4- Tsedeq
8	7	5- Madim
	9	6- Chemech
	10	7- Nogah
		8- Kokav
		9- Levanah
		10- Relem Iesodot

Meditate for a few moments. Relax and listen to the sound of your own breathing. After breathing quietly for a little while, visualize a triangle of gold, engraved with the four sacred letters of the divine name (the Tetragrammaton) directly in front of you:

Yod ('), He (ה), Vav (ו), He (ה)

Listen to the sound of your breath as it flows in and out, while you continue to focus your attention on these four letters.

When you feel ready, light each of the candles in ascending order, as explained in the chart below. Each time you light a candle, you must pronounce (or vibrate) the corresponding sacred word, which is on the right side of the chart. You will do the same for the ten spheres.

Sequence		Sacred names to pronounce (Yetzirah)
	10	10- Chaiot hakodech
8	9	9- Ophanim
6	7	8- Aralim
	5	7- Rachmalim
3	4	6- Séraphim
	2	5- Melerim
	1	4- Elohim
		3- Tarchichim
		2- Keroubim
		1- Achim

Meditate until you feel ready to continue. Breathe deeply, rhythmically, and empty your mind.

Now imagine that you are standing in front of an altar of white marble that is two cubits high. On the top of this altar you see a triangle of agate engraved with the four letters of the Tetragrammaton (described above). Contemplate this jewel until you feel ready to continue, and then cease all visualizations.

Imagine that you are looking up at the sky. Visualize the starry arch of the heavens as the ceiling of your temple. The vast expanse of this starry arch is the vaulted ceiling that surmounts all beneath it. This is the first veil. Maintain this visualization and pronounce the words:

Eïn Soph Aor

Visualize yourself penetrating the veil. Continue your journey across this starry expanse, on to the next veil. When you are directly in front of it, pronounce the words:

Eïn Soph

Imagine yourself penetrating this veil. Continue on until you reach the third veil. When you are directly in front of it, pronounce the word:

Eïn

Imagine that you are now floating in a vault of empty and silent space. Your respiration is the only thing that connects you to your physical body. Meditate on this feeling and experience for as long as you like. When you feel your concentration on this experience decreasing, bring your attention to the sensations of your body and open your eyes.

Take the candle snuffer and extinguish the candles in the order shown in the chart below. When you extinguish a candle, pronounce the word and visualize the color associated with this sphere (see table below). Take your time moving through this sequence, gradually progressing from one sphere to the next. The duration of your stay at one sphere may differ from your stay at the next sphere. This is normal and it is a good indication of the work you are doing. This work is connected to your spiritual and invisible bodies, and different aspects of your spiritual and physical bodies need a different amount of time to accomplish the necessary work.

Sequence		Sacred names to pronounce (Briah)	Colors
	1	1- Metatron	1- White brillance
3	2	2- Ratziel	2- Dynamic nacreous vortex of all spectrum colors
5	4	3- Tsafkiel	
	6	4- Tsadkiel	3- Indigo
8	7	5- Kamael	4- Blue
	9	6- Raphael	5- Red
	10	7- Haniel	6- Yellow
		8- Mikael	7- Green
		9- Gabriel	8- Orange
		10- Sandalphon	9- Violet
			10- Citrine, olive, russet, black

When all the candles are extinguished, breathe deeply and meditate briefly with your eyes closed. Begin to enjoy this darkness, recognizing it as benevolent. You realize that there is an eternal flame inside you. This inner light can never be extinguished. Enjoy the sensation of your breathing gently in and out; listen to your heartbeat; experience all the sensations emanating from your physical body.

When you feel finished enjoying this inner peace, pronounce the sacred names in ascending order, as indicated in the table below. As you pronounce the name, visualize the associated color.

Sequence		Sacred names to pronounce (Atziluth)	Colors
	10	10- Eieh	10- Brilliance
8	9	9- Iah	9- Ultraviolet
6	7	8- Yod-He-Vav-He Elohim	8- Dove gray
	5	7- El	7- Lilac
3	4	6- Elohim Guibor	6- Amber
	2	5- Yod-He-Vav-He Eloah	5- Pale greenish yellow
	1	4- Yod-He-Vav-He Tsébaot	4- Greenish blue
		3- Elohim Tsebaoth	3- Yellow ochre
		2- Chadai El Rai	2- Red-purple
		1- Adonai Meleur	1- Purple-brown

After you have completed the pronunciation of the ten sacred words, relax for a few moments. When you feel ready to begin the closing, remove the candles and the representation of the Qabalistic Tree. Use your notebook to record your feelings, comments, and any ideas you received during this ritual.

THE SYMBOLIC STORY OF THIS DEGREE

It might be interesting for you to know the myth that is related to this degree. The information in this myth will help you to understand the relationship of some of the history of the world with the individual practice of this degree.

A long time after the deaths of Hiram, Solomon the King of Jerusalem, and all the people of their generation; after the armies of Nebuchadnezzar had destroyed the kingdom of Judah and the city of Jerusalem; after they had razed the Temple to the ground and taken the survivors into captivity; when the mountain of Zion was no more than an arid desert where a few skeletal goats grazed, three travelers arrived one morning, riding their camels. They were magi, initiates from Babylon, and members of the universal priesthood, who came to this place on a pilgrimage, to explore the ruins of the ancient sanctuary.

After a frugal meal, these pilgrims began to walk around this devastated place. The ancient walls and columns that had fallen on the ground helped them to imagine the borders of the Temple. They started to look more closely at the engravings on the capitals, and to examine some of the stones that were strewn about, trying to find special inscriptions and symbols.

As they were searching under an overturned wall in the middle of a huge network of brambles, they discovered a hole in the ground. The hole was located in the southeast corner of the Temple. They immediately began to clear away the brambles around this opening. After a period of work, the eldest, who appeared to be their leader, lay down on his stomach and peered into the hole.

It was midday, the Sun shone at its zenith, and its rays of light penetrated almost vertically into the well. The magus saw something that looked like a shiny object at the bottom of the well. He called his companions to check this glimmer of light reflecting up from the earth. As the elder had done, they, too, laid down and looked. Undoubtedly, something was sparkling beneath them, flashing with fire like a sacred jewel. The three pilgrims decided one of them should go down into the well. To make a rope so the chosen member could climb down, they undid their belts, linked them together, and threw one end into the well. Two of them then held one end of this leather rope, helping the third to climb down into what now seemed like a very dark cave. Their leader disappeared into the shadows.

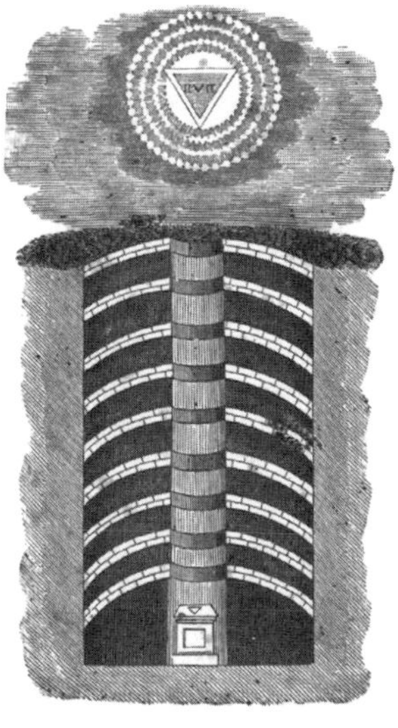

Using his hands and feet, the magus rappelled into the depths of the cave. As he progressed, he noticed that the

Figure 39: Structure of the well in the Royal Arch Degree in the Scottish Rite

wall was divided into several cylinders or columns that were each made of stones of many different colors. The dimension of these different stones was around a cubit each in height. When he finally reached the floor of the well, he realized that there were ten rings. He looked around at the floor. At the center of this circular floor, he saw what he recognized as the jewel of Hiram. Picking it up, he looked at it more closely and saw with a flood of emotion that the holy sacred name was engraved in it. As a perfected initiate, he recognized this sacred word. In order to prevent his companions from seeing this word (because they had not yet received the full initiation necessary), he placed the jewel on his chest, with the engraved side touching his skin, thus hiding the engraved side, as had Master Hiram.

He looked around and saw a gap in the wall that seemed large enough to walk through. He entered, stumbling in the darkness like a blind man. His hands touched a surface that he imagined was made of bronze. He moved back and called his companions to help him climb out of the well.

Seeing the jewel on the chest of their chief, both magi bowed to him, guessing that he had just received an important initiation. He explained to them what he had seen and spoke about the bronze door. They thought that a holy mystery was connected with this place and decided that all of them would climb down into the well.

They put one end of the rope made of the three belts under a flat stone near the well. On this stone, the word *Jachin* was engraved. They rolled a broken column over to the other side. The word *Boaz* was engraved on this column.

Two of the men made a sacred fire by rolling a stick of hard wood between their hands. The stick was set into a hole one of them had made in a soft piece of wood. Tinder was set around the wood. When the friction of this action on the wood caused sparks to ignite the tinder, they blew on it to increase the flame. Meanwhile, the third man lit one of the three torches of resin they had brought with them, and used it to scare away any wild animals near the mouth of the well. Next, each of the torches was successively ignited with the sacred fire. Each magus, holding a torch in his hand, used the rope to descend to the bottom of the well.

Once there with their chief, they entered the hall and made their way to the bronze door. The old magus raised his torch and attentively examined the door. At its center, he saw a raised pattern that looked like a royal crown. A circle of twenty-two points surrounded the crown.

The magus closed his eyes and meditated deeply on this image for some time. Opening his eyes, he looked at the door and pronounced the word *Malkuth*. Suddenly the door opened.

The explorers were standing in front of a staircase that led down into the earth. They began to descend, counting the stairs as they went. After three stairs, they encountered a triangular floor. On their left, they saw another staircase. They continued to progress in this fashion, and, after five stairs, found themselves on another triangular floor, of the same form and dimensions as the first. Another staircase appeared on their right, where they noticed seven steps continuing down into the earth.

Having crossed the third floor, they next descended nine stairs where they stopped in front of a second bronze door.

The old initiate took a look at it and saw that there was also a raised pattern on this door. It was composed of a right angle set in stone at the center of circle formed by twenty-two points. He vibrated the word *Yesod* and the door opened.

The magi entered into a large vaulted circular space. On the walls, nine lines were engraved that formed rays from the center of the vault to the outer edge of the circular floor. They looked around to see if there was another door, but they were unable to find anything. Looking more carefully between the lines, the old initiate saw a new gate in the darkness of the cave and the symbol of a shining sun at the center of a circle of twenty-two points. Powerfully, he pronounced the word *Hod* and the door opened onto a second room. Successively, the explorers crossed through five other hidden doors, always discovering another crypt beyond each new door.

On one of these doors, there was a wonderful engraving of a moon, and thereafter, the head of lion, a soft and gracious curve, a ruler, a scroll of the law, an eye, and, finally, a royal crown.

At every door the wise initiate successively pronounced the words *Netzach, Tiphareth, Geburah, Chesed, Binah, Chokmah,* and *Kether*. When they entered the ninth arch, the magi stopped—surprised, dazzled, and scared. The other passages had been dark. By contrast, this place was brilliantly lit. At the center of the ninth arch, there were three candleholders with candles in them, each eleven cubits high. Each candle had three branches. These lamps, which must have burnt for all the intervening centuries since the destruction of the holy Temple, shone with a wonderful brightness. They illuminated the entire area with a soft yet intense light, revealing all the details of its marvelous architecture. The vault was carved directly into the rock.

The pilgrims extinguished their torches, setting them by the door. They removed their shoes, as one does in a holy place, and then they moved forward, bowing nine times toward the colossal candles.

At the base of the triangle formed by the three candelabra rose a cubic altar two cubits high, made of white marble. On the right side, near the summit of the triangle, the tools of the Craft were represented in gold: the ruler, the compass, the square, the level, the trowel, and the mallet. On the left side, there were geometric symbols: the triangle, the square, the five-pointed star, and the cube. On the right side, numbers were engraved: 27, 125, 343, 729, and 1331. Finally, on the remaining side, the symbolic Acacia was represented. On top of this altar, a stone of agate was set. Its dimensions were three palms wide. At its base, the letters of the word *Adonaï* were engraved in gold.

Both the younger magi bowed before the name of God. But the elder initiate raised his head and said to them: "It is now time for you to receive the last teaching. This initiation will transform you into perfect initiates. You must remember that this name is also a vain symbol, which does not express the concept of supreme understanding."

Holding the stone of agate in his two hands, he turned round to face to his companions and said to them: "Behold! The supreme understanding is here. You stand at the center of this understanding."

The followers spelled out the letters of the words that make up the Tetragrammaton, Yod, Heh, Waw, Heh, and began to open their mouths to pronounce the final word. But the old initiate stopped them, saying: "Silence! This is the ineffable word, which must not be pronounced."

Figure 40: The Tetragrammaton

Then he put the stone of agate on the altar, took the jewel of Master Hiram from his chest, and showed them that the same signs were also engraved on it. "Now you must know," said the Master, "that it was not Solomon who created this hypogeum, nor did he create the other eight rooms, nor is it he who hides the sacred stone. This holy symbol was put here by Enoch, the first of all initiates, the master initiator, who did not die, but survives in all his spiritual sons. Enoch lived a long time before Solomon, even before the flood. Nobody knows when the first eight arches were built, nor when this one was dug directly in the rock."

However, the new grand initiates were looking all around this room, eager to understand the secrets and sacred teachings of this place. They walked up to a carefully hidden door, on which they saw the symbol of a broken vase. They called their master and said to him: "Open this door for us. There must be another new mystery behind it."

"No," he answered them, "we should not open this door. There is a mystery there, but it is a terrible mystery, the mystery of death."

"Aha," they said. "You want to hide something from us, to keep it for yourself. But we want to know everything. We will open this door ourselves." They started to pronounce all the words that they had heard from the mouth of their master. As these words had no effect, they began to pronounce all the words they could remember. These, too, had no effect. Just when they were about to give up, one of them said, "We cannot continue like this *ad infinitum*." He spoke one more word.

At the sound of this word, *En Soph* (in Hebrew), the door opened violently and the two new initiates were knocked across the floor. A howling wind blew in the arch and the magical lamps were blown out. The master rushed to the door, calling to his followers to help. They ran to him and united their efforts to close the door again. The door did not close, and the lights did not relight.

The young magi stood in the deepest darkness, impossible to imagine. They heard the voice of their master saying: "Alas, this terrible event, the consequence of your imprudence, was written of long ago. Now we are all at a terrible risk of perishing in these unknown, underground caverns. Let us try to leave this place. We must cross the eight arches and go back up through the well by which we came down. We must form a chain with our hands in order to make it safely to the exit. We must search for the gate in every room until we arrive at the foot of the staircase of twenty-four stairs. Let us hope that we will reach it in safety."

They began the tedious and frightening journey back. Hour after hour they toiled in fearful unity toward their goal. They were filled with fear at every step, struggling to find their way. At last, they arrived in front of the staircase of twenty-four stairs. They climbed slowly upward by counting nine, seven, five, and three until they stepped out, once again at the bottom of the well. It was midnight. The stars shone in the firmament. The rope of belts was still there.

Before they began the climb to freedom, the master showed his companions the circle of the sky created by the edges of the well. He said to them: "The ten circles we saw in this well also represent the arcs of the staircase. This last circle corresponds to the number 11, where the wind of disaster blew. It is the infinite sky, the lights we can never hold in our hands."

The three initiates climbed up out of the well. They once again rolled the column from its place, without seeing the word *Boaz* that was carved on it. They detached their belts and, without exchanging a word, began a deep, silent meditation under the starry sky. In the middle of this nocturnal silence, they rode their camels back to Babylon.

Figure 41: Representation of the Rose-Cross symbol in a plate from Kunrath

Chapter of Rose Croix
Knight of the Rose-Croix (18th Degree)

In the last chapter, I revealed the names of several Rose-Cross orders that existed in the past. Historically, in Freemasonry, several rituals are more or less related to the Rose-Cross. The 18th Degree, Knights of the Rose-Croix, developed in several versions, according to the influences, understanding, and goals in different countries. Those details that were of lesser importance ultimately disappeared. The individual practice found here is rooted in the most accurate and effective origins, so that you will achieve an immediate and powerful connection with this egregore and spirit.

For this practice, it will be necessary to use certain images related to this ritual, which you will be able to find in the appendix, and some required images will be placed beside the relevant part in reduced size, in order to fit the page.

Prepare your room for the practice as you did for the Masonic meditation (Chapter Six).

On your altar, place two items: (1) a printed representation of a pentagram surrounded by Hebrew letters, crowned by a triangle, with the Tetraktys at the center, and (2) a black veil large enough to cover your head. (If you don't have one, you can visualize it during the practice.) Optional items to place on the altar are a bell or five tealight candles (place one candle on each of the points of the pentagram).

Put the symbol of this degree (the compass, rose-cross, and pelican) to the east of your altar or on the eastern wall. If you have the apron or collar of this degree, you may wear them.

When everything is prepared, sit down on your chair and relax for a while. Remain in this position for a few moments, breathing quietly, with your eyes closed or slightly closed. Be attentive to your breathing; listen to the flow of your breath, in and out. Watch your chest rise and fall. Remain quiet, breathing gently in and out. Breathe in through your nose and out of your mouth. Relax for a while until you are deeply comfortable.

Maintain your state of relaxation. Make sure you are comfortably seated and that your back is as straight as possible. Place your hands flat on your thighs, breathing quietly for a little while.

After a moment of silent relaxation, stand up. Put the palm of your right hand on your solar plexus and exclaim: "O thou who art the creator, the preserver, and the father of all mankind, O beneficent and merciful one, please guard us in thy holy keep; guide our footsteps, that we may not stray from thy truth into the paths of error! If we, in our hearts, desire of thee anything whatsoever that is not good for us to have, deny it unto us! If we fail to ask for anything that we ought to ask at thy hands, give it unto us, we beseech thee, out of thy exceeding goodness. Chasten us for our sins, that we may, by thy discipline, learn wisdom. Make us useful unto others and content with the lot which thou assignest unto us; and may we so labor here and elsewhere, as to deserve thy favor and benefit our fellows. So mote it be!"

Relax your arms and sit down. Put the veil on your head, covering your face and your eyes. Visualize a dark place all around you. The light is just adequate for you to see the details of the place where you stand. The floor is strewn with broken columns and fragments of Masonic working tools. There is a pillar in front of you, to the east. The word *Faith* is engraved on it in violet paint. On your right, to the south, another column is engraved with the word *Hope* painted in scarlet red. On your left, to the north, the third column is engraved with the word *Charity* painted in sky-blue.

In front of you, to the east, an altar is covered with a black cloth strewn with white flames. On the altar in your mind, visualize the symbol you placed on the altar at the beginning of this practice. Pick up the bell with your right hand, or just use the palms of your hands to clap, making a sharp noise, similar to a knock. This is a "battery."

While you hold the visualization of this place in your mind, knock thirty-three times. Stand up, remove the veil from your eyes, and light the five small candles clockwise, beginning with the candle nearest you on the left.

With your body, you will form a pentagram by lifting your arms so they are on the horizontal plane, with your palms facing the floor. (Your legs should be shoulder width apart.) Visualize your solar plexus filling with a bright rose-colored light. Feel the vibrations coming from your solar plexus, the light and heat.

Visualize the five Hebrew letters on the five parts of your body: Yod—י (red): left foot; He—ה (blue): left hand; Shin—ש (bright white light): head; Vav—ו (yellow): right hand, He—ה (dark brown): left foot. If you are unable to visualize the Hebrew letters, hold the colors and their positions on your body in your mind. Feel the presence and power of each center.

Breathe deeply and relax. Increase the intensity of your visualization.

Holding this position, pronounce (vibrate) the first letter Yod. Pronounce this letter five times. During each inhalation, increase the visualization of the letter. If you are unable to visualize the letter precisely, just stay focused on the feeling in that part of your body.

Repeat this process for each of the following letters, with five vibrations of each letter. The order is: Yod, Heh, Shin, Vav, Heh.

When this sequence is complete, relax your arms on either side of your body, with your legs in contact, or very close together. Breathe normally for a while, without visualization. Remove the black veil from your head.

Figure 42: Pentagram and the invocation direction

With your right forefinger in front of you, draw a clockwise pentagram of invocation beginning with the top point of the pentagram. During this movement, pronounce the sacred name "Yeshua" (Yod-He-Shin-Vav-He). The pronunciation must start when you begin the pentagram and stop before you complete it.

Turn right to face south. Draw the same pentagram, pronouncing the same sacred name.

Proceed in the same way, turning to the west, and then the north. Face east to complete and close the circle. You have drawn four pentagrams to the four directions. These invocations have increased the light of your aura and the subtle light of this place.

Place your right hand on your solar plexus, and your left hand on top of your right hand.

Vibrate the same sacred name "Yeshua" six times.

Visualize your aura increasing in brightness. After you have completed these six vibrations, lower your arms and relax them, then kneel.

Visualize again a dark place all around you. You are in a small, square room. The walls are black. You feel a frightening aura and the presence of human skeletons all around you.

Figure 43: Symbolic representation of the Rite Rose Cross developed in this part of the book

Breathe slowly and focus on your inner soul, the essential and immortal part of your being.

Cross your arms on your chest, left over right, the palms of your hands in contact with your body. Your eyes are closed. After a short period of silence and meditation, pronounce each letter of the Hebrew alphabet. At the same time, visualize the creation of a wall of light all around you, revolving clockwise. If you don't know the alphabet, just read this list, with your eyes slightly closed. (The letters are: Alef, Bet, Gimel, Dalet, Heh, Vav, Zayin, Cheth, Tet, Yod, Kaf, Lamed, Mem, Nun, Samekh, Ayin, Peh, Tsadi, Qof, Resh, Shin, Tav.) Don't worry about pronouncing the letters correctly. Focusing on the alphabet and the wall of light will be enough to create this subtle reality on the spiritual plane.

Meditate in this place of light for a while, and then stand up.

Resume your seat and breathe in silence.

Visualize the chamber of the chapter created by your last invocations. Imagine that the hangings surrounding the chamber are crimson red. The chamber is lit by thirty-three candles. Three candlesticks each hold eleven candles, and these candlesticks are placed to the east, south, and west, respectively.

To the east, you see the image of the compass, the rose cross, and the pelican. Take your time and focus on each symbol. Imagine that your altar is covered with a white cloth, or look at your altar with your eyes slightly closed. Visualize the symbols you placed on it.

Exclaim: "More than any other, a Knight of the Rose-Cross must know himself—he must find his inner balance and renounce all disgraceful behavior. May the divine powers help me to clearly see the secret of my being!"

Pause.

Exclaim: "May the divine powers be invoked by their sacred names, sealing my deep and true desire!"

Invoke the four sacred names:

1- "Yod-Heh-Vav-Heh Eloah Vedaat"

2- "Raphael"

3- "Malachim"

4- "Chemech"

Visualize the lights of the candles increasing.

Focus for a while longer on the symbol of the pelican, then say: "*Lux e Tenebris*" ["Light out of darkness"].

Pause.

Pronounce the Greek words, which are keys of this degree: *Pistis* [faith], *Elpis* [hope], and *Agape* [charity, love].

Breathe rhythmically and relax.

When you feel ready to continue, stand up and return to the pentagram posture. With your arms on the horizontal, turn your palms to face the east. Close your eyes and breathe rhythmically. After a moment of silence, exclaim: "*In hoc signo vinces!*"

After a short pause, continue:

"As true Knight of the Rose-Cross, I will always put my higher ideals before every-thing else. I know the weakness of my human nature. I know that desire and will are the only powers allowing me to progress beyond my physical limitations. In order to become the Knight of the Rose-Cross that I truly want to be, I understand that self-sacrifice must be at the core of my dedication. At every moment of my life, I need to learn a way to live simultaneously in this world and in the spiritual world, illuminating the one by the divine fire of the other."

Lower your arms and relax them. Visualize a rose as large as you are, directly before you. Imagine that the rose progressively surrounds you. You are at its center, and this mystical flower illuminates your aura. Feel its energy and peace.

With your right forefinger, draw a horizontal line in front of you from left to right while you exclaim: "*Ego Leukothea Eïmi!*" Feel this balanced power deeply within your aura.

With your right forefinger, draw a vertical line in front of you from top to bottom (approximately the same size as the first line) as you exclaim: "*Ego Melanotheos Eïmi!*" Feel deeply that you are on the vertical axis between the earth and sky.

Breathe rhythmically and relax.

Place your hands on your solar plexus. Visualize the heart of the rose (your own heart) becoming more and more luminous. You are surrounded by rays of light. In front of you, the pelican and the surrounding scene comes alive, receiving the sunlight of your hidden rose, the light of your noble desire.

Breathe rhythmically and relax for a while, holding on to this feeling and visualization in your mind. Exclaim: "*Igne Natura Renovatur Integra!*" [My entire nature is renovated by fire!]

Visualize the light increasing again. Exclaim: "*Ego Agathodaïmon Eïmi!*"

Spread your arms out wide on either side of your body, with your palms open and facing the sky. Exclaim: "May the rose of my soul illuminate the cross of my body!"

Maintain this position for a few moments.

Relax your arms and be seated for a moment of silent meditation. When you feel ready to stop, open your eyes and blow out the candles. Remove your apron if you have one. Record your feelings, remarks, experiences, and thoughts about this practice in your notebook (which must be reserved for this purpose).

Council of Kadosh

Knight of the Sun (27ᵗʰ Degree)

Numerous books and studies have been published in several languages regarding the Knight of the Sun (27ᵗʰ Degree). It is considered to be one of the most significant degrees, with regard to understanding the Ancient Mysteries. Although it is possible to find many lesser influences that are associated with this degree, over the centuries Mithraism has become increasingly established as the major tradition from which it sprang. In the first few chapters, I established the importance of this tradition for Freemasonry. Freemasonry and Mithraism are very closed allied.

The worship of light (the Sun) is one of the central elements of Mithraism. The Sun is called *Sol Invictus*, which means "Sun undefeated." The journey of the soul through the seven veils of the planets, as described in the Ancient Mysteries, is present in the structure and meaning of this degree.

This respectable tradition is very old. Evidence of its existence and character may be found in the recorded history of the Chaldean civilization. Some time after the Renaissance, the scale used in Mithraism was associated with the Qabalistic Tree of Life and the spheres called Sephiroth. The soul's journey was described in Mithraic mythology as being constituted during its descent into the material world. As the soul descended through the heavens, each of the seven planets, consecutively, added its influence in the form of the symbolic "clothing" that is uniquely related to each of those planets. Thus, each planet gives the soul a specific influence characteristic of that planet, and the unique combination of these seven influences yields the human personality. In this way, the incarnated soul is composed of the various powers acting on it.

In Mithraism, there is both a theological and Esoteric justification for astrology. Its origin in this ancient religion demonstrates its value as much more than a simple predictive art. Astrology is also rooted in the Hermetic tradition. Thus, the goal is not to learn astrology in order to know your destiny in some passive way. You can learn how to use these astrological symbols in order to have a dynamic influence on your life. At every moment of your life, you receive influences from your external circle of friends, family, and associates—your outer world. At the same time, on the inner planes, there are many influences coming through your unconscious mind that deeply affect your everyday life. For psychologists, the unconscious is composed of memories that are hidden from us from birth. Other theories, such as the theory of hypnotic regression, demonstrate that you do have memories that predate your birth, and perhaps even predate the current incarnation of the soul and the appearance of this individual consciousness. For esotericists, the early memories are composed of specific, precise influences that are balanced somewhat differently for each incarnate human being. Of course, these influences may also be seen as hidden memories. This notion is compatible with the astrological theory that emphasizes the existence of symbolic inner characters that are represented by the planetary divinities. The Hermetic Tradition accepts this occult structure of the human being and has devised a special method that allows the initiate to be aware of these influences in order to balance them. From a passive position, the initiate become an actor of his own destiny. This knowledge was transmitted under the veil of symbols, which was introduced early on into the Masonic Tradition.

Regarding the influence of Hermeticism in the Italian Renaissance, the (then) new *Academia Platonica*, which was established in Florence by Marsilio Ficino, was directly responsible for developing this aspect. The esoteric science called theurgy was used to develop a good inner balance between all the influences received during one's journey and descent. To accomplish that, they used the theory of correspondences and signatures. I partly developed these concepts in the section on symbols in order to convey that the material world retains footprints (signatures) of the invisible influences with which it has had contact. There is a connection between that which is above and that which is below. A perfume, a color, or a stone really can be linked to spiritual and divine spheres and divinities. A yellow flower and a gold nugget are inevitably connected to the Sun, as well as the gods Helios and Apollo. No gap can exist in this vision of a global universe or a global planet. In this we see that such ideas are really very modern, and they are currently in use as part of some of the most advanced scientific theories of our time. (They are used to explain global warming, and are central to the concept that is called the butterfly effect).

These signatures and symbols are the foundation of the Hermetic rituals that were developed in the Renaissance. By using these secret ceremonies, early Hermetists were able to balance their invisible bodies. Since the invisible body also has an effect on the physical body, this ritual work was also used to heal physical illnesses. This relationship between the invisible body and physical body and the doctrine of signatures was associated with special diets and a real hermetic regimen was composed and developed. As a physician, Marsilio Ficino, who was also the Chief of the Academy, was well aware of such necessities. His vision is a primary principle in the Hermetic way: work to improve both the outer and the inner self in order to have a long and healthy life. These rules, as developed by Ficino, are well deserving of a complete study in and of themselves.

Using these laws of universal interrelatedness, those early initiates also worked to ascend to the spiritual planes, and thereby to return to their divine origin. Happiness in this material world is possible by achieving balance in this inner dimension.

These symbolic and ritual elements were a part of the amazing heritage of Free-masonry. The heart of this 27th Degree is on the border between theurgy and symbolic ritual. The practice I will provide for you here will allow you to achieve much more progress, so that you will be able to feel and to increase your inner connection to the archetypes present in your unconsciousness. In order for you to continue your progress, it would be necessary to perform a more complete ritual, including a group ritual.

Visualization, meditation, and the vibration of sacred words are used in the same way in this practice as in the previous practices. These practical keys will enable you to establish immediate contact with the archetypal and divine entities. Remember that these classical divinities are just aspects of the different manifestations that originate with the Great Architect of the Universe, the hidden One. Yet these powers will have an immediate, deep, and lasting effect on you.

Of course, you must not expect a complete and immediate transformation, nor a miracle. This practice will affect you, just as a drop of water falling regularly on a stone will ultimately change the stone that you are. Even a hard rock can be pierced by persistent action. If you persist, these practices will bring you to the center of your stone and they will show you the way to see the pure light from which you came.

THE INDIVIDUAL PRACTICE

To begin, I will present several correspondence charts that are intimately connected to the esoteric practices of this Masonic degree. Don't be surprised by the differences you will find between the rituals and symbolic attributions (such as colors or names) that you are used to and those provided here. There are many versions of ritual texts and the charts I have provided offer very traditional associations rooted in the most ancient traditions. They will establish the coherence needed for this kind of work.

Planet	Symbol	Day	Color	Spirit	Divinity	Greek Vowel	Sephirah on the Qabalistic Tree
Saturn	♄	Saturday	Indigo	Michael	Cronus	Ω Omega	Binah
Jupiter	♃	Thursday	Blue	Gabriel	Zeus	Υ Upsilon	Chesed, Gedulah
Mars	♂	Tuesday	Red	Ouriel	Ares	O Omicron	Gueburah
Sun	☉	Sunday	Yellow	Zarakiel	Helios	I Iota	Tiphareth
Venus	♀	Friday	Green	Hamaliel	Aphrodite	H Eta	Netzach
Mercury	☿	Wednesday	Orange	Raphael	Hermes	E Epsilon	Hod
Moon	☽	Monday	Violet	Tsafkiel	Selene	A Alpha	Yesod

MITHRAISM		
Grades, Translation	Planet	**Symbolic Meaning,** Symbols
Corax, crow	Mercury	Messenger crow, caduceus, small vessel
Nymphus, fiancée, spouse	Venus	Alliance lamp, bridal torch, diadem with crescent moon
Miles, warrior	Mars	Soldier of Mithra helmet, pilum (spear), bag
Leo, lion	Jupiter	Celestial fire, power of purification spade, sistrum, bolt of lightning (attribute of Jupiter)
Perses, Persian	Moon	Fecundity, Guardian of the fruits sickle, sword, crescent moon
Héliodromus, Messenger of the Sun	Sun	Courier of the Sun torch, crown with rays and ribbons, whip of the Sun
Pater, father	Saturn	Command, authority Phrygian cap, pruning knife of Saturn, wand of command

Heliocentric position of the planets	
Position of the planets according to the symbol of the hexagram	Qabalistic sequence
♄ ♃ ♂ ☉ ♀ ☿ ☽	♄ ♃ ♂ ☉ ♀ ☿ ☽

Set up the ritual space just as you did for the Masonic meditation (Chapter Six). In the appendix, you will find the image of the hexagram and the planets. You will need to copy these and place the hexagram on your altar. You will also need seven tealight candles; place one candle on, or next to, the symbol of the planet on the hexagram. You may also use incense if you like. To the east of your altar or on the eastern wall, place the symbol of this degree: the pentagram surrounded by an ouroboros. If you have the apron or collar of this degree, you may wear it.

When everything is ready, be seated, and just relax for a while. Remain in this position for a few moments, breathing quietly, with your eyes closed or slightly closed. Be attentive to your breathing; listen to your breath flow in and out. Watch your chest rise and fall. Remain quiet, breathing gently in and out. Breathe in through your nose and out through your mouth. Relax for a while longer, until you feel comfortable.

Maintain your state of relaxation. Make sure you are comfortably seated, and that your back is as straight as possible. Place your hands flat on your thighs, breathing quietly for a while.

Begin to think about the journey of your soul, when it began its journey earthward for this incarnation, passing through each of the seven planets.

Relax and continue to breathe rhythmically.

Stand up and move both arms in front of you, with your forearms on the horizontal plane and your palms facing the heavens. Your back must be straight, your shoulders relaxed, your eyes turned up to look at the sky. Hold this position and exclaim:

"From the depth of my being, my soul desires to return to the light where it was at the beginning. I am meditating in order to know myself. I am studying the sacred book of nature. I am progressing toward the light. I already know that the Sun, which is the origin of daylight, along with the practice of virtue, is the safe guide who aids me in this ascent."

Breathe deeply for a while and say: "Divine power who animates this world and my being, hear my voice and help me to ascend from this cave. *Ex Tenebris Lux!*"

Relax your arms and light the first tealight candle (the one closest to you). This is the symbol of the Moon. Continue to light the candles by following the order given below.

Visualize a violet light all around you. Hold this visualization in your mind for a while. Then light the first candle. When the first candle has been lit (representing the Moon), focus on the image of Selene. Exclaim: "O shining and sure guide through the illimitable realm of dreams, most gracious opener of the way to those who venture into worlds unseen! Thou maker and destroyer of illusions, thou who knows the tides of ocean, the furthest distances of the mind and the dark places of unreason: hail to thee!"

Visualize the color violet becoming more intense. After a time, allow the color to disappear gradually into a light mist.

Visualize an orange light all around you. Hold this visualization in your mind for a while. Light the second candle (to Mercury; see numbered chart above). Focus on the image of Hermes. Exclaim: "O thou swift and unconstrained traveler in the ways between the worlds, divine imparter of secret tidings to the gods and humankind, bountiful bestower of aid in the art of magick! Knowledge and skill, rite and high result are thine to impart! Thine are the tongues and the numbers, thine the signs and the sigils and the words of power. Thine it is to heal, and to teach, and to watch upon the way. Hail to thee!"

Visualize the color orange becoming more intense for a while, and then allow it to disappear into a light mist.

Visualize a green light all around you. Hold this visualization in your mind for a while. Light the third candle (to Venus; see chart above for placement). Focus on the representation of Aphrodite. Exclaim: "O thou radiant giver of love, ruler of the forces of life, divinely robed in light and girded with invincible beauty! Perfect harmony and concord are as the perfumes of thy presence, and thou it is who dost create those rhythms whose pulsations call into life the sacred dance. O thou who ever sendest forth all delight, hail to thee!"

Visualize the color green becoming more intense for a while, and then allow it to disappear into a light mist.

Visualize a yellow light surrounding you. Hold this visualization in your mind for a while. Light the fourth candle (to the Sun; see chart above for placement). Focus on the image of Helios. Exclaim: "Far-riding ruler of days, all-seeing arbiter of the planetary powers! Thine is the wisdom of prophecy, the rapture of music and poetry, the upward surging force of mystical endeavor. Thine is the vision which sees beyond all change and chance, and the clear perception of truth which dispels all shadow. In the rising and in the incomparable luster of the Day-Star, thou givest a sacred image to magical ascendence, even as thy power enkindles a glory within us and elevates us to accomplish that which we seek. Hail to thee!"

Visualize the color yellow becoming more intense for a while, and then allow it to disappear into a light mist.

Visualize a red light surrounding you. Hold this visualization in your mind for a while. Light the fifth candle (to Mars; see chart above for placement). Focus on the representation of Ares. Exclaim: "All-powerful defender of justice and truth, thou noble inspirer of courage and endurance and of bold resolve! Inculcator of loyalty, giver of the joy which springs from shared endeavor. Thou divine patron of fruitful debate and of good order, thou who dost confirm the steadfast heart and the unfaltering hand! Thou mighty adversary of the powers adverse, hail to thee!"

Visualize the color red becoming more intense for a while, and then allow it to disappear into a light mist.

Visualize a blue light all around you. Hold this visualization in your mind for a while. Light the sixth candle (to Jupiter; see chart above for placement). Focus on the representation of Zeus. Exclaim: "Royal and magnanimous giver of abundance from a cup unfailing, shepherd of the golden stars, lord of the tides of fortune! Glorious dispenser of mercy, divine patron of paternal and filial love! Thou dost bless peace and amity between all beings; thou great father of benevolent rule and of priesthood, and of that loving wisdom which sublimates authority! Hail to thee!"

Visualize the color blue becoming more intense for a while, and then allow it to disappear into a light mist.

Visualize an indigo light all around you. Hold this visualization in your mind for a while. Light the seventh candle (to Saturn; see chart above for placement). Focus on the representation of Cronus. Exclaim: "Sublime and shadowed one, austere awakener of high aspiration and mystic hope! Thou art giver of the silent will to endure, thou art patron of the spirit's creativity and of the forces of preservation and of renewal. In thy keeping are alike the scythe of the reaper and the instruments of the builder in stone; thine, too, is the open scroll of the past, and thine the sealed scroll which holds the mysteries of the future. Hail to thee!"

Visualize the color indigo becoming more intense for a while, and then allow it to disappear into a light mist.

Be seated as before and meditate on this ascent. Above your head, visualize a starry sky. Imagine that you grow in size until your consciousness ascends into this mystical vault. Your spiritual body grows larger and larger, until it includes the whole universe. From your heart there is an outpouring of rays of an intense light of pure gold. Your entire body is irradiated by this divine light. Breathe deeply and relax, totally illuminated by this intense light. Invite your feelings, thoughts, etc.

When you feel the moment is right, stand up and exclaim: "A true initiate of the Sun cannot remain in contemplation. He must take action and return to the world to help his fellow human beings in their difficult task of achieving material and spiritual happiness. May the work I undertook at the creation of the world be accomplished this day."

Use the candle snuffer (or whatever you use to extinguish the candles) and extinguish the candles in the reverse order from which they were lit, following the chart on the next page.

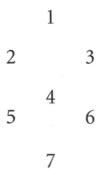

Before extinguishing the candle of Saturn, exclaim: "May the power of the divine Cronus, represented by the Pater, allow his balanced indigo light to remain with me as I go about my day. By the power of the sacred sound Ω [the letter Omega must be vibrated as the letter *o* as in *only*]. So mote it be!"

Extinguish the first candle.

Before you extinguish the candle of Jupiter, exclaim: "May the power of the divine Jupiter, represented by Leo, allow his balanced blue light to remain with me as I go about my day. By the power of the sacred sound ϒ [the letter Upsilon must be vibrated as the German letter *ü*, which sound like the *eu* in *eunuch*]. So mote it be!"

Extinguish the candle.

Before you extinguish the candle of Mars, exclaim: "May the power of the divine Ares, represented by Miles, the warrior, allow his balanced red light to remain with me as I go about my day. By the power of the sacred sound O [the letter Omicron must be vibrate as the *o* in *hot*]. So mote it be!"

Extinguish the candle.

Before you extinguish the candle of the Sun, exclaim: "May the power of the divine Helios, represented by Heliodromus, messenger of the Sun, allow his balanced light of pure gold to remain with me as I go about my day. By the power of the sacred sound I [the letter Iota must be vibrated as the *ee* in *meet*]. So mote it be!"

Extinguish the candle.

Before you extinguish the candle of Venus, exclaim: May the power of the divine Aphrodite, represented by Nymphus, the fiancée, allow her balanced green light to remain with me as I go about my day. By the power of the sacred sound H [the letter Eta must be vibrated as the *a* in *care*]. So mote it be!"

Extinguish the candle. Before you extinguish the candle of Mercury, exclaim: "May the power of the divine Hermes, represented by Corax, the crow, allow his balanced orange light to remain with me as I go about my day. By the power of the sacred word E [the letter Epsilon must be vibrated as the *e* in *set*]. So mote it be!"

Extinguish the candle.

Before you extinguish the candle of the Moon, exclaim: "May the power of the divine Selene, represented by Perses, the Persian, allow her balanced violet light to remain with me as I go about my day. By the power of the sacred word A [the letter Alpha must be vibrated as the *a* in *father*]. So mote it be!"

Extinguish the candle.

Breathe rhythmically, relaxing inwardly.

Place your right hand on your solar plexus, and your left hand on top of the right hand. Breathe quietly for a while, then exclaim: "A Knight of the Sun promises to be a tireless worker, to always fight for the triumph of the light, to persist in maintaining right thoughts, right words, and right actions in every part of his life. May the love of beauty, truth, and justice be established in every moment of my life, under the aegis of the powerful divinities that I have just invoked in this sacred rite. So mote it be!"

Meditate for a few more moments. When you feel ready, remove your apron if you have one. Record your feelings, remarks, experiences, and thoughts about this practice in your notebook (which must be reserved solely for this purpose).

THE MYTH OF MITHRA

Mithra was associated with the Sun very early on in the history of mankind. Eastern mythology described the god Mithra as appearing suddenly out of the starry sky, which was symbolically connected with the rocky vault of a cave. In other versions of this story, Mithra appeared from a stone, with a Phrygian cap on his head, a knife in one hand, and a torch in the other. Darkness cannot enter him.

The shepherds who witnessed his birth worshipped him as a child of the divine and brought him the first pick of their herds and the first fruits of the land. They dressed him in fig leaves they cut for that purpose. Dressed in those leaves, Mithra began his journey to fight the evil powers that are in the world.

His first adversary was the god of the Sun. The solar power was obliged to withdraw in the presence of the invincible strength of the young Mithra. Magnanimous, Mithra crowned the solar god with a brighter crown. From that day forward, the Sun continued

Figure 44: Representations of an initiation in the Mithraic Mysteries

to wear the crown that Mithra gave him, during his daily journey across the skies. After that, Mithra sealed the bargain with the Sun, their hands joined in friendship.

Mithra's most important feat was his fight with a giant bull. This wild and powerful animal was grazing in the mountains. Mithra found him, grabbed his horns, and jumped on his back. Furious, the bull stampeded, but Mithra resisted, holding on to his horns until the bull fell, totally exhausted. Lifting the bull by its legs, he brought it to a cave, but the bull escaped into the countryside. The Sun god asked a crow to be his messenger and carry this message to Mithra: catch the bull and kill it.

Fearfully, our hero obeyed his ally, the Sun god. Once again he found the bull and caught it. Controlling it with one hand on its snout, Mithra stabbed the bull in its shoulder with his hunter's knife. From the cadaver of the bull, many herbs and useful plants appeared, spreading across the countryside. From its spinal column came cereal grains, which would be used for the

Figure 45: Mithra and Sol

bread eaten during spring celebrations. Its blood was changed into wine and became the sacred beverage of the land. In order to put a stop to these beneficent actions of Mithra, the spirit of evil sent various impure animals to poison the source of the bull's life force: a scorpion, an ant, and a snake tried to eat the bull's testicles and to drink its blood. But the evil spirit failed. The Moon, who is the wife of the Sun, purified the bull's sperm in order to create from it many useful animals. The bull's soul ascended to the divine plane and became a protective divinity for all the cattle of the earth. Thus, because of his prowess as a hunter, Mithra became the creator of all the plants and animals living on our planet, and from this killing came a beneficent outcome: a new, more abundant and rich life for all.

Around this same time, the god Ahura Mazda had created the first humans. He gave Mithra the task of protecting humanity. The powers of evil attempted to destroy Mazda's creation by sending diseases and suffering to humanity. However, Mithra was alert to these attacks. The evil powers opposed him by sending famine and starvation, killing the crops with drought. Mithra shot an arrow into a rock and a fountain of water gushed forth, giving a new life to all the dying creatures. But the flow of water became cataclysmic, flooding every country on the planet. Fortunately, the gods informed someone, who built an ark and saved a male and female of each animal. With this construction, humanity and all the animals were saved. Mithra succeeded in the mission he had been charged with by the supreme being, and when his feats were completed, he met with his friend the Sun for a last solemn meal. When the meal was finished, Mithra ascended to the heavens where he resides to this day, watching over his initiates and protecting them from evil creatures.

Consistory
Sublime Prince of the Royal Secret (32nd Degree)

MYSTERIOUS HEREDOM

The 32nd Degree (which is the second of the Consistory degrees) summarizes all the preceding degrees of the Ancient and Accepted Scottish Rite into a single coherent "holy doctrine" based on the fundamental truths and symbols common to major cultures throughout the ages.

Albert Pike connected this degree to the ancient spiritual traditions of the Vedas in India and the Zend-Avesta of pre-Islamic Persia. Of course it was impossible for him to know the different contemporary Hermetic and symbolic documents.[2] A complete study of the Hermetic and classical sources of this degree would shine a wonderful light on those symbolic elements that have always been a part of the tradition, even if they are less emphasized today. This is a good indication of the presence at the higher level of the Scottish Rite of several interesting spiritual elements of the Western Tradition. You will notice some of these elements in the individual practice of this degree (provided later in this chapter).

It may be interesting to the reader to focus on some of the issues surrounding the origins of this degree, which are connected both to Dan Brown's *The Lost Symbol* and the esoteric dimension of this initiation.

The first "Regulations and Constitutions of the Sublime Knights of the Royal Secret, Princes of Masonry" were established in Bordeaux, France in the eighteenth century by the "Order of the Emperors of the East and West," with a view to aggregating selected and independent degrees within the Rite of Perfection, a.k.a. the Rite of Heredom. The current 32nd Degree was, then, the supreme degree, which held the highest authority over the whole Scottish Rite.

Figure 46: Symbolic representation of the 32nd Degree called the "Camp"

The Rite of Heredom (of Kilwinning) has many Hermetic and Rose-Cross influences. You must also remember that the Royal Order of Heredom was equivalent to the higher degree of Masonry in Scotland. It is clear that Dan Brown used these elements in placing this word *Heredom* at the top of his mysterious pyramid.

2. In the texts found in *Nagh Hammadi*, for example, there is a remarkable text called "The Discourse on the Eighth and Ninth," which is very helpful to your understanding of the dark sayings of this degree.

Figure 47: Symbolic representation of the nine-pointed star, center of the symbolic representation from Kircher

Figure 48: Detail of the frontispiece of a book from the Qabalist Athanasius Kircher

This mysterious name *Heredom* was first connected to the medieval Latin word *hoeredum*, signifying "heritage." As Edward L. Hawkins noted in the *Encyclopedia of Freemasonry*,[3] the most plausible derivation is one given in 1858. *Heredom* is a word composed of two Greek words: *Ieros*, "holy," and *Domos*, "house." Consequently, *Heredom* means that (symbolically) Masonry is the holy house or the temple. As Hawkins wrote, the title of "Rose-Croix of Heredom" would signify the "Rosy Cross of the Holy House of Masonry."

The study of such definitions is interesting on the etymological level. Still, even more can be learnt from some of the elements that are present in the practice itself. I previously stated that the 32nd Degree was the highest degree of the Rite of Heredom. This means there is a strong connection between these elements and the belief that this 32nd Degree is the holy house, which summarizes the entire Masonic system. A thorough analysis of this degree shows clearly that this is actually the case. Its central

---

3. The *Encyclopedia* was supervised by Albert G. Mackey.

symbol, which is called "the camp," presents the complete Masonic structure and leads the new initiate through the different degrees he has already received. You will recall the previous mention in this text of the ancient practice called "the art of memory." This practice gave birth to an important part of the rituals and the initiatic progression in Freemasonry. Every room (degree) contains different symbols that are connected to its meaning, goal, and purpose. The visualization and memorization allows the candidate to deeply integrate these unique archetypes in his psyche, so that he may be able to achieve another level of transformation. In the original art of memory, the orator mentally visits each room of the house during his oration. Every Masonic degree is likened to a single room in this house. At this juncture, the initiate has been raised to this high degree, into the holy house of Freemasonry, the 32nd Degree. His hidden abilities have been developed and he is able to visit the complete building, in its entirety, as a whole. This kind of mental control is not easy, but if the esoteric practices of each degree have been well learned, he is now able to maintain his awareness during this special journey. The control of this inner meditation will allow him to balance every aspect of his character and every element proper to each degree. This is not an inspection. This is a reminder, a balancing of forgotten parts, a real fulfillment of potential. It is clear that such a highly esoteric level must be practiced several times, as a complete Masonic meditation, before one could expect to achieve an actual victory in this matter.

Now you understand that Freemasonry can be understood and used as a deeply powerful initiatic system, which is not limited to its surface appearances. Just as you will find various dark-sounding portents in various sacred texts, including the Bible, there are similar "dark sayings" in Freemasonry. I do not wish to develop all the details of the occult level of this degree in this text, but I will provide you with some of the important exercises and teachings that will enable you to partially open this mystical gate.

The symbolic representation of this degree shows us various different geometrical elements, which are connected to both the Masonic building and the structure of the cosmos. Such representations (pictures, images) come directly from an esoteric tradition of the Hermetic representation called the mandala in the Eastern traditions. In the Western tradition there is a clear statement of the origin of this hidden teaching. The frontispiece of a book by Athanasius Kircher (1665) called *Arithmologia* reveals a precious key to us. Kircher gives us indications that convey the elements in images that are clearly geometric, arithmetic, and spiritual. The representation of the cosmos in the *Arithmologia* is consistent with the same design in the Hermetic Tradition. From the

Figure 49: Frontispiece of a book from the Qabalist Athanasius Kircher

center of the central sphere (which is a symbol of Earth) and extending outward, there are the seven planets, the ogdoad composed of stars in the night sky, followed by the divine level, the ennead. In this design, it is interesting to see an ennead design that is so similar in design to the one composed by Albert Pike, when he wrote of a union of three triangles, which are precisely numbered. At the center of this union of three triangles, there is another triangle (just as we find in the symbol of the 32nd Degree) and a central eye. At each center of the triangle, there are two Hebrew letters that are often used to write the sacred name of the Great Architect: Yod, He. In the symbols used in the 32nd Degree, the equivalent symbol shows us a crow, a phoenix, and a dove.

Another interesting key is shown in the magical square in the upper-right side of the drawing. This kamea is composed of the nine numbers, from 1 to 9. These numbers correspond to the ennead of "the camp" and the divinity expressed by the ennead. Thus, you have the seven planets, the ogdoad (represented by the number 8), and then the Great Architect (the number 9), which is the divine manifestation of the One, and is above all, even the ogdoad. This kamea reveals a Qabalistic key to us, because the number of vertical and horizontal lines adds up to 15. This number in Hebrew is written with two letters: Yod, Heh (which, as I mentioned above, is a reference to the Grand Architect). Of course, the letters Yod and Heh are a confirmation of the ineffable presence at the center of the inner triangle. However, the supreme central point must not be overlooked: the eye. There is an interesting connection here between the eye at the supreme central point and the eye at the center of the pyramid (triangle), which is connected with the representation of the unfinished pyramid (also on the dollar bill). The spiritual meaning is the same in both cases and we are reminded of this fact by the numbers at the bottom, which define the divine Tetraktys (1–2–3–4) and show that the Tetraktys is always geometrically represented on the shape of a triangle, (which brings forward its relationship to the pyramid.

Now I will pick up the thread I started at the beginning, with the idea that this degree is connected to the Rite of Heredom. The jewel of the 32nd Degree is a Teutonic cross of gold with arms frosted. At the center of this jewel are the letters "XXXII," surrounded by a green wreath. Different variations of this cross are found in several previous degrees. However, it is important to emphasize that this cross was called the Hermetic cross in the Rite of Heredom. In that instance, the purpose is explained and connected to a precise symbolism. As the texts of this rite explain, the "Hermetic cross is very precious because, in the clearest way possible, it explains the elements we must know in order

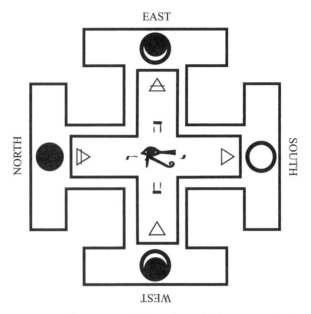

Figure 50: Representation of the Hermetic Cross from old documents in the Rite of Heredom

to perform the Great Work." The teachings of this rite explain that the Hermetic cross (see the image above) may be associated with Saint Andrew's cross. There are some very interesting elements in this image. Note the central eye, as well as the mention of the three mysterious animals present at the center of the degree: the crow, the dove, and the phoenix. These three birds represent the most important spiritual and initiatic Western traditions that formed the heritage received by Freemasonry: the Egyptian Tradition, the Mithraic Tradition, and the Biblical Tradition. The Egyptian Tradition is represented by the phoenix, which is mentioned many times in the Hermetic Egyptian teachings. The crow is the symbol of the first step in the Mithraic Tradition, which is always connected with the caduceus. The last one is the dove, which is present in Genesis and in Christianity as the manifestation of the divine fire.

I hope it is increasingly obvious to the reader that the 32nd Degree is a wonderful example of what Freemasonry is able to offer the aspirant at the highest level: a beautiful fusion of the kaleidoscopic aspects of this ancient tradition, combined with the necessary keys to continue one's progress along the spiritual path.

THE INDIVIDUAL PRACTICE

Prepare your room for this ritual just as you did for the Masonic meditation (Chapter Six), then prepare your altar in the following manner. Cover the altar with a purple cloth. At the center place of the altar, set or draw three intertwined equilateral triangles of gold forming a nine-pointed star, with a triangle at the center. Optional items to use are a bell and nine tealight candles (you will place one candle on top of each of the points of the star).

Put the symbol of the degree (the camp) to the east of your altar, or on the eastern wall. If you have the apron of this degree, you may wear it. If you have the cross of this degree (or even a printed representation), also place it on your altar.

When all is ready, sit down on your chair, and then relax for a while. Remain in this position for a few moments, breathing quietly, with your eyes closed or slightly closed. Be attentive to your breathing; listen to your breath flow in and out. Watch your chest rise and fall. Remain quiet, breathing gently in and out. Breathe in through your nose and out through your mouth. Continue relaxing until you feel ready to begin.

Maintain your state of relaxation throughout the ritual. Make sure you are comfortably seated, and that your back is as straight as possible. Place your hands flat on your thighs, breathing rhythmically for a while.

After a moment of silent relaxation, stand up, and exclaim: "May the spiritual journey of the 32nd Degree, under the auspices of the Great Architect of the Universe, begin!" (You may proceed to the Masonic journey in your reading of the text, or you may make a recording of that part and listen to it at the appropriate moment, or you may proceed with your memorization of the whole process.)

Visualize yourself immersed in blue light. Breathe and feel this light inside of you, permeating every cell of your being and completely surrounding you. You are in the first room of the holy house of Freemasonry, of Heredom, which is the foundation of the whole pyramid. Visualize the altar at the center of the lodge. The book of the sacred law is closed and set upon it. On the book you can see the compass and the square.

Imagine you are standing right in front of this altar. Open the book and then intertwine the square and the compass as you did in the 1st Degree. Continue to feel the blue light within you and all around you.

Place your right hand on the three lights (the square, the compass, and the book) and say: "May the first step in Freemasonry be accomplished!"

Feel your right hand in contact with this powerful Masonic symbol. Remove your hand.

Visualize yourself intertwining the square and the compass as before in the 2nd Degree. Again, put your right hand on them and proceed in the same way with the second declamation: "May the second step in Freemasonry be accomplished!"

Visualize yourself modifying the position of the tools again, so that they are in the position of the 3rd Degree. Proceed in the same way for the third declamation: "May the third step in Freemasonry be accomplished!"

Stand up, then perform the symbolic signs of this degree. (Alternatively, instead of these signs, you may remain seated and knock.) If you are standing, sit down again.

Visualize the blue light becoming brighter and brighter. This color is progressively replaced by a green light. Just as you did in the first room, breathe rhythmically, relax, and hold this precise color in your mind for a while.

You are in the second room of Heredom. Here are gathered the Secret Masters, and the Perfected Masters, who are there in order to protect the secrets of the 4th and 5th degrees.

While you focus on the green light, place your right hand on your solar plexus and exclaim mentally (or in a low voice): "By the power of the sacred word, may the mysteries of the second room of Heredom be unveiled!" (Hold a short pause in silence before continuing.) "So mote it be!"

Knock once.

Visualize the green light becoming brighter and brighter. This color is progressively replaced by a mixture of red and green lights. You are in the third room of Heredom. Here are gathered the Intimate Secretaries, and the Provost and Judges in order to protect the secrets of the 6th and 7th degrees.

While you focus on the mixture of red and green lights, place your right hand on your solar plexus, and exclaim mentally (or in a low voice): "By the power of the sacred word, may the mysteries of the third room of Heredom be unveiled!" (Hold a short pause in silence before continuing.) "So mote it be!"

Knock once.

Visualize the red and green lights becoming brighter and brighter. This color is progressively replaced by a mixture of red and black lights. You are in the fourth room of

Heredom. Here are gathered the Intendants of the Building, in order to protect the secrets of the 8th Degree.

Be focused on the mixture of red and black lights, put your right hand on your solar plexus, and exclaim mentally (or in a low voice): "By the power of the sacred word, may the mysteries of the fourth room of Heredom be unveiled!" (Hold a short pause in silence before continuing.) "So mote it be!"

Knock once.

Visualize the mixed red and black lights becoming brighter and brighter. This color is progressively replaced by a dark light. You are in the fifth room of Heredom. Here are gathered the Elus of the Nine, the Elus of the Fifteen, and the Elus of the Twelve, who are here in order to protect the secrets of the 9th, 10th, and 11th degrees.

While you focus on the dark light, place your right hand on your solar plexus, and exclaim mentally (or in a low voice): "By the power of the sacred word, may the mysteries of the fifth room of Heredom be unveiled!" (Hold a short pause in silence before continuing.) "So mote it be!"

Knock once.

Visualize the dark light becoming brighter and brighter. This color is progressively replaced by a mixture of red and black lights. You are in the sixth room of Heredom. Here are gathered the Master Architects, and the Royal Arch of Solomon, who are here in order to protect the secrets of the 12th and 13th degrees.

While you focus on the mixture of red and black lights, place your right hand on your solar plexus, and exclaim mentally (or in a low voice): "By the power of the sacred word, may the mysteries of the sixth room of Heredom be unveiled!" (Hold a short pause in silence before continuing.) "So mote it be!"

Knock once.

Visualize the red and black lights becoming brighter and brighter. This color is progressively replaced by a red light. You are in the seventh room of Heredom. Here are gathered the Perfect Elus in order to protect the secrets of the 14th Degree.

While you focus on the red light, place your right hand on your solar plexus, and exclaim mentally (or in a low voice): "By the power of the Sacred Word, may the mysteries of the seventh room of Heredom be unveiled!" (Hold a short pause in silence before continuing.) "So mote it be!"

Knock once.

Visualize the red light becoming brighter and brighter. This color is progressively replaced by a pale green light. You are in the eighth room of Heredom. Here are gathered the Knights of the East, and the Princes of Jerusalem, who are here in order to protect the secrets of the 15th and 16th degrees.

While focusing on the pale green light, place your right hand on your solar plexus, and exclaim mentally (or in a low voice): "By the power of the sacred word, may the mysteries of the eighth room of Heredom be unveiled!" (Hold a short pause in silence before continuing.) "So mote it be!"

Knock once.

Visualize the pale green light becoming brighter and brighter. This color is progressively replaced by a pale white light. You are in the ninth room of Heredom. Here are gathered the Knights of the East and West, and the Knights of the Rose Croix, who are here in order to protect the secrets of the 17th and 18th degrees.

While you focus on the pale white light, place your right hand on your solar plexus, and exclaim mentally (or in a low voice): "By the power of the sacred word, may the mysteries of the ninth room of Heredom be unveiled!" (Hold a short pause in silence before continuing.) "So mote it be!"

Knock once.

Breathe and relax for a while, keeping in mind the first step of this spiritual journey. All these powers have been sealed in the secret of your heart and they will grow in good balance.

Now you may open your eyes (or keep them slightly closed) and stand up. (If present, light the nine tealight candles surrounding the nonagon in the sequence indicated by the numbers.) Exclaim: "May the powers of the Great Architect of the Universe be manifested in the nine rooms of Heredom!"

Close your eyes and meditate for a while.

Exclaim: "The cosmos was created in seven days and organized by seven divine [planetary] powers. From the highest level of the divine, our soul descended through seven veils, receiving each of their influences in its descent. All these powers have been sealed in my invisible and visible bodies and are sometimes unbalanced. By the help of the immortal divinities and the supreme being, may this inner and essential balance be restored!"

Breathe in silence for a while, and then declaim (in a low voice) the seven sacred Greek vowels [O-U-O-I-H-E-A]. Each time you pronounce a vowel, touch each point of the heptagon, with your right forefinger, moving in a clockwise direction. During this invocation, imagine feeling that you are moving closer to the center of your being.

Be seated. Breathe rhythmically in silence. Relax. Do not focus on any ideas during this period.

Visualize the red light becoming brighter and brighter. This color is progressively replaced by a pale green light. Exclaim mentally (or in a low voice): "By the name of Amariah, guardian of the first upper region of Heredom, may the mystical gates be opened!"

Visualize the Ark of the Covenant directly in front of you, set on a stone altar. The ark is surrounded by two lit torches and two palms. Here are gathered the Grand Pontifs, and the Masters of the Symbolic Lodge, who are here in order to protect the secrets of the 19th and 20th degrees. Exclaim: "By the power of the sacred word Yod, may the mysteries of the first upper region of Heredom be unveiled!" (Hold a short pause in silence before continuing.) "So mote it be!"

Knock once.

Visualize the pale green light becoming brighter and brighter. This color is progressively replaced by a golden light. Exclaim mentally (or in a low voice): "By the name of Garimont, guardian of the second upper region of Heredom, may the mystical gates be opened!"

Visualize a black ox directly in front of you. Here are gathered the Noachites, and the Knights of the Royal Axe, who are here in order to protect the secrets of the 21st and 22nd degrees. Exclaim: "By the power of the sacred word Heh, may the mysteries of the second upper region of Heredom be unveiled!" (Hold a short pause in silence before continuing.) "So mote it be!"

Knock once.

Visualize the golden light becoming brighter and brighter. This color is progressively replaced by a green light. Exclaim mentally (or in a low voice): "By the name of Mahuzem, guardian of the third upper region of Heredom, may the mystical gates be opened!"

Directly in front of you, visualize a silver double-headed eagle with a gold crown, a sword in its right talon and a bleeding heart in its left. Here are gathered the Chiefs of the Tabernacle, the Princes of the Tabernacle, and the Knights of the Brazen Serpent, who are here in order to protect the secrets of the 23rd, 24th, and 25th degrees. Exclaim: "By the power of the sacred word Shin, may the mysteries of the third upper region of Heredom be unveiled!" (Hold a short pause in silence before continuing.) "So mote it be!"

Knock once.

Visualize the golden light becoming brighter and brighter. This color is progressively replaced by a white light. Exclaim mentally (or in a low voice): "By the name of Ooliab, guardian of the fourth upper region of Heredom, may the mystical gates be opened!"

Directly in front of you, visualize a flaming heart with two wings and a crown of laurel. Here are gathered the Princes of Mercy, the Knights of the Sun, and the Knights Commander of the Temple, who are here in order to protect the secrets of the 26th, 27th, and 28th degrees. Exclaim: "By the power of the sacred word Vav, may the mysteries of the fourth upper region of Heredom be unveiled!" (Hold a short pause in silence before continuing.) "So mote it be!"

Knock once.

Visualize the white light becoming brighter and brighter. This color is progressively replaced by a blue light. Exclaim mentally (or in a low voice): "By the name of Bezaleel, guardian of the fifth upper region of Heredom, may the mystical gates be opened!"

Directly in front of you, visualize a gold lion with a gold key in its mouth and a gold collar on which "SQS" is written. Here are gathered the Scottish Knights of Saint Andrew, and the Knights Kadosh, who are here in order to protect the secrets of the 29th and 30th degrees. Exclaim: "By the power of the sacred word Heh, may the mysteries of the fifth upper region of Heredom be unveiled!" (Hold a short pause in silence before continuing.) "So mote it be!"

Knock once.

Breathe and relax for a while, while holding the first step of this spiritual journey in your mind.

Stand up and open your eyes (or keep them slightly closed).

Visualize a sphere of subtle energy all around you. Feel this special and radiant energy.

Directly in front of you, using your right forefinger, draw a triangle beginning at the uppermost point and continuing in a clockwise direction. As you draw this figure, you may pronounce the sacred word IAO. Exclaim: "Here are gathered the visible and invisible guardians of the Masonic tradition. May the higher superstructure of Heredom be opened!"

Within the triangle points, you will now visualize the three mysterious birds: the dove, the phoenix, and the crow. Breathe and relax for a while. Pick up the cross on your altar, hold it in the palm of your hands facing the heavens, and exclaim: "By the power of the four directions, may this cross manifest my dedication to the Great Work! May the divine powers bless me as I swear to participate in the enlightenment of humanity! So mote it be!"

Either in your visualization or in actual reality, place the cross upon your solar plexus and sit down.

Meditate for a moment.

When you feel ready, extinguish the candles and remove your apron if you have one. Record your feelings, remarks, experiences, and thoughts about this practice in your notebook (which must be reserved for this purpose).

chapter eight
GETTING TO KNOW THE POWERS IN WASHINGTON DC

The Mind's Energy and the Egregore

In Chapter Six, I described the powers of the mind and the use of visualization. You should now be well aware of the inner energies present in your being and their possible uses.

Centuries ago, the idea of a universal invisible magnetism was already well known. Albert Pike wrote: "Paracelsus, the great Reformer in medicine, discovered magnetism long before Mesmer, and pushed this luminous discovery to its ultimate conclusion. Really, it would be better to call this discovery an initiation into the magic of the ancients, who understood the great magical agent better than we do; they did not believe that the Astral Light, Azoth, the universal magnetism of the Sages [. . .] emanates only from certain special beings."[1] Here I am describing an invisible energy that is present everywhere in the universe. Today I might describe this energy as electricity, terrestrial magnetism, or as a flux of particles moving throughout the cosmos. All these modern scientific fields are parts of the intuition or insight of the ancient initiates. There are several astrological and/or alchemical texts that strongly suggest such an identification. However, in several other cases, the description of the invisible energy used in rituals cannot be reduced to those fields that have already been discovered. This energy seems different in some way from what science has identified; it is more subtle. When Albert Pike used the words "Astral Light," his purpose was to intimate the existence of a higher quality of

---

1. Albert Pike, *Morals and Dogma*, "The Knight of the Sun" chapter.

energy, which is nearly identical to the original pulse, the creator of all things. According to spiritualists (and those with psychic vision), this astral energy is the fluid that gives life to human cells, providing health by causing a good balance and circulation at the different levels of one's being. Initiates from every period in human history, living on every continent, have written about these "bodies of light." Every religion describes a penumbral light surrounding the figures of their wise or holy men and women. This is just as true in shamanic ceremonies as in the mystical Christian transfiguration. Something universal is perceived here. Someday in the future, it may be possible to explain more clearly and scientifically the essence of this subtle energy, but for now, it is important to understand that we do not have to wait for this level of clarification to use this subtle energy. Simply put, no one needs to study the laws of electricity in order to learn to flip a light switch and turn on a light. If such were the case, I am afraid we would be in the dark for a very long time! Therefore, it is crucial to clarify the difference between scientific principles and practical application. With this clearly understood, we may easily understand the main principles that enable us to use this energy, even if the scientific explanations have not yet evolved. That is what I will teach how to do in this book, by following the teachings and explanations of the ancient masters.

The most important concept taught by the ancients is the interconnection between the universe and each of us. *The Lost Symbol* shows this relationship, using the Hermetic aphorism many times in order to emphasize this union between that which is above and that which is below. We live every day of our lives in the matrix of these universal energies. It is similar to being surrounded by water when swimming in a lake or breathing the air that is present everywhere we go. The ancients taught that these energies are both inside and outside of us; they are a real part of us, and yet they are simultaneously a real part of the universe. In the same way that we constantly exchange air with the air in our environment, there is a constant exchange of this energy inside of us with the energy of the universe.

At this point, I assume that you will simply accept the hypothesis of the existence of these subtle and spiritual energies, just as you accept the possibility of the flow of electricity before you turn on a light. The only way to know whether a house is connected to the main power source is to turn on the light and see what happens. The same is true in this case. You can engage in an endless argument about the existence of this subtle energy, or you can try to use it and see what happens. The results are convincing!

The best way to use the mind's energy is to follow the process described in the Masonic meditation. Visualization and pronunciation of sacred names are very good ways to begin using your mind's energy. This meditation will have a positive effect on your aura, your psyche, and even on your physical body. Of course, the purpose of this inner process is first to control your mind, to balance your energies, and to increase the level of your consciousness. However, any regular meditation will also have a positive effect on your whole body, just as your spiritual life has a potent effect on your health.

This is an important step, but not the definitive one. In fact, this energy is spiritual, and consequently not limited to your bodily limitations. You are part of this spiritual world; the act of meditating builds a bridge for us between these visible and invisible dimensions.

As the ancient masters explained, this energy is a part of a "cosmic consciousness," which is outside the confines of the body (and, therefore, not subject to its limitations). This is the theory developed by noetic science. Every human consciousness is a part of this cosmic consciousness, which is not limited to humankind. When the wise men spoke about the cosmos, they described it as a large architectural structure integrating every conceivable dimension. Just as in the physical world, everything is interdependent, and each thought has an effect on the whole cosmos. To understand this, consider a grain of salt in the sea. It is impossible for us to feel each microscopic grain of salt in the ocean. You understand that the accumulation of all these grains in the water results in the existence of the ocean. You also know that, if I remove a few grains, the sea does not cease to exist. However, if I continue to remove grains of salt, eventually the sea will be affected by these changes. It will shrink, and, if no more grains of salt replace the lost grains, there may be a chain reaction. The consequences of complete desalination of the ocean would have tremendous effects on the entire planet. It would affect our weather and even, ultimately, the ability of life to endure on Earth.

Likewise, if you imagine that every grain of salt is a human consciousness, you can see that one person's effort to elevate his or her consciousness is not enough to bring about global changes. Of course, it will have an effect, but not enough to be felt globally. However, if a group meditates regularly, or if a fraternity works with the same powerful ritual, something will happen. Just as a cosmic wave or tsunami gathers energy until it reaches tidal wave force, the power of the focused thoughts of this fraternal group will change things in the "common human consciousness" and (ultimately) this will affect the "cosmic consciousness."

The common thread in these phenomena is the power of the union of many minds with a single thought. When these thoughts are coordinated, something happens on the invisible plane and this result can have an effect on physical matter. Quantum physics, one of the most advanced sciences, has demonstrated that a human presence (human thoughts) can change the behavior of particles. It is interesting to note that a phenomenon such as the invisible wave created by a union of wills or thoughts does not disappear after the first impulse. This phenomenon is similar to what happens in an earthquake. After the initial "slide" and the formation of the first wave, that wave of energy will continue surging through the ocean (or even on land), continually gaining in power. Once this wave has been generated, it becomes an independent form that obeys the laws of nature.

In fact, the way that a wave of energy is built or generated is a good representation of how a thought-form or an egregore is created. Through different spiritual practices (prayer, invocation, meditation, ritual, etc.) a reaction is set in motion by each individual unconsciousness and this sets up a chain reaction that gives birth to an invisible presence, and the resulting effect on the physical plane. In reality, the egregore is not just the common essence of a group. It is something much larger that can interact with the whole planet. When a Masonic lodge is performing a ritual for the good of an initiate and humanity, they are not merely wishing; they are creating a reality on the spiritual plane. Perhaps this fact alone is a good enough reason to ask Masons to believe in the existence of the spiritual plane and the Great Architect of the Universe. Thus, this spiritual "common body," which is activated by each ritual meeting, constitutes the egregore of the lodge.

What is harder to understand is the fact that the egregore persists even when the meeting is disbanded. The afterglow of a television screen after it is turned off might help us understand why this happens. When you turn off a television, energy remains present for a while before it disappears completely. Perhaps an even more obvious example is what happens when you turn off the heat in an oven. The heat takes a while to dissipate.

The more rituals the group works, the more likely the egregore will endure. At some point, the spiritual egregore will remain active between meetings. Somehow, in this way a new spiritual existence has been created. This egregore becomes a powerful aid, adding measurably to the effectiveness of the ritual life of the lodge and to the realization of its purposes. There is a sentence in Hermeticism that says, "With the participation of all, our action will never disappear." The egregore is the spiritual illustration of the truth of this declaration.

As I explained in Chapter Five, the Grand Lodge is the structure that manages every lodge in its state. An egregore of the Grand Lodge exists as well. Each member and each lodge help give birth to and regularly activate this special thought-form.

According to the theory espoused by Spiritualists, we are children of both the earth and sky. They teach that we are composed of two distinct aspects: the human aspect and the divine aspect. This spiritual (divine) aspect works to help us become enlightened, and it participates in the energetic animation of our physical bodies. The result of our participation in this work is a real body of light that is capable of illuminating us. This light surrounds us as the aura. Modern parapsychology borrowed the ancient Greek word *aura* to describe this invisible body. The Western and Eastern traditions have developed several (sometimes conflicting) explanations about the different parts of this spiritual dimension. What I am calling magnetism in this book is the conscious, intentional use of some levels of this special energy of light. There are fields in parapsychology and noetic science that are now devoted to the study of the effect of this magnetism. The research carried on by various initiatic orders demonstrates that they are able to make conscious use of magnetism in their rituals. For example, they teach that is possible to use this magnetism on someone else in order to increase his power (for healing and strength). They also teach that you can do the same thing with other living things, such as animals and vegetables. Sometimes this exchange of energy occurs unintentionally. It is possible for anyone to give or receive this energy without intending to do so (without a conscious intention to exchange this energy or transfer it). In other words, giving and receiving magnetic energy does not depend on your will to do so. One example of this phenomenon is the situation in which the initiate is in a temple, doing the work of experiencing the Ancient Mysteries or, as another example, the initiate might receive a transmission. Both of these examples demonstrate the transmission and reception of this energy.

Obviously, you are not alone in the world. Surrounding you at every moment of your life are other people, animals, vegetables, stones, manufactured items, etc. All of these living and apparently nonliving things are composed of a visible and an invisible dimension. Everything has a body of light surrounding its physical form. It is, perhaps, easier to believe that this is true for living beings, and perhaps even for plants. Still, it is necessary for us to realize that the exact same thing is true for inanimate objects. Of course, the process of exchange is different for living beings than it is for inanimate objects. An inanimate object does not have a soul that extends to it from heaven, so these "things" are not alive in the way that human beings are alive. However, every inanimate object really does have an invisible aspect, an aura. Most of the time, the aura surrounding inanimate objects has an external origin. For example, everything you touch and use as you go about your day receives, stores, and records the energy it receives from you. During the course of a day, imagine that you pick up and use a cup, a mug, a pen, and a hat. Some of these items will have more contact with you than others, but each will record all your smells, feelings, thoughts, etc. Some of what the objects receive can be perceived on the physical level. For example, you might be able to smell the scent of a person who has worn a hat long enough. Yet there are other invisible energies you have transmitted to your coffee mug, your pen, and everything else you had contact with during the day. This transfer of energy is how magnetism works. The object progressively develops its own aura as a result of everything it recorded during its contact with animate beings. As you might well imagine, this process is much more efficient and powerful if it is the result of a conscious will to make it happen. Such is the case when an initiate imbues the special tools or symbols used in rituals with this energy. These are all examples of the use of magnetism.

As I previously explained, cornerstones contain different items and receive a particular consecration prior to being installed in a temple. Somehow this ritual action creates a life form, a sort of dormant memory in the cornerstone. Every thought that is focused on this stone will be captured by it and integrated into it. I am talking about it receiving and holding these thoughts and memories in an invisible and spiritual dimension. There is no difficulty about the issues of distance, time, or any of the normal physical limitations. Over the years, each such stone will become more and more powerful. Its aura will progressively increase and will have a positive, beneficial effect on everyone around it. These principles apply equally well to the items and tools used in rituals. The Freemasonry mallet, apron, and sword, as well as a chart of foundation are all examples of ritualistic symbols that are impregnated by the magnetism of the initiates using them or even by the egregore of the group. The sacred book that rests at the center of the temple is a good example of this principle. In fact, this is equally true of every religious and spiritual tradition. The invisible body connected to these objects continues to exist as long as the object exists. Even if its owner disappears, the object continues to have a life, and people in contact with that object will participate in its invisible development.

The beautiful thing is that we can feel the energies that these objects retain. Somehow we can interact with the object and receive some information from the recording that represents this living memory. It may be an indistinct feeling or a precise intuition. This inner ability is called "token-object reading," and is also known as psychometry.[2] Extrasensory perception allows us to make contact with the invisible part of an object in order to obtain information about its owner(s). Generally, simple contact with the tool or object is enough to begin the process so that we may receive information and develop a conscious or unconscious exchange with it. A few years ago, I had the opportunity to touch the ritual clothes and tools of a dead shaman from Mongolia. The feeling was powerful and quite amazing. I didn't receive any mental impressions, smells, or sounds, but I felt a powerful energy in my hands and arms. It was like touching a live electric wire or a hot iron. This physical feeling continued to be present in my arms for a period of more than two hours. I felt a sort of contact or attraction that lingered all during the night, which I experienced as a strong desire or need to be close to, or in direct contact with, this clothing. However, I was unable to do that.

Another example of this sort of experience occurred during a Masonic ritual. Some years ago in Paris, I conducted an initiation using General Lafayette's Masonic sword. Again, it was amazing. The feelings were more intimate than the shamanic example, but it was like being helped by something larger than me. Of course, many people believe that such feelings are just the creations of their imagination. But parapsychology and new fields like noetic science are progressively demonstrating the reality of the existence of such phenomena. There is no doubt that, in the coming years, new research and experiments will confirm the reality of these phenomena. For now, I find it useful and interesting to accept this traditional knowledge and to work individually and in groups to discover the best way to use our abilities in order to consciously interact with the most powerful artifacts. You may say that this initiatic process is constituted of several steps: (1) accept the existence of this invisible reality in all things (animated or inanimate); (2) work to increase your inner ability to perform "token-object readings"; and (3) use this inner contact to assist others in their practices and rites.

In Chapter Two, I wrote about the design of the buildings of the capital in the District of Columbia. I wish to add another element. Besides the design itself, there is another

---

2. The word *psychometry* is gradually being replaced by the term *token-object reading* to avoid potential confusion with the branch of psychology called psychometrics.

aspect of importance: there is power in the shape of objects, buildings, structures, etc. A field called radionics was developed in the nineteenth century. One of the beliefs central to that field of learning is that every shape has a special effect. Sometimes this effect is psychological; sometimes it may be more than that. To easily understand this concept, imagine that you are sitting on your favorite chair. An arrow has been placed on the table in front of you, and it is pointing in your direction. Some people will find this position uncomfortable. They might find it impossible to remain in front of the tip of this arrow. I might offer many explanations. Some would be psychological, but radionics explains this phenomenon by saying that this discomfort is directly connected to the shape of the arrow and the fact that it is pointing directly at you. Just as a magnet has a special energy and special characteristics that you can sense, every shape has a unique energy and set of characteristics. A cube, a pyramid, and an octagon each have a specific energy; the subtle shape of their auras is different. You may be consciously or unconsciously sensitive to these energies. The color of the object is another component that influences its aura.

This phenomenon also occurs when you are surrounded by a variety of artifacts. All day long you are interacting with your environment on both the visible and invisible planes. From the time of the ancient Mediterranean civilizations, our Western Tradition has known how to work with the power of the land, how to find and organize special areas using these principles. In modern times, the inner ability to feel and detect energies of the land, their orientation, clumps of energy, and special shapes is called radiesthesia. This knowledge allows initiates to organize special areas, which are then dedicated to certain specific purposes. You see a graphic demonstration of this principle in the District of Columbia and the choices regarding the best places to build specific buildings. This modern use of geobiology can be seen as a practical Western feng shui. Our system is different from the Chinese system, which is adapted to the Eastern subconscious mind and their style of architecture. The Western system is connected to the deepest roots of our culture and ethnic heritage. These principles are a part of what the Founding Fathers and the builders of the capital understood and utilized. The Roman example I used in Chapter Four, which was founded on texts by Vitruvius, provided significant elements of this knowledge.

At this point, it is worthwhile to admit that Freemasonry contributed significantly to the earliest plans for the new American nation. The ideals developed in the Declaration of Independence and the other founding documents of this new country are completely in harmony with the ideals of Freemasonry. It would be completely inaccurate to say that the United States is a Masonic nation, but I may certainly say that Masonry and the American people share common goals, a unique way of seeing the world, and a kind of insight that seems peculiar to both groups. Freemasonry in America developed specific and very special characteristics that are not found elsewhere around the world. Totally rooted in its traditions, aware of modern challenges, American Freemasonry is a beautiful evolution of an ancient fraternity. This permanence of ideals allows the Craft to demonstrate its heritage in the most contemporary way. However, these ideals are not just something written in texts that are gathering dust somewhere. On a spiritual level, they have given life to an archetype of this nation. This hidden elaboration was the result of a conjunction of different elements including fostering good will, influencing the design and directional placement of the buildings of the city and their layout, contributing to the architectural styles and positions of the main buildings, and participating in the Masonic dedication of each of the cornerstones. Undoubtedly, Freemasonry held the role of an esoteric guardian of the American soul. I described earlier the creation of a spiritual egregore for various groups, such as a lodge or a Grand Lodge. The process could equally be applied to a large city or to the capital (as, in fact, it was).

There can be no doubt that certain cities around the world, such as Washington DC, have a uniquely special history. Some such cities are built near large natural bodies of water, volcanoes, and other amazing features of the earth. A city that is located in the desert, near the ocean, or near any other natural wonder is affected by that location, and develops a special personality as a result of its geographic proximity to these unique geographical features. People who live near a fault line (such as the people in Los Angeles), or those who live near a volcano, develop a different way of life than people who do not live near these features. At the same time, each of these cities is connected to its own history. Sometimes the weight of history is so heavy in such locations that it is nearly impossible to innovate or to initiate change. The flow of new people to these cities is also a part of their development and history. Someone who lives on the West Coast is somehow very different from those who live on the East Coast.

Throughout the history of this nation, some cities have evolved special functions, a special character or specific purpose that is identified with that city. Some examples might be cities that are the hub of political influence, cities that are very innovative, each state's capital, etc. These geobiological influences also created a conjunction of all the thoughts of its inhabitants. Every visitor is able to feel this special energy, which can sometimes cause a real fascination in some people. Of course, the place one feels the most connected to is different for everyone, but something irrational can happen when you are walking around or visiting such a city for the first time. More than the physical dimension of the architecture or the land, there is something larger you might call the egregore of the city. Somehow, this is the real soul of the city, with an archetype that has been progressively developed and sometimes consciously crafted by initiates. Undoubtedly this is true for Washington DC, as I have been at some pains to point out in this book. You might imagine this archetype as an invisible power that is presiding over the city and keeping alive the original intention and will of its creators. Furthermore, the main planetary characteristics may be found in specific cities. In other words, one city manifests the characteristics of the Moon, another the Sun, and so on.

Still, the specific character of a city does not exist in isolation, separate from other external influences. An important part of the power of a city comes from foreign countries. It is easy to understand how this process occurs. Imagine how many times the White House has been seen on television all around the world. Every single day, the Capitol building, the president, or the White House (with its red, white, and blue flag flying proudly) are on television in Asia, India, the Middle East, Europe, America, etc. Everyone around the world who sees this building knows immediately that this is the center of American power, the building that represents the United States. All these thoughts consciously or unconsciously, are turned and focused on Washington DC. Every day, all year long, human thoughts, wills, desires, and fears are focused on these central symbols. This reality is not just an abstraction, an allegory to describe the presence and the symbolic power of America. The energy of thoughts is a spiritual reality. Like the previously described tsunami, these thoughts create waves of energy flowing from every point of the planet and moving like a giant wave toward this symbolic center of the Capitol surmounted by the statue of freedom. This works so effectively because the esoteric layout of the city was created according to the traditional rules of Freemasonry. The Mall and all the buildings that were dedicated in accordance with the principles of Masonic rituals created the most powerful radionics system conceivable! It would be impossible today to create such a system and (at the same time) to cause this system to draw energy from around the world to itself so that all the powers generated all around the world are directed to one place. It is amazing to even think about the existence of such an energy flow as you find present on the Washington Mall. The obelisk focuses this power and disperses hate and other dark intentions.

Of course, most of the time people living and working in Washington DC are not aware of these powerful energies. Even if they became aware of the invisible powers focused on this place, they would be very disappointed if they tried to use these energies for themselves. It is important to know about their existence, but their best use is for the protection and development of this nation and, even more importantly, for the good of the world. Generally, when such energies are not continually used, they are progressively dissipated. Once again, the shape and the design of the city prevent this from happening. Its hidden shape and the arrangement of the buildings cause the capital to act as a capacitor. Centuries ago, Saint Augustine wrote a book describing what he called the city of God. The human construct, the city of men, was the darker representation of a divine model—the city of God. Similarly, you might imagine the capital with an invisible doppelganger. There is the visible city you can visit and walk around in, and there is an invisible, energetic city built and supplied by the world's thoughts. These twin cities are not separated from their birth; they are intimately connected at all times. Dan Brown was correct when he spoke of a hidden portal in *The Lost Symbol*. There are several gates in Washington DC that allow the transfer of the energy that is accumulated on the spiritual plane to be directed to a gate in Washington DC in the physical world. Of course, each gate has a special key. Moreover, its design restricts its use to the beneficial intentions I outlined above. This process and its associated keys are true for other cities; other processes and keys are specific to an individual city.

In Washington DC, these keys, the gates, and the process I have been discussing are intimately connected to Freemasonry. The purpose is not to argue such against such assertions. I believe that a better understanding of these traditions and the knowledge dispersed by emerging scientific fields (such as radionics and noetics) will allow us to make the leap from arguing about their existence or worth, to describing and teaching their immediate and effective use.

Practical Work and Places to Practice

I have already described the Masonic meditation and some of its uses. Now I will teach how to use these basic elements for a specific purpose. As in every working that involves the use of subtle energies, this practice can be either beneficial or self-centered and contrary to the health and well-being of others. There is an esoteric and Hermetic rule that says if you are working for the good of others, you will receive the positive consequences of your actions and thus good things will come to you too. Of course, your intentions in working this ritual must be sincere, not contrived to manipulate the system. You cannot fool your own higher nature!

Remember that every spiritual working or ritual could have one or more of several purposes: (1) to help you to raise the level of your consciousness, (2) to facilitate the use of your inner abilities, and (3) to enable you to use your knowledge and abilities for the good of other people. As you will see during your use of this ritual, it is very often the case that points 1 and 2 occur simultaneously, or point 2 follows very close on the heels of point 1.

It is also important to point out that some rituals may be performed by a single person working alone, and that others require a group. Obviously, performing group practices in crowded public areas is not always easy to manage. Certain kinds of spiritual work do require some privacy, but you may adapt some of these practices to your needs, and you will find them both powerful and effective once you develop a familiarity with this system.

Spiritual Practices at the Mall

At the end of Chapter Two, I explained the symbolic connection between the Washington Mall and a lodge. In a Masonic temple that is oriented to the four directions, the four directions are associated with the positions of the main ritual officers. The altar is well represented by the Jefferson Pier Stone.

One characteristic of a symbol is that it is not limited to one interpretation. In Chapter Four, the study of the ancient architectural principles of Vitruvius allowed us to identify the Capitol Building with the temple of the gods, which is the protector of the city; I also identified the temple of Hermes with the Library of Congress. You will be able to use these identifications in your ritual practices.

In esoteric traditions, the geocentric vision of the universe was an important part of the initiatic process. I previously explained the meanings of the terms *macrocosm* and *microcosm*. In this case, the orientation of Washington DC, which is especially visible when you are at the Mall, may also be linked to the cardinal directions. This is the reason why some practices are connected to precise periods of the year, and, even more importantly, to specific cosmic events.

The practices in this part of the book allow you to use specific symbols and to connect those symbols with the energy of Washington DC. Of course, this will be much clearer if you are able to stand in the Mall and follow the directions given in the following pages. However, it is important to remember that subtle energies exist on the vibratory planes, and these energies are not limited by space and time. Consequently, it is possible for you to use meditation to accomplish these practices, no matter where you are living, even if you live in another state or even abroad. If you must use meditation because you are unable to be physically present, it would be advisable for you to print out the images of the symbols and the different monuments so that you have them directly in front of you during your ritual. During meditation, your mind and astral body will be connected to the place you are focused on.

Initiatic Journey at the Washington DC Mall

This practice is designed to be used at the Washington DC Mall (or in meditation, as described above). It is an initiatic journey that will allow you to ascend progressively to the light, using the Mall as a symbolic place as described and explained here. This journey requires the use of a Masonic grid, but every sincere person will also be able to use it. If you are already an initiate of Freemasonry, you can perform this ritual while holding the first step of Freemasonry in your mind. If you are not initiated, this journey will help you to understand what kind of inner experience the Freemasons are trying to achieve in their rituals—in other worlds, what the attempt to reach a higher level of consciousness is like. Of course, you may use the energies present in this ritual in precisely the same way.

This "pilgrimage" is based upon various destinations in the Mall. The morning is the best time to begin this journey, so that you reach the "fourth rest stop" at around midday. If you want to increase the inner power of this pilgrimage and you are already initiated into the Craft, you may perform this ritual on the anniversary of your initiation. You will find that this ritual can be a very powerful tool for the enhancement of your inner Great Work. If you are an initiate of another initiatic tradition, you will have an equally profitable experience by performing this spiritual journey on your initiation anniversary.

Remember that the complete journey required for this ritual is approximately 4.9 miles. If you are unable to walk that far, just grab a cab between the different rest stops.

Rest Stop 1. The first stop will be in front of the White House at the north point of this invisible temple. Of course, it isn't easy to get inside the building itself.[3] Instead, begin by looking at the White House as a tourist would; just stand in front of it. Remain for a while, and just be aware of the importance this symbolic building has for millions of people everywhere. Imagine its visual presence all around the world. This building is one of the best known buildings in the world. Naturally, a large part of the invisible magnetism of this area is concentrated at this point. Think about someone in Asia, Africa, etc., focusing his or her thoughts on this special center of power. Imagine the energy in the air all around this place. This is an important center of power—not just political power, but spiritual power as well.

Turn right to face south. You may remember that the District of Columbia is oriented along this north/south axis. A hidden explanation for this orientation may be found if you look at some research that describes a grid surrounding the Earth. In 1951, the physician and radiesthesist Dr. Ernst Hartmann discovered a radiation grid surrounding the Earth. He called it the "global-net grid." Today it is called the "Hartmann grid" or the "first grid." This electromagnetic grid pattern consists of naturally occurring charged lines that are magnetically oriented, and they run along lines that form a north/south and east/west grid.[4] At this juncture, you are standing on a special magnetic line. Its power starts to become focused a few miles to the north, at the uppermost marker stone of the District of Columbia. Your first exercise involves connecting these two energies: one energy flowing from above (from the thoughts around the world that are focused on this special center), and the second energy flowing from below, coming up out of the earth and following the magnetic line along the north/south axis. In order to connect these powers, breathe rhythmically while you look to the south, toward the Jefferson Memorial. Your eyes should be slightly (half) closed. Relax for a while, breathing rhythmically and receiving this energy. In Freemasonry, the northwest or north is the place where the Great Architect of the Universe is invoked at the beginning of the initiation.

---

3. Check the White House website for visitor information: http://www.whitehouse.gov/about/tours-and-events.

4. The Hartmann grid appears as a structure of radiations rising vertically from the ground like invisible, radioactive walls. Alternate lines are usually positively and negatively charged, so where the lines intersect it is possible to have double positive charges and double negative charges, or one positive and one negative charge. It is the intersections that are seen to be a source of potential problems.

You are now standing in the place where you can invoke the Grand Architect with the following declamation (or any text with the same intention):

O Grand Architect of the Universe, I invoke you! Please hear my voice calling out to you, as I begin this spiritual journey. This special place was organized by the Founding Fathers of this nation and there are potent forces concentrated here. May the president of the United States receive an ample portion of your divine wisdom! May the Great Work I accomplish this day on the visible and invisible planes be an expression of my will to participate in the evolution of beneficence, truth, and justice for all human beings. So mote it be!

Visualize the power all around this place increasing and becoming more luminous and benevolent. Focus for a while on the necessity of everyone working for the highest good. Imagine that this energy is able to help that work and that it will increase and aid the president in having the right understanding of whatever work he is involved with. Do not specify any precise intentions; just organize the energy so that it is directing good and wisdom to this place.

Now you may walk, following the east side of the ellipse, toward the south. Follow 15th Street and continue your walk on the east side of the tidal basin until you reach the Jefferson Memorial. This involves a long walk (1.5 miles) so take your time and enjoy your experience of the area.

Rest Stop 2. When you have reached the Jefferson Memorial, walk around it clockwise, and then stand in front of it and spend some time in reflection. Remain standing in front of the Memorial for a while, concentrating on the dreams and hopes of people all around the world who think of this as a symbol of freedom. Even though it is less well-known than the White House, the spiritual energy flowing from north to south creates a special link between these two points. All those worldwide aspirations for greatness are now shared with this place, because the builders chose wisely and erected this memorial to Thomas Jefferson as a true archetype of these primary virtues.

Next, you will organize and focus the stream of thoughts that are present in this place. To do that, just walk into the building, just in front of the northern opening, facing the White House. Breathe for a while, visualizing this energy as coming from the north. Imagine that you are surrounded by this powerful flow of energy. It is part of you and it is part of this peaceful place.

Turn right and walk to the northeast panel (which is situated between the White House and the Capitol). Stop, breathe rhythmically, and, as a silent invocation to yourself, read the text, which is engraved on the wall:

God who gave us life, gave us liberty. Can the liberties of a nation be secure when we have removed a conviction that these liberties are the gift of God? Indeed I tremble for my country when I reflect that God is just, that his justice cannot sleep forever. Commerce between master and slave is despotism. Nothing is more certainly written in the book of fate than that these people are to be free. Establish a law for educating the common people. This is the business of the state on a general plan.

Move clockwise so that you are facing the eastern opening. Breathe deeply and rhythmically for a while, without any specific thoughts; just feel the sensations received by your body in this beautiful place.

Continuing to move clockwise, stop in front of the southeast panel. Breathe deeply and rhythmically for a while, and then read the text engraved in the wall quietly to yourself as a silent invocation. Adopt this text as your own.

I am not an advocate for frequent changes in laws and constitutions, but laws and institutions must go hand in hand with the progress of the human mind. As that becomes more developed, more enlightened, as new discoveries are made, new truths discovered and manners and opinions change, with the change of circumstances, institutions must advance also to keep pace with the times. We might as well require a man to wear still the coat which fitted him when a boy as civilized society to remain ever under the regimen of their barbarous ancestors.

Move clockwise so that you are facing the southern opening. Breathe deeply and rhythmically for a while, without any specific thoughts; just feel the sensations received by your body in this beautiful place.

Continue to move clockwise. Stop in front of the southwest panel. Breathe deeply and read the text engraved in the wall quietly to yourself as a silent invocation. Adopt this text as your own.

We hold these truths to be self-evident: that all men are created equal, that they are endowed by their Creator with certain inalienable rights, among these are life, liberty, and the pursuit of happiness, that to secure these rights governments are instituted among men. We solemnly publish and declare that these colonies are and of right ought to be free and independent states. And for the support of this declaration, with a firm reliance on the protection of divine providence, we mutually pledge our lives, our fortunes, and our sacred honor.

Move clockwise so that you are facing the western opening. Breathe deeply and rhythmically for a while, without any specific thoughts, and just feel the sensations received by your body in this beautiful place.

Continue moving clockwise; stop in front of the northwest panel. Breathe rhythmically and read the text engraved in the wall as a silent invocation to yourself. Adopt this text as your own.

Almighty God hath created the mind free. All attempts to influence it by temporal punishments or burdens . . . are a departure from the plan of the Holy Author of our religion . . . No man shall be compelled to frequent or support any religious worship or ministry or shall otherwise suffer on account of his religious opinions or belief, but all men shall be free to profess and by argument to maintain, their opinions in matters of religion. I know but one code of morality for men whether acting singly or collectively.

Move clockwise to face the northern opening. Breathe deeply and rhythmically for a while, without any specific thoughts, and just feel the sensations received by your body in this beautiful place.

Turn toward the tidal basin and continue walking in this direction. Visualize the line you are walking on as linking the energies of the White House to the Thomas Jefferson Memorial. Visualize this energy flowing from the north point of the District of Columbia to the south point far behind you.

Rest Stop 3. You will now walk to the Lincoln Memorial, which is northwest of the tidal basin.

You should now be west of the Mall and for the first time in your spiritual journey you will be stopping on the axis of the Sun, facing east (toward the rising Sun). Take the time to visit this monument. When you are ready, sit down on the stairs that face east, toward the Washington Monument and the Capitol. Relax and breathe deeply and rhythmically for a while. You are in a very special place. You are facing east, just as the ancient Pythagoreans faced when they worshipped the rising Sun. The place where you are standing at this very moment is the central axis of the invisible temple you are walking through. This central axis is the place where all the forces you have been working with are to be balanced. This occurs both inwardly and outwardly.

The obelisk in front of you is the living symbol of the journey of your soul from heaven to earth and its return to the realm of nature. (You may review these concepts in Chapter Four, at the end of that chapter). High in the sky at the vertex of the Washington Monument, the forces are focused in the invisible pyramid created by the shape of the District of Columbia. Visualize these powers flowing up to the vertex of the Washington Monument and flowing directly from there to the Sun.

If you are lucky, or have timed your journey well, the Sun will be directly in front of you. Stop and feel the power of the Sun on your body. Visualize its ability to transform the powers it has received from the energetic center of this Mall into good vibrations that empower and bring about the promises you have claimed as your own from the many declarations you have read.

You may exclaim the following hymn mentally, or you may substitute an equivalent hymn that has meaning for you:

O benevolent Sun, whose immortal eye shines down on all, hear me!

Your golden rays give life to all the earth; you are the brightest star in the firmament; you are immortal, tireless—a sweet vision to every living creature; hear my voice!

You orchestrate the harmonious clockwork of all the bodies in the cosmos.

You are the master of the beauty in all that we do; you are the youth who brings about the changes in the seasons.

You are the master of the universe, and the sound of your flute accompanies the lighting of the circle of fire.

O you bearer of light, dispenser of life, provider of the bountiful fruits of the land, hear my hymn!

You are the spherical eye of the cosmos, which spreads its beautiful rays of light to all who live on this earth.

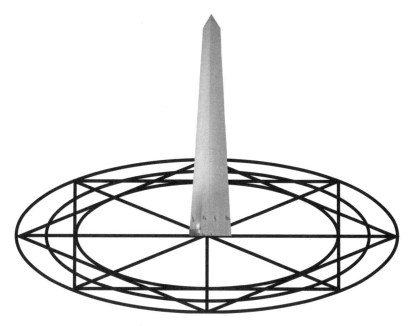

Figure 51: The Washington Monument as symbolic axis (gnomon) of the city

Eye of justice; O light of life that rises daily in our sky, give to your initiates the sweet life they seek, and grant to the people in charge of our government, who are working at the center of this great nation, bravery, insight, and wisdom.

May your power bring enlightenment to the hearts and minds of the people all around the world!

So mote it be!

After a moment of silent meditation, you may continue your journey in an easterly direction, as you walk to the symbolic central altar, which is the Jefferson Pier Stone. From it, you will enter in the triangle formed by the White House, the Jefferson Memorial, and the Capitol Building.

Rest Stop 4. As you read earlier in this text, the Jefferson Pier Stone is a very special place. It is the meeting place of the two axes (north/south and east/west) and is at the center of the District of Columbia, which is surrounding you. This is a very good place to meditate on the symbol of the center, on the hidden stone, on your heart. This symbolic stone is interesting because its shape is a reminder of something Dan Brown emphasized in *The Lost Symbol*: the relationship between the cube and the unfinished pyramid.

Whether you are a Freemason or not, you can effectively associate this stone with the most sacred altar at the center of your inner temple. Visualize the sacred book that corresponds to your beliefs open atop this stone. Above the book, visualize the symbols of the Craft: the square and the compass. If you are a Freemason, you can visualize these tools intertwined, according to your level or degree. Breathe rhythmically for a while. Then, if you can do it discreetly, put the palm of your right hand on the top of the stone (if you are unable to do that, simply visualize this action). Visualize your palm as being in direct contact with the tools and your sacred book. Visualize the sunlight everywhere around you and then exclaim your Masonic obligation quietly to yourself. If you are not a Freemason, make this simple declaration: *"May the divine light illuminate this place, giving wisdom, strength, and beauty to all people working for the good of humanity! May all the powers focused on this special space bring peace and insight to all the people around the world! So mote it be!"* (If possible, remain in contact with the stone during your silent exclamation. In order to be discreet, you may withdraw a reasonable distance once you have made contact with the stone. After you withdraw, you may make the exclamation as a silent invocation in your mind.)

Rest Stop 5. Before you continue your journey back to the Capitol Building, which is the highest point of the Mall, stop at the Washington Monument. Walk clockwise around the obelisk while you think about the meaning of this symbol and the double square I described previously. The double square is the symbol that is drawn using eight points. (See Figure 51 on the previous paragraph).

Rest Stop 6. There is a special place to the east of the Mall. As I previously explained, a triangle is an important symbol and generally the letter G (or Yod) is written at its center in Masonry. According to the theory of radionics, the energy of this shape is focused on its center. The center of this letter "G" is on the central axis, just in front of the entrance to the Arts and Industries Building.

If the weather is good, it would be a good idea to sit on or near this point for a while, facing east. Once you are seated, meditate on the meaning of the triangle and the letter G, which is a half-square in the shape of the Greek letter Gamma (Γ).

Visualize your aura surrounding you. Feel a real connection to the energy of this place, a connection to the earth beneath your feet and the sky above you. Visualize this aura glowing with life and light and imagine that you are receiving the best energies available here. Each time you inhale, imagine that you are absorbing this energy. After a few minutes of enjoying your contact with the elements and feeling the glow of your aura pulsating with energy, mentally exclaim:

The Sun must always be at its zenith to spread the light of Freemasonry all around the planet. By the help of the Great Architect of the Universe, may this enlightenment be accomplished!

May the rays of the divine shed their benign influence upon me, and enlighten me in the paths of virtue and science! May the power of the mysterious word be manifested today in this place, in order that order may be victorious over chaos for the good of all people everywhere!

Extend your right hand directly in front of you. Imagine that you are engraving the shining sacred letter G in the Greek shape of a square (Γ) into the aura of this place. In the same way, engrave a triangle of fire around this letter.

Relax and breathe rhythmically, without focusing on anything. Stand up and walk toward the Capitol. As you walk up this hill in reality, you are also accomplishing an important symbolic action. According to Vitruvius, this ascent is a symbolic illustration of the inner progression of your soul, emulating the Sun as it rises toward Mount Olympus, the residence of the divinities.

Rest Stop 7. You will now enter the Capitol Building. The final part of your spiritual journey requires that you walk along the vertical axis at the center of this building. First, walk to the crypt under the rotunda. As you will see, there is a golden star at the center. Relax, breathe rhythmically, and make one circle clockwise, encircling this room. If possible, walk into the center of the golden star. At the center of the star, project your consciousness deep into the earth so that you are connected to the powers of this place. When you are ready, look up above your head. Exactly above you is the center of the rotunda. Project your consciousness from the floor, ascending in your mind up the vertical axis towards the heavens. You will now mentally invoke the four guardians of the four directions in order to increase the potentiality of the energy where you are. Face east: the star on the floor will aid you in orienting.

Begin by saying (in your mind): "*Tu es . . . Regnum . . . et potentia . . . et gloria . . . in saeculis.*" On your right, to the south, visualize a brilliant red light with scintillating sparks of green and mentally invoke: "Ashiel."

In the west behind you, visualize a sparkling blue light merging into highlights of orange. Mentally invoke: "Miel."

On your left, to the north, visualize an indigo light that gleams with flashes of pale gold. Mentally invoke: "Auphiriel."

Mentally exclaim:

"From the portal of earth to the portal of fire, from the portal of air to the portal of water, from the center of power to the encompassing adamant, let this sanctuary be established within the black rose. So mote it be!"

You may now respectfully leave this place and go upstairs to the rotunda. Take your time walking around the rotunda; then, if you can, walk to the center. Look above you at the painting of the apotheosis of George Washington surrounded by the Olympian divinities. This is not an easy place to perform a ritual practice. However, you can always visit the place and take the time to visualize and perform an inner ritual.

Stopping to contemplate the beauty of this place is very close to stopping to perform an inner visualization. So feel free to do this next part with tact and discretion.

Stop in the middle of the rotunda or any place that seems appropriate to you. Face east. Begin saying: "*Tu es . . . Regnum . . . et potentia . . . et gloria . . . in saeculis.*" Turn your thoughts toward your aspiration to ascend to the prime source of light and life. In this contemplation, allow your imagination to expand to a constantly increasing vastness as your desire is magnified in being and power by adherence to the object of this highest and inmost desire: union with the prime source. Imagine your body ascending to the sky, to the highest level of the dome. Holding this sense of vastness in your mind, visualize a powerful light radiating inwardly and outwardly. You are the cosmos! The bright light of the vertical axis is streaming through your body, linking the deepest levels of the earth to the uppermost levels of the sky.

Still aware of this splendor, look at the symbolic apotheosis of George Washington, who is the archetype of your own ascent to your own divinity. Maintaining the extension of your consciousness (if you memorized it), you may now mentally exclaim the hymn to all the gods by Proclus, by which you will be worshipping the divinities protecting this place, this Capitol, and this nation. (If you don't know this text, print it out beforehand.) Maintain this feeling and read this text anywhere in the rotunda that seems appropriate:

O Gods, You who hold the rudder of sacred wisdom, who light in our human souls the flame of return, bring us back among the Immortals, and by the inexpressible

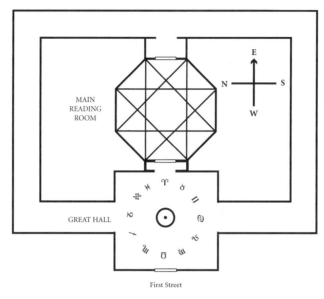

Figure 52: Symbolic structure of the Library of Congress

initiations of the Hymns, give us the capacity to escape from our dark caves and to purify ourselves. Grant this to me, O powerful liberators! Grant me, by knowledge of the Divine writings, by dispersing the darkness which surrounds me, a pure and holy light. Allow me to perfectly know the incorruptible God, and the man [or woman] that I am.

May a wicked djinn never overcome me by pains, or indefinitely hold me captive under the rivers of oblivion.

May I never be held captive in the jail of life, for the frightening expiation, with my soul fallen in the icy flows of the river of regeneration, where I never want to wander too long.

So, O gods, sovereigns of the radiant wisdom, grant to me and reveal to one who hastens on the ascending path of return, the holy ecstasies and the initiations which are at the heart of the divine words!

At the conclusion of your ascension, mentally exclaim: "*E pluribus unum!*"[5] Put your right hand on your solar plexus and go meditate in silence for a while.

---

5. Latin for "Out of many, one."

Figure 53: Pavement of the Great Hall of the Library of Congress

Rest Stop 8. The Library of Congress will be the final stop on this spiritual pilgrimage. Since this eighth step is a different level of the previous step of ascension of the soul, you may choose to complete it at another time. To do so, simply return to this place at another time and complete this part. Of course, if you wish, you may finish it now, right after your experience at the Capitol.

As I mentioned in Chapter Four, the Jefferson Memorial is really a temple of Hermes, which integrates many elements from the Hermetic and Ogdoadic Tradition. Its architecture reminds us of this inheritance.

The first step will be your walk through the Great Hall. Following the old traditions, you must circumnavigate the zodiac that is set into the floor. Naturally, you will begin at Aries, continuing around with Taurus, Gemini, Cancer, Leo, Virgo, Libra, Scorpio, Sagittarius, Capricorn, Aquarius, and Pisces. You will stop at each sign of the zodiac. When you stop at these signs, breathe rhythmically and take time to relax during your circumambulation. When you come back to Aries, turn and walk to the central golden sun. Face east, in the direction of the Main Reading Room. Mentally exclaim the Ogdoadic oath: "*En*

Figure 54: General view of Capitol Hill

Giro Torte Sol Ciclos Et Rotor Igne!" Visualize a pulsating golden aura all around you. You are at the center of the Sun, which is shining from the core of your own being.

Breathe and walk to the east, where you will enter a corridor to the Main Reading Room of the Library of Congress.[6] After acquiring a book, for example the *Corpus Hermeticum*, sit down and relax. You are in the center of a beautiful traditional octagon. For thousands of years, this shape has been associated with the Hermetic Tradition. Above your head, Isis raises her veil. If you have the *Corpus Hermeticum* in front of you, open it to Book 13, which is titled *The Secret Discourse*. Raise your consciousness to Hermes Trismegistus and mentally exclaim the text called "The Secret Hymn":[7]

Ye powers that are within me, hymn the One and All; sing with my Will, Powers all that are within me!

---

6. You must have a Reader Identification Card issued by the library before to attempting to enter.

7. *Corpus Hermeticum*, Book 13:17–18.

O blessed Gnosis, by thee illumined, hymning through thee the Light that mind alone can see, I joy in Joy of Mind. Sing with me praises all ye Powers!

If you have this book with you, you should now read the complete section on "The Secret Hymn" 17–18. After this reading, take some time for meditation. Mentally say:

Konx Om Pax! My spiritual pilgrimage has been achieved. May the divine powers I solemnly invoked today participate in my spiritual enlightenment and bring about the establishment of peace and wisdom all over the world. So mote it be!

Now might be a good time for you to write some personal notes about this experience and this real pilgrimage. This experience is an amazing way to make personal contact with the egregore of the Capitol Building and to participate inwardly in the growth of the light around the world.

The Seasons at the Mall

As previously explained, the cardinal points are important with regard to the powers that are present in the earth, but they are also significant for celestial movement. In this place, the movement of the Sun is easy to understand.

At the equinoxes,[8] the sunrise is exactly on the east/west axis. If you are standing in front of the Lincoln Memorial, the Sun will rise above the Capitol and the statue of freedom. At noon, the Sun will be at the highest point in the sky, and the sunset will be behind you, exactly on this axis.

At the winter solstice,[9] the sunrise will be on the right side of the Capitol, in the southeast. The Sun will progress across the southern quadrant during the day and the sunset will be on your right, to the southwest. The highest point at noon will be in the south.

At the summer solstice, the progression across the sky is reversed. The sunrise is at the left of the Capitol, on the northeast; at noon the Sun is at the northernmost point; and at sunset, the Sun is in the northwest.

The benefits of these observations include the ability to choose precise and specific moments to perform these rituals and thus to connect to these potent energies. Each

---

8. Spring equinox: approximately March 20. Fall equinox: approximately September 22.
9. Approximately December 21, the day of shortest daylight.

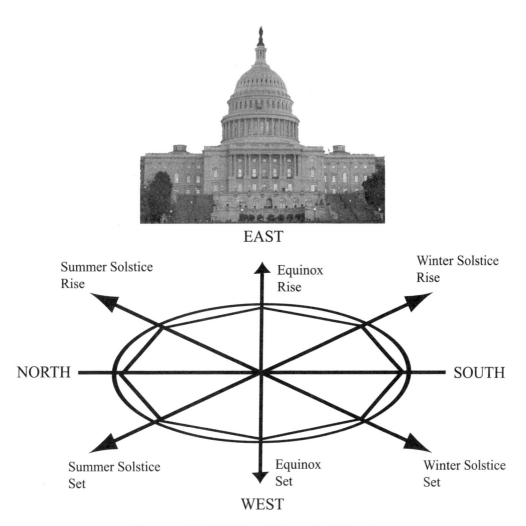

Figure 55: Capitol Hill and the cardinal directions

location has a particular season during which the energy is at its peak in that place. The best moments for focusing these powers are: (1) the White House—summer solstice; (2) the Jefferson Memorial—winter solstice; (3) the Capitol Building—the morning of either equinox; (4) the Jefferson Pier Stone and the Washington Monument—noon of either equinox; (5) the Lincoln Memorial—the afternoon of either equinox.

In the description of this spiritual journey on the Mall, I described various practices and visualizations at these locations. You will find it very interesting to make a special visit to one of these monuments at the astronomical peak of its energy (as outlined above). During these periods, these energies are undoubtedly at their peak, and you will be able to perform the most effective esoteric ritual. Of course, to accomplish this task, it is not necessary to complete an entire pilgrimage again. In fact, if you are unable to be physically at the Mall, you may use a photo of the monument you have chosen and perform this ritual at home.

If you are a Freemason who is eager to associate your knowledge of the Craft with these practices, I suggest that you mentally repeat the ritual text of your function at the place that is symbolically associated with it, as follows: (1) the White House—Chaplains; (2) the Jefferson Memorial—Junior Wardens; (3) the Capitol Building—Worshipful Master and Past Masters; (4) the Jefferson Pier Stone and the Washington Monument—Worshipful Master and Past Masters; (5) the Lincoln Memorial—Senior Wardens. The other officers can choose the symbolic location closest to their office in the lodge and can research the best moments of the year to perform these practices.

Of course, in the tradition of ancient Freemasonry, men who come together as members of a lodge may join their hands together to form a chain (a circle created by joining their hands together). This will be a powerful moment for members of a lodge.

Rebirth of the Sun and the Moon: December 2010

In Chapter Two, I described the central Masonic symbols of the Moon and the Sun. You are reminded that the teachings regarding the potency of such symbols comes from old pre-Christian traditions and, more precisely, the Mithraic and Hermetic Traditions. The symbolic and potential powers of these two lights in the sky are ancient and very important. From the most ancient times, astronomical and astrological events have been considered as relevant phenomena. In the Western Tradition, stars crossing the sky were not thought of as physical planets or suns as you understand them today. Even if some earlier philosophers knew and understood the physical aspects of these observations, they connected such astral movements to powerful archetypes.

As a point of fact, initiates always considered what is above the earth as divine. The sky and all things in it were considered the divine plane. Consequently, in their world, the stars were thought of as good symbolic representations of the divinities. Their color, movement, and brightness were a source of powerful symbolism to the ancients, who gave birth to the archetypes that have been an enduring part of our unconscious mind right up to the present moment. Western people (though they are mostly unfamiliar with this concept) are composed of these archetypes, and our unconscious uses this hidden mental grid when we try to think about the big questions of life: birth, death, life after death, the meaning of life, etc. The traditional divine stories are always a part of us, as a hidden divine presence walking beside us during the whole of our lives. Everything in the universe is alive, and the divine is very close to us.

Among all these divine presences, the Moon and the Sun may be the most powerful. Life on Earth began with the help of the Sun. Life cannot continue unless the Sun is its rightful position. On the other hand, the Moon is really the companion of the Sun, receiving his power. Sometimes considered to be female (Selene), sometimes male (Thoth), the Moon is the closest divinity to us on Earth. The Moon has been described as the first divinity, in the sequence of the seven others (Mercury, Venus, Sun, Mars, Jupiter, and Saturn). The physical action of these two divinities, the Moon and the Sun, is visible all around the world. They cause all: life, tides, moon cycles, etc. The Egyptian Tradition understood this powerful archetype and used it in several divine representations. The Mythraic Mysteries used them as well. In all their temples (called Mithreum), the Sun and the Moon were shown on each side of Mithra as his divine companions. This is exactly what has been used right from the beginning in many Masonic temples.

For the Hermetist in the Renaissance, the movements of the Sun and the Moon were good opportunities to balance the power of the psyche. As archetypes of all divinities and celestial phenomena, it was possible to use the movements of the Sun and the Moon in order to perform an inner spiritual work that would balance these powers within the Hermetist. Of course, some periods of the year were better, more powerful. This is the case during the phases of the Moon. This is also the case at specific moments in the apparent movement of the Sun, such as the equinoxes and the solstices. When specific meditations are performed at these moments of the year, they may link the initiate to these cosmic bodies and act as a real activation of these unconscious archetypes. Better still, if these connections are especially potent, timed with cosmic events and occuring at a specific location, the result will be even more powerful, allowing the initiate to make much greater progress. It is possible to imagine (as Dan Brown's *The Lost Symbol* describes) a union of minds focused on the nation and the world with the intent of drawing good, peace, and progress to the place of this unity. The mind (or minds) is/are capable of having a physical effect on the material plane. If the minds are focused during a critical planetary configuration, the result is enormously spiritual and can be very philanthropic! I have described a mythical time during which it is possible to imagine such a focus of the wills and minds at a powerful moment of astral conjunction. Washington DC's architectural landmarks and history emphasize the Masonic symbols, and in this year, 2010, there will be an actual and amazing opportunity to witness just such an astral conjunction live. Undoubtedly, the energies and the powers of the symbols will be at their maximum.

This special moment will occur on a very unique date: December 21, 2010. This day will be a very special one for Masons everywhere and, of course, for everyone involved or interested in esoteric traditions. This is the exact date in 2010 of the winter solstice, which will occur at 6:38 PM local time. That is the moment when the days are the shortest. According to the Mythraic Tradition, this is the exact moment of the fight between Mithra and the bull. The victory of Mithra allows the Sun to begin its ascent into the sky. This is called *Sol Invictus*. This story is symbolic of the Scottish Rite 27th Degree, Knight of the Sun.

However, this date is very special for another reason. From 8:13 AM on, there is a full moon on Washington DC. This connection between the solstice and the full moon is extremely rare, and this symbol is esoterically relevant. Still, you may go even further and assign to this date an exceptional character. On December 2, at midnight, this full moon will be obscured by a total eclipse! This celestial phenomenon will be visible above Washington DC for several hours.

To see a similar conjunction between the solstice, the full moon, and a total eclipse, you must wait until December 21, 2094. The last conjunction like this was in 1638.

Such astral events have always been used by initiates to rebalance the inner powers and to focus their minds on the best outcome for humankind. The deepest archetypes will be invoked by this visible astral event of 2010, and we will be able to change things for the better because we will be able to send a positive impulse to the world from this special place, Washington DC, just as every initiate has the power and the duty to do.

Stars and astral movements are not something that just happen in the heavens. On the contrary, such divine conjunctions, and our intentional connection to them, can be an opportunity for us as humans to become more spiritual and to help overcome the challenges facing today's modern world.

APPENDIX

Masonic Decalogue

Excerpt from Albert Pike's *Moral and Dogmas*.

"Masonry has its Decalogue, which is a law to its Initiates. These are its Ten Commandments:

1. God is the Eternal, Omnipotent, Immutable WISDOM and Supreme INTELLIGENCE and Exhaustless LOVE.

   Thou shalt adore, revere, and love Him!

   Thou shalt honor Him by practising the virtues!

2. Thy religion shall be, to do good because it is a pleasure to thee, and not merely because it is a duty.

   That thou mayest become the friend of the wise man, thou shalt obey his precepts!

   Thy soul is immortal! Thou shalt do nothing to degrade it!

3. Thou shalt unceasingly war against vice!

   Thou shalt not do unto others that which thou wouldst not wish them to do unto thee!

   Thou shalt be submissive to thy fortunes, and keep burning the light of wisdom!

4. Thou shalt honor thy parents!

   Thou shalt pay respect and homage to the aged!

   Thou shalt instruct the young!

   Thou shalt protect and defend infancy and innocence!

5. Thou shalt cherish thy wife and thy children!

   Thou shalt love thy country, and obey its laws!

6. Thy friend shall be to thee a second self!

   Misfortune shall not estrange thee from him!

   Thou shalt do for his memory whatever thou wouldst do for him, if he were living!

7. Thou shalt avoid and flee from insincere friendships!

   Thou shalt in everything refrain from excess.

   Thou shalt fear to be the cause of a stain on thy memory!

8. Thou shalt allow no passions to become thy master!

   Thou shalt make the passions of others profitable lessons to thyself!

   Thou shalt be indulgent to error!

9. Thou shalt hear much: Thou shalt speak little: Thou shalt act well!

   Thou shalt forget injuries!

   Thou shalt render good for evil!

   Thou shalt not misuse either thy strength or thy superiority!

10. Thou shalt study to know men; that thereby thou mayest learn to know thyself!

    Thou shalt ever seek after virtue!

    Thou shalt be just!

    Thou shalt avoid idleness!"

Marcus Vitruvius
De Architectura, Book I—Chapter 6

6. Let a marble slab be fixed level in the centre of the space enclosed by the walls, or let the ground be smoothed and levelled, so that the slab may not be necessary. In the centre of this plane, for the purpose of marking the shadow correctly, a brazen gnomon must be erected. The Greeks call this a gnomon. The shadow cast by the gnomon is to be marked about the fifth ante-meridianal hour, and the extreme point of the shadow accurately determined. From the central point of the space whereon the gnomon stands, as a centre, with a distance equal to the length of the shadow just observed, describe a circle. After the sun has passed the meridian, watch the shadow which the gnomon continues to cast till the moment when its extremity again touches the circle which has been described.

7. From the two points thus obtained in the circumference of the circle, describe two arcs intersecting each other, and through their intersection and the centre of the circle first described draw a line to its extremity: this line will indicate the north and south points. One-sixteenth part of the circumference of the whole circle is to be set out to the right and left of the north and south points, and drawing lines from the points thus obtained to the centre of the circle, we have one-eighth part of the circumference for the region of the north, and another eighth part for the region of the south. Divide the remainders of the circumference on each side into three equal parts, and the divisions or regions of the eight winds will be then obtained: then let the directions of the streets and lanes be determined by the tendency of the lines which separate the different regions of the winds.

The Hermetic Tree of Life

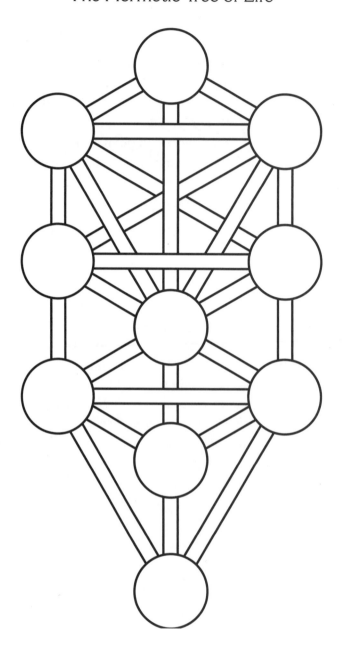

Symbol for the Practice: Knight of the Sun

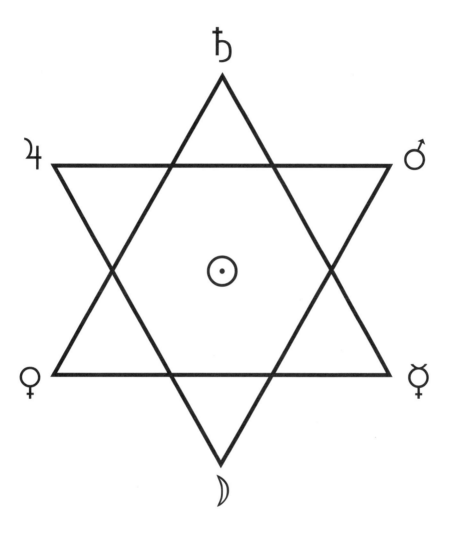

Masonic Ciphers

Several different ciphers are used in Freemasonry. The one used by Dan Brown in *The Lost Symbol* is called the Pigpen cipher (sometimes called the Masonic cipher, or Freemason's cipher). This cipher was developed and used by the Freemasons in the early eighteenth century. The example (below) shows how the letters are assigned to a grid.

The word *Freemasonry* is shown in Latin characters and, below it, it is shown in encrypted form. As you can see, the position of the letter in the grid gives the shape of the code that was used. If the letter is in the middle of the grid, the code of the letter is a square. If the letter is in the middle and it has a dot in it, the code of the letter is a square with a dot in its center.

Down through the centuries, several Masonic ciphers have been developed all around the world, based on this same grid.

Below, you will find an English Masonic cipher.

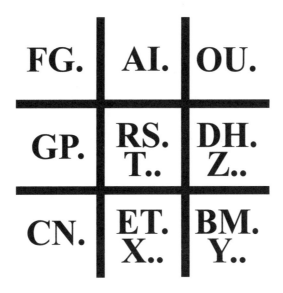

Below you will find a Continental Masonic cipher.

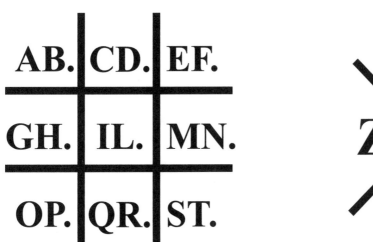

Below, you will find a Masonic cipher that was developed after the eighteenth century. The use of the three points (dots) is symbolically interesting. They may indicate a European origin, because three points (dots) in a triangle are frequently used in Freemasonry.

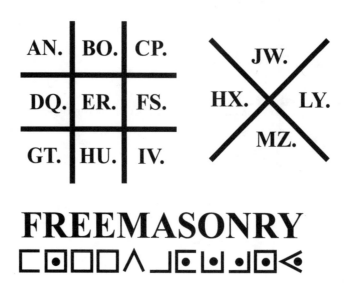

Below you will find a Masonic cipher from the United States. As an illustration, the word *Freemasonry* is shown in Latin characters. Below it, the encrypted form is shown. You may notice that this encryption is different from the first one demonstrated. This example demonstrates why the code is essential for the decryption of the message.

GLOSSARY

Note: All entries from Dan Brown's *The Lost Symbol* are followed by an asterisk. The others (without an asterisk) are from this book only.

Abramelin*

The *Book of Abramelin* (*Book of the Sacred Magic of Abramelin the Mage*) is a fifteenth-century grimoire written by Rabbi Yaakov Moelin, a German Jewish Talmudist. The text describes an initiatic journey from Germany to Egypt. A magician and Qabalistic Master, Abramelin teaches his secrets to his son Lamech. This volume is composed of four books: (1) the initiatic journey, (2) materials from the practical Qabalah, (3) magical practices, and (4) more magical practices.

The text describes an "Invocation to Visible Appearance of the Holy Guardian Angel." A long preparation is required (between six and eighteen months). This angelic manifestation is supposed to give high magical secrets to the magician. This book (translated by Mathers) became a central mystery in the Order of the Golden Dawn.

In this book, Abramelin provides an oil recipe, which was referenced by Dan Brown. The formula reads as follows: "Take one part of the best myrrh, half a part of cinnamon, one part of cassia, one part calamus (*Acorus calamus*), and a quarter of the combined total weight of good, fresh olive oil."

Alchemy*

Alchemy can be seen as the origin of modern chemistry. However, the purpose of the alchemists was (and is) not just a study of chemical reactions. For them, everything in the universe is connected. The human body is a representation of the cosmos. Many people believe that the main purpose of alchemy is to make gold. In fact, the long process of working with plants and stones is meant to simultaneously accomplish an inner spiritual work. If you are inwardly pure, you will achieve a connection between the inner life and the outer world that enables you to obtain such results as the alchemical elixir. Further, all of the external work is just a representation of the ascension of the soul. Alchemy cannot be understood or practiced independently of the spiritual alchemy that is the real transformation of the soul.

Alexandria*

Alexandria is the famous city founded by Alexander the Great in the Nile Delta in Egypt. The first famous library of Alexandria was built there. It was the central hub of a great cultural network involving all the religions and cultures of that time. It was the place where the Bible was translated from Hebrew to Greek. When Christianity emerged and became a political power, the philosophical schools were shut down and the initiatic traditions went into hiding.

Alexandria, Virginia is a city in the United States that is located very near Washington DC. It was named in honor of John Alexander. This is the site where the Masonic Memorial to President George Washington was built in the shape of the lighthouse of Alexandria, Egypt.

All-Seeing Eye*

The all-seeing eye is also known as the eye of providence. One of the first uses of this ancient symbol was found in the writings of ancient Egypt. The eye of Ra is drawn on the walls of many ancient Egyptian buildings. It represents the divine presence and power among all the peoples of the world and all living creatures. The eye of Ra was ultimately connected with the Christian god, but was not depicted as having any relationship to Christianity prior to the medieval era. The Christian Trinity was eventually symbolized by a triangle with the divine eye at the center, resulting in this specific symbol. It has been used in many documents: political, Masonic, religious, etc. as a primary symbol of divine providence. In 1782, it was engraved into the top of the reverse of the Great Seal of the United States.

Altar*

At the time of the earliest beginnings of many religious traditions, the central altar was very often a piece of stone that was employed for offerings and sacrifices. Depending on the religion (or philosophical mystery teaching), the altar was placed variously, including at the center of the temple, in the east, or in front of the eastern wall. There is no set rule for the shape of these altars. They may be circular, cubic, rectangular, etc. However, despite the variations, it is quite impossible to imagine a temple, or a church, without such an altar.

Apocalypse*

This is the name of the last book of the Christian Bible. The original text was in Greek, and the word *apocalypse* means "revelation." These visions were received by the Apostle John on the island of Patmos, Greece. Even if the text can be explained by an analysis of the political and religious issues of the time, these writings are deeply symbolic and can be interpreted in many ways. The text predicts an important development at the "end of the age" and was (is) used as a basis for the apocalyptic groups that crop up around the millennium, which are extant even today.

Apotheosis*

This word means "to become divine," or "to ascend to a divine level." The origins of this concept are found in the historical writings of many ancient religious and theurgic traditions. In ancient civilizations like Sumer, Greece and Egypt, the king was divinized and considered as the earthly manifestation of a god. The French monarchy also used this same principle. In theurgy, the apotheosis occurs when, as a result of the soul's contemplation, it is raised to the highest level of consciousness. Theurgic rituals are performed in order to ascend to this divine world.

Christian theology attempted to associate this concept of "becoming God" with the absolute distinction between the unique God and its creatures. The resulting use of the term *apotheosis* by that group is closer to an act of "partaking of the divine nature," rather than a real revelation of one's own divinity.

The Apotheosis of Washington*

In works of art, the term *apotheosis* is used to indicate a specific genre that depicts the subject of the work of art in an exalted manner. The purpose of this godlike representation is to glorify the ideal that the artist is trying to represent. You can find this sort of glorification in many sculptures and paintings. The painting on the canopy of the Capitol in Washington DC is an example of this kind of idealization. It deifies one of the Founding Fathers of the new nation, by surrounding him with Olympian deities. George Washington becomes Zeus himself, in order to govern well, and so that he can direct the power of the divine onto the people of the nation.

Ashlar*

An ashlar is a large stone rectangular block, larger than eleven inches. It has square edges. In Freemasonry, the term *ashlar* has two primary meanings. The stones, which represent Masons themselves at various stages of their development, are described as either "rough ashlars" or "smooth ashlars." These two blocks are part of the decor in every Masonic temple. They represent the two states of the inner work of every Mason: the entered apprentice and the master mason. This stone is also a symbol of the philosopher's stone, which is hidden. The philosopher's stone is used to transform basic materials into precious metals. This alchemy is a symbol of an inner transformation (see the entry for *alchemy* for further information).

Aura

According to the main spiritual traditions of both the East and West, our physical body is surrounded by a subtle energy field that is usually invisible. This energy is a manifestation of the life force in all living things, and can be found in every living being (plants, humans, etc.). This energy, called *prana* in India, constantly surrounds us and is continually being absorbed by our energetic centers. Special spiritual states of consciousness reveal this aura as an intense light surrounding the head or entire body. (This is the origin of the halo depicted by artists around the heads of saints, and the penumbral light around some saints' bodies.) The aura is seen by clairvoyants as a colored light that is egg shaped, which surrounds the physical body. These colors may reveal interesting information about the person.

Breathable Liquid*

This is an oxygen-rich liquid, which could be used in the treatment of patients with pulmonary and cardiac trauma. It is expected to be used in deep sea diving and space travel too. In both of these instances, the goal is to balance the extreme external pressure of deep sea and space conditions that would break the ribcage of an unprotected human being. The pressure of the liquid in the lungs prevents this problem. However, the completely successful application of a breathable liquid has not yet been established. In Dan Brown's novel, this breathable liquid was used in conjunction with an isolation chamber, so that the person could forget about his or her physical body and achieve a higher (more spiritual) state of consciousness.

Capstone*

A capstone is a stone with a very specific shape. The capstone completes a structure and is placed at the top of a building, wall, etc. When it is used to complete an obelisk, the shape of the capstone is generally pyramidal. Its symbolism is important, and it generally symbolizes the highest level of consciousness.

Chamber of Reflection*

This is a special room that is often used in European Freemasonry to isolate the uninitiated person prior to his initiation. The profane person (that is, someone who has not yet been initiated) is locked in this chamber to meditate on his intention, purpose, and reasons for undertaking the initiatic path. This chamber is very dark (lit with just a single candle). Its walls are painted black with symbolic representations of death. Alchemical mottos and symbols (mercury, salt, sulphur, and bread) are provided to the person as support during this meditation. The origins of this place can be found in the ancient Mediterranean Mysteries.

Cipher*

A cipher is a type of code that may be used to encrypt or decrypt a text. It substitutes characters, words, or phrases in the body of a text in order to preserve its meaning, while keeping that meaning hidden from those the author did not intend to understand it. In a cipher, the encoded text contains all of the original information. The Masonic cipher is such a code, and there are many different Masonic ciphers.

Codes were often used in esoteric texts and teachings. The reason is not well known. In some cases it was to keep the texts secret, and in other cases it was to use the symbols for magical or talismanic purposes. Magical squares are a good example of that use of codes.

Circumpunct*

The circumpunct is an ancient solar symbol of the Egyptian god Ra. The image consists of an encircled dot or a circle with a point at its center. This symbol is also a Neoplatonic representation of the soul in the spiritual world, and its relationship to the One (to beauty, justice, and truth).

However, this ancient symbol has even more to offer us. There is an important topic represented in the paintings of the Christian Tradition: the two Saints John, or the Holy Saint John. Generally these are depicted as being on each side of the Virgin Mary with her baby. Freemasonry chose Saint John the Apostle and Saint John the Baptist as their patron saints. Gradually over the years, Freemasons began using the circumpunct (composed of a circle with a central point and two vertical lines touching each side) as a symbol of the two saints, and also the Sun and the solstices. The circumpunct's center dot represents the Sun, and the lines on either side represent the solstices. Furthermore, the dates of the solstices are close to the dates of the celebrations related to the two sainted Johns.

Aleister Crowley*

Aleister Crowley (1875–1947), born Edward Alexander Crowley, was an English occultist. He was a very complex person: a writer, poet, mountaineer, etc. He was an initiate in the main Western initiatic traditions. What really set him apart from other magicians of his day was that he was a very active initiate who actually practiced the rituals he received. (The reality is that most of the people who talk about rituals are not really practitioners; they are just "intellectual magicians.") Crowley was a real magus and theurgist. He developed his own method from the materials of the Golden Dawn and other fraternities to which he belonged. Many of his studies and writings are interesting, but most of his writing is only useful within the context of his own system. Unfortunately, many people try to repeat what he did, when it was only good for Crowley himself. His practices and teachings are difficult and may even be dangerous to his followers, and must be read and studied with a prudent spirit.

Cube*

In Dan Brown's novel, a two-dimensional cross is folded to make a three-dimensional cube. For more information on this aspect, see the *ashlar* entry of this glossary.

Dollar Bill*

The first dollar bill in its present design came off the presses in 1957. According to the U.S. Treasury Department, that is when the motto "In God We Trust" started being used on paper money. The two circles present on the front side represent the two sides of the Great Seal of the United States: the unfinished pyramid and the eagle. Both representations are allegories for the intended development of the new nation. As archetypal symbols, they have been interpreted as having various meanings by different groups of people, including political, ideological, Masonic, satanic, etc. Of course, it is only accurate to connect these symbols to the first three interpretations. The "satanic" interpretation seems immaterial.

Albrecht Dürer*

Albrecht Dürer (1471–1528) was a German painter, printmaker, and theorist. His work follows the Renaissance philosophy and many of his paintings and writings contain interesting Hermetic symbols, which can be considered as esoterical keys. In relationship to *The Lost Symbol*, it is relevant to highlight his study and comments about Vitruvius, his painting titled *Melancholia*, and his graphic interpretations of the Tarot of Mantegna.

Eastern Star*

This is an initiatic group that has a direct relationship to Freemasonry. Its rituals were written by a Freemason who was eager to start an initiatic tradition that would be open to women. Consequently, the Order of the Eastern Star is a part of what are called the Allied Masonic Organizations.

Elohim*

Elohim is one of the holy names of God in the Torah. In Hebrew, the suffix "im" indicates that the word is plural. For this reason, some esotericists believe that this word indicates the plural nature of God. Of course, this suffix can also be seen as a plural that is intended to emphasize respect and reverence. In this case, the unique nature of the God of the Bible (as the One indivisible) remains undisputed.

Eukharistos*

This Greek noun (in English, "Eucharist") means "good, grateful" or "thanksgiving, grace." It is found in the major texts of the Bible that describe the Lord's Supper. In the Catholic faith, the pronunciation by a priest of Christ's words at the Last Supper act as magical words. By the power of these words, the essence of the bread and wine are really transubstantiated into Christ's blood and flesh. The appearance of the bread and wine remains the same, but their essences are changed by this action. When Catholic followers consume the transubstantiated bread and wine, they actually absorb the real Christ's blood and flesh. This idea also existed in some pre-Christian groups and is sometimes used in magick.

Exotericism

This word is opposite in meaning to *esotericism*. The phrase "esoteric teachings" means "teachings from the inside," or "knowledge that is hidden from the public." In the mystery school of Pythagoras, students were divided into noninitiates and initiates. From this separation came the idea of an inner circle and an outer circle. Thus, exotericism provides the outer (mundane) explanations of private knowledge.

Eight Franklin Square*

The early American scientist Benjamin Franklin (1706–1790) created bent-diagonal magic squares. In his lifetime he published several magic squares: one to the order of 8 and the other to the order of 16, as well as a magic circle. These squares are combinations of numbers in a geometric figure, by which one may obtain the same sum horizontally, vertically, or diagonally. In the Western Tradition, such squares were considered magical according to their numerological connection to the planets: Moon = 9, Mercury = 8, etc. Magical squares are also used with sacred alphabets such as Hebrew, Greek, and Enochian, which provide an opportunity to link oneself to the invisible power that is associated with these planets or spiritual powers. For further reading, I suggest the following article: Paul C. Pasles, "The Lost Squares of Dr. Franklin: Ben Franklin's Missing Squares and the Secret of the Magic Circle," *The American Mathematical Monthly*, 108:6, June–July, 2001.

Geobiology

Geobiology can be seen as an interdisciplinary field that explores interactions between the earth and the heavens. I might say that geobiology is the Western version of feng shui. Even if the word seems new, this knowledge is ancient and was used by Egyptian, Greek, and Roman architects. They used their knowledge of cosmo-telluric radiations and geobiology to determine the location of their cities, homes, rooms within the rooms, etc. They also utilized the services of waterwitches, or dowsers.

This knowledge still exists in the writings of the ancient masters of the Western Tradition.

Grand Architect of the Universe*

This is the name given by Freemasonry to the supreme being. Any male may join Freemasonry without confessing membership in any religious denomination. This allows the believers of every religion in the world to be initiated in the famous brotherhood.

Great Seal of the United States*

The Great Seal was created in 1782, between the creation of the Declaration of Independence and the Constitution. It can be found on many official documents. See the *dollar bill* entry of this glossary for more explanations. For further reading: http://www.greatseal.com.

Great Work*

In alchemy, the Great Work is the realization of the philosopher's stone, which allows the alchemist to have a long (eternal?) and healthy life. At the same time, the realization of this stone accomplishes the manifestation of the ascent of the soul to a higher level of consciousness.

Hand of the Mysteries*

The emblematic hand of the mysteries is a representation from Montfaucon's *Antiquities*. This hand, covered with numerous symbols, was shown to the neophytes when they entered into the Temple of Wisdom. As Manly P. Hall wrote in *The Secret Teachings of All Ages*: "An understanding of the symbols embossed upon the surface of the hand brought with it Divine power and regeneration. Therefore, by means of these symbolic hands the candidate was said to be raised from the dead."

Heredom*

The Masonic rite called Heredom (of Kilwinning) has many Hermetic and Rose-Cross influences. This mysterious name "Heredom" was first connected to the medieval Latin word *hoeredum*, signifying "heritage." As Edward L. Hawkins noted in the *Encyclopedia of Freemasonry*, the most plausible derivation is the one given in 1858. *Heredom* is a word composed by two Greek words: *holy* and *house*. Consequently Heredom means (symbolically) that Masonry is the holy house or the temple. As Hawkins noted, the title of "Rose-Croix of Heredom" would signify the "Rosy Cross of the Holy House of Masonry."

Hermes Trismegistus

It is possible that Hermes Trismegistus was the fictional representation of a Master. Many teachings and writings (probably by several other authors) were attributed to him. These teachings and writings were developed in Egypt during the Ptolemaic period and expanded over the first few centuries of that period. Later, the god Hermes was linked by the Hermetists to the divine figure of the Egyptian god Thoth. The *Corpus Hermeticum* (his remaining collected teachings) is considered to be a sacred book by all Hermetic initiates. If we compare this book with the books of other religions, we find that this text is one of the very rare sacred books that contains no violent writings and no exhortation to intolerance.

Hermeticism and Hermetism*

This is one of the most ancient Western traditions from Chaldea and Egypt. The teachings and mysteries of Hermes were assembled in a book called the *Corpus Hermeticum*. It provides philosophical, spiritual, religious, and theurgic teachings that have been used by Hermetic initiates for centuries. One of the main elements of this tradition is an open mind. It is very close in spirit to Freemasonry because it allows everyone to work cooperatively with its sacred knowledge, so that all can make progress in their search for the divine. Today, those who inherited these initiatic and theurgic teachings are referred to as ogdoadic orders (*ogdoadic* means "of, or related to, the number 8") or Hermetic orders. Anyone interested in more information may contact the *Ordo Aurum Solis* or write the author.

House of the Temple*

The famous Masonic temple, which is called the House of the Temple, is located at 1733 Sixteenth Street NW, in the District of Columbia. This monumental building has been the national headquarters of the Supreme Council 33rd Degree, Scottish Rite in America, since 1915. Its architecture is an adaptation of the famous Mausoleum at Halicarnassus, one of the Seven Wonders of the Ancient World.

Illumination*

The meaning of this word is different in the Eastern and Western traditions. In the Mediterranean, pre-Christian, and Western Hermetic traditions, the term *illumination* is used to mean "a contemplation of the divine." In this spiritual contemplation, the soul partakes of divine beauty, wisdom, and truth. However, this process does not entail the dissolution of the soul. Rather, the soul's own essence is preserved. The Western Tradition provides a variety of practices intended to facilitate the ascent to this level, including prayer, meditation, ritual, theurgy, etc.

Kryptos*

Kryptos is the name of the sculpture by American artist Jim Sanborn located on the grounds of the Central Intelligence Agency (CIA) in Langley, Virginia, USA. This sculpture is composed of four encrypted panels. Today, only three are partially decrypted.

Magic Square*

See *Eight Franklin Square.*

Magic, Magick, Theurgy*

A belief in the existence of inner human abilities and invisible powers in the universe that gave rise to numerous esoteric methods that enable the practitioner to develop and use these abilities. Magic, sometimes spelled magick, is the occult use of the invisible powers present in the human being and the universe. High magic and theurgy use the same principles, however, the purpose of this work is the obligation to use the knowledge to ascend to the divine. This practice is always connected with high moral development.

Magnetism

Magnetism is an invisible energy present everywhere in the universe. One might describe this energy as electricity, terrestrial magnetism, or as a flux of particles moving throughout the cosmos. According to spiritualists (and those with psychic vision), this astral energy is a fluid that gives life to human cells, providing health by causing a good balance and circulation at the different levels of our being. Initiates from every period in human history, living on every continent, have written about these "bodies of light." (See the entry *aura* in this glossary.)

Masterpiece*

In the Masonic Tradition, the "masterpiece" is the physical and visible realization of mastery. In creating this masterpiece, the Mason must master the tools of the craft, and also must manifest his abilities in the fellow-craft. In Freemasonry, this realization may also be seen as an inner process. One becomes a masterpiece when all of one's unbalanced desires are integrated into a balanced life, which is manifested as the Masonic ideal of a good man. Naturally, this inner work is associated with a balanced spiritual life as well.

Meditation

Meditation is an inner process that allows us to create a more balanced life and helps us to develop the spiritual dimension of our lives. The Eastern and Western traditions have evolved different methods for meditating. There are some similarities and some marked differences in the two systems. The fundamental differences in these two systems are the result of the differences in the unique cultural heritages and archetypal subconscious of these two groups of people. As explained earlier, Freemasonry has its own tradition, which provides its adherents a very interesting and original system for learning to meditate.

Mithraism

Mithraism is an initiatic tradition that originated in Persia. Its mysteries and rituals were developed around the first century CE and were spread by the Roman Legion throughout the Roman

Empire. This tradition is still known today by the unique style of architecture of its buildings, and is very close to Freemasonry in many aspects, such as male initiation only, architecture of the temples, and symbolism of different degrees.

Mysteries and Mystery Schools*

In ancient Greece (approximately 2000 BCE), there were several groups of highly developed initiates. These groups were generally created around their interest in a particular divine story, such as Orpheus, Demeter, Mithra, Isis, etc. These myths emphasized teachings about the afterlife and personal destiny. Special rituals and initiations allowed the candidates to directly experiment with these teachings, in order to achieve an inner knowledge of these "truths." After these ceremonies, personal fears regarding destiny and death were resolved (being no longer traumatic) and the initiates were able to prepare for the end of their physical lives and rebirth through reincarnation (metempsychosis).

Myth

A myth is a story that describes the life of and background surrounding a god or goddess (or gods or goddesses). Even though some myths may have certain historical events as part of their storyline, the fundamental characteristic of myths is that they utilize potent archetypal (universal) symbols to evoke certain states and to teach. Myths are the foundation of the sacred books or teachings of every religion, including Christianity, Hinduism, etc. Other myths gave birth to the various mystery schools. The myth of Demeter in the Eleusinian Mysteries is one such example.

Newton Scale*

In *The Lost Symbol*, the novel's hero used the Newton scale in order to find the correct temperature of water that would be required so that the code would be revealed once the stone had been plunged into the pan containing the water. This is a reference to the scale Newton created and used for a while. The two primary scale markers Newton used were 0°, when ice melts (at standard pressure), and 33°, when water boils (at standard pressure). This scale was a precursor of the Celsius scale, which uses the same temperature references.

Noetic Science*

The word *noetic* comes from the Greek word *noetikos* ("mental"), which is itself a combination of the words *noein* ("to think") and *noûs* (for which there is no exact equivalent in English). The original noetics was only concerned with a philosophical study of the mind and a study of intuition (a philosophy of the mind). Noetic science, in general terms, is the combination of new models in neuroscience and quantum physics, with a refined definition of parapsychology.

Numerology*

In several ancient alphabets (Greek, Hebrew, Latin, etc.), the letters were also used to represent numbers. For example 1 = A = Aleph = Alpha, 2 = B, etc. Thus, a sequence of letters that formed a word might also have a numerical value that would yield further meaning about the word, by comparing it to other words that had the same value. This comparison offered valuable information that would otherwise be hidden. Numerology evolved from this characteristic of ancient alphabets. Numerologists attempt to extract hidden meanings from words by comparing words with equivalent numerical value. Numerologists also (conversely) use words to find the hidden meaning in numbers that occurs in sacred works and other important documents. The main problem with numerology is that it does not have a consistent table of correspondences that can reliably be used to relate the various ancient alphabets. This problem is due to the fact that ancient alphabets do not have an equal number of letters, and Hebrew (and some other ancient languages) has only consonants. Thus, modern numerology has invented correspondences that are not always perfectly logical.

Obelisk*

The obelisks of the Egyptian Tradition stood at either side of the entrance to their temples. These pairs of stone columns also stood at the entrance to many oriental sanctuaries, such as the ones at Khorsabad, Tyre, and Hieropolis. The obelisk is a symbolic of resurrection. The first obelisks were built in the center of a large open space, in front of the temples of the Sun god Ra.

The shape of the obelisk indicates that its primary functions include dispersing negative forces, piercing the night sky, and attracting higher order energies into this symbol of petrified light.

Ouroboros*

The ouroboros is a symbol depicting a serpent (also sometimes a dragon) with its tail in its mouth. The word *ouroboros* comes from the ancient Greek, and literally means "one who bites his own tail." The serpent biting its own tail symbolizes a self-enclosed cycle of evolution. The term also conveys the ideas of movement, continuity, self-generation, and, consequently, eternal rebirth. Lastly, the circle is a potent symbol of the sacred, and of unity.

Pagan*

In the year 356 CE, Constance II, successor to Constantine, forbade the celebration of traditional rituals and ordered that all temples be closed. Christians were looking for a name for the traditional believers in the immortal divinities, and they called them "pagans" (meaning "peasants"). However, the essence of one religion cannot be legitimately classified by another religion. No belief system is superior or inferior to another. Consequently, the immortal divinities continued to be immortal and their believers continue to exist today. They may be called Wiccans, Hermetists, etc. The essence of this religious tradition is tolerance. Pagans consider all nonviolent religions to be respectable ways of searching for the divine.

Parapsychology*

The use of the scientific method to classify various aspects of traditional knowledge and to measure the attempts to extend human abilities. Using experiments, we can measure and record valid instances of telepathy, clairvoyance, psychometry, etc.

Philosopher's Stone*

See the entry *Great Work* in this glossary.

Phoenix*

An Egyptian mythological bird with gorgeous plumage, which is sacred to the Sun. The phoenix is reborn from the ashes of the funeral pyre that it makes for itself, whenever it completes its life span of five hundred years. It has become a universal symbol of rebirth. The phoenix does not eat grains (it is not grain fed, as other birds). It lives on frankincense and the sap from plants.

Potomac Lodge*

Potomac Lodge No. 5 is the oldest Masonic lodge in the District of Columbia. First chartered as Lodge No. 9 of Maryland on April 21, 1789, it was renamed as Potomac No. 5 in 1811, when the Grand Lodge, F.A.A.M. of the District of Columbia was consecrated. It has been well authenticated that President George Washington, President Thomas Jefferson, Marquis de La Fayette, and Pierre Charles L'Enfant visited this lodge, whose members met at Suter's Fountain Inn for several years after it was chartered.

Psychometry (Token-Object Reading)

Every creature on Earth, and every single object as well, has what has been termed an invisible internal memory storage, a kind of invisible mark that can be read by those who are sensitive to it. Some human beings have an ability called token-object reading, also known as psychometry. This extrasensory perception allows a person who is sensitive to contact the invisible part of an object in order to obtain information about its past and/or present owner(s). Generally speaking, simple contact with the object is enough to initiate this process and receive the desired information. The sensitive person accomplishes this by having a conscious or unconscious exchange with the object or creature.

Qabalah

The Qabalah is a set of esoteric teachings about the Torah. This tradition has several aspects. Some are focused on a kind of spiritual meditation, others on magical practices. However, all of them are founded on texts, such as the *Sepher Yetzirah* and the *Zohar*. The use of gematria with the Hebrew alphabet allows its students to achieve a deeper understanding than is available from the meaning of the literal text. They study the texts in order to understand the occult or hidden sayings within the body of the work, which not visible to the untrained.

Just as this system uses the gematria of the Hebrew letters and numbers, other forms of the Qabalah exist that use other alphabets and the gematria related to that alphabet. These systems include the Hermetic Qabalah, the Greek Qabalah, etc.

Radiesthesia

Radiesthesia (also called dowsing) is the study of the distribution of energy at and around various locations. The word *dowsing* was invented in 1890 by an abbot named Father Bouly; *radius* and *aisthêsis* are close in meaning to the word *sensitivity*. Radiesthesia is the modern development of several very ancient dowsing practices called pallomancy (dowsing with a pendulum) and rhabdomancy (dowsing with a rod or stick). There is evidence of the use of radiesthesia from the earliest historical records of humanity, right up until today.

Various esoteric and initiatic groups are still using this knowledge in order to divine the best location for rituals that are held outdoors.

Radionics

The field known as radionics became prominent in the nineteenth century. The practitioners in this field believe that every shape has a specific effect on the environment. This effect may be psychological, physical, or other. A cube, a pyramid, and an octagon, for example each have a specific energy according to this system of beliefs, and the subtle shape of the aura of each of these shapes is unique. Whether we are conscious of these effects or not, we may be sensitive to these energies. Different systems have been developed in order to focus these energies and then use them to cure people or make other uses of the special effects that are related to that particular shape.

Revelation*

See the entry for *apocalypse* in this glossary.

Rose-Cross*

This term refers to certain esoteric groups that came into being after the publication in Germany (1614–1616) of the fundamental writings of the Rose Cross by John Valentin Andreae and his circle of friends. After these publications, the Rose Cross was developed along two main lines:

one was Masonic, the other one Hermetic. In the twentieth century, several other initiatic Rose-Cross orders were created (see Chapter Five of this book).

Sanctum Sanctorum*

The term *Sanctum Sanctorum* literally means "Holy of Holies." This expression was used to describe the most holy place in the Temple of Solomon. It is used universally in both religious and occult orders. The Sanctum Sanctorum is generally used in a religious context, to describe the place where the divine powers are manifested. This same term is used similarly in temples that practice magick and Hermetism.

Scottish Rite*

The complete name of what is referred to as the Scottish Rite is, in fact, the Supreme Council, Ancient and Accepted Scottish Rite, Southern Jurisdiction, USA (commonly known as the Mother Supreme Council of the World). It was the first Supreme Council of Scottish Rite Freemasonry. The Scottish Rite is a set of thiry degrees. The number thirty does not mean that there are not thirty-three degrees. The first three degrees in the Blue Lodge are 1st Entered Apprentice, 2nd Fellowcraft, and 3rd Master Mason. After that there are thirty degrees, beginning with the 4th Degree (Secret Master) and ending with the highest degree—the 33rd (Sovereign Grand Inspector General).

   The Scottish Rite is also the name of a specific rite performed in Blue Lodges.

Shriner*

Despite its name, the Shrine (Ancient Arabic Order of the Nobles of the Mystic Shrine) is in no way connected to Islam. The Shriners International is a fraternity managed by Master Freemasons that supports the Shriners Hospitals for Children. This is an international health care system of twenty-two hospitals dedicated to improving the lives of children by providing special needs pediatric care, innovative research, and outstanding teaching programs.

Symbol*

A visual image, which may help the practitioner of Hermetism, or other systems to understand the meaning of very arcane concepts that are part of texts, myths, or rituals.

Talisman*

A pictorial representation composed of geometric symbols, sacred characters, or magical squares, etc. It is possible for this drawing, engraving, or painting to have an effect on the invisible plane.

33rd Degree*

This is the last and highest degree of the Scottish Rite: Sovereign Grand Inspector General. Several symbolic interpretations are connected with this number.

Thought-forms

Theosophical expression invented by Helena P. Blavatsky. As an archetype, a thought-form is the result of a conjunction of wills, thoughts, and ritual actions. Over many years, this sort of archetype can sometimes become autonomous (see also *egregore*).

Vesta*

In ancient Rome, the vestal virgins were the virgin priestesses of Vesta, goddess of the hearth. Their main duty was to maintain the sacred fire of Vesta. This fire was the real heart of the city, the light of its life. It had to be preserved with care and dignity.

Visualization

An ancient esoteric practice for controlling and focusing the mind. It allows the practitioner to conduct effective rituals and meditations. Effective visualization requires a precise process, which is outlined and described in Chapter Six of this book.

Zohar*

The *Zohar* is the Hebrew name for a collection of writings titled the *Book of the Splendor* (or *Radiance*). It contains esoteric and mystical commentaries on the Torah (the five books of Moses). It also contains a discussion on the nature of God, the universe, human souls, etc. This is one of the main corpuses of the Hebrew Qabalah.

Mottos and Meanings

*Laus Deo**: "Praise be to God" (written on the east side at the peak of the Washington Monument in Washington, DC).

*Annuit coeptis**: "He approves (or has approved) our undertakings."

*Tempus fugit**: "Time flies."

*Ordo ab chaos**: "Order out of chaos."

*Jeova Sanctus Unus**: "One true God."

*Vitriol**: "*Visita Interiora Terrae, Rectificandoque, Invenies Occultum Lapidem*" (Visit the interior of the earth, and rectifying it, you will find the hidden stone).

*E pluribus unum**: "From many, comes one." (Usually translated "Out of many, is one." This is the motto of the United States of America.)

Novus Ordo Seclorum: "New Order of the Ages."

INDEX

Art Credits

Page xviii: Official pin of Nevada's Grand Master, Carl L. "Bud" Banks reprinted with permission.

Page xx: Executive Chamber of the Supreme Council 33rd Degree Southern Jurisdiction, in the House of the Temple. Reprinted with permission by Executive Director Admiral Sizemore.

Page 19: Bust of Plato in the Library of the Scottish Rite, Washington DC. Reprinted with permission by Executive Director Admiral Sizemore.

Page 26: Masonic representation of Hiram's grave. Redrawn from the book "The True masonic Chart". Reprinted with permission of the Scottish Rite Library.

Page 29: Bust of Pythagoras in the Library of the Scottish Rite, Washington DC. Reprinted with permission by Executive Director Admiral Sizemore.

Page 31: Masonic representation of an Egyptian goddess with the blazing pentagram. Artwork is a personal drawing by the author.

Page 40: The sacred delta in the center of the ouroboros, symbol of eternity. Artwork is a personal drawing by the author.

Page 49: House of the Temple, Washington DC. Reprinted with permission by Executive Director Admiral Sizemore.

Page 50: Entrance door of the House of the Temple, Washington DC. Reprinted with permission by Executive Director Admiral Sizemore.

Page 54: The Pentagram and its attributions to the five elements. Redrawn by the Llewellyn art department.

Page 56: Ancient representation of Mithra and the ox sacrificed. From the book "Mithra, ce dieu mystérieux" by Martin Vermaseren.

Page 57: Symbolic representation of the Chamber of Reflection subject by the author of this book. Artwork is a personal drawing by the author.

Page 60: Masonic Lodge. Redrawn by the Llewellyn art department.

Page 63: The Capitol. Personal photo by the author.

Page 64: The Capitol. Personal photo by the author.

Page 81: Representation of the eight-pointed star and the ziggurat from the Aurum Solis tradition. Symbol from an Aurum Solis Degree, authorized by The Grand Master I am. Redrawn by the Llewellyn art department.

Page 82: Main symbol of the Ogdoadic Tradition today called "Aurum Solis". Symbol from an Aurum Solis, authorized by The Grand Master I am. Redrawn by the Llewellyn art department.

Page 89: Florence's Baptistery. Artwork is a personal drawing by the author.

Page 95: Vitruvius's gnomon traditionally used to organize a new city. Artwork is a personal drawing by the author.

Page 111: The sacred book, present on every central altar of the Masonic Temples. Artwork is a personal drawing by the author.

Page 115: Jewel of a Master of a Lodge using Egyptian symbols. Artwork is a personal drawing by the author.

Page 118: Circumpunct. Artwork is a personal drawing by the author.

Page 121: Symbols representing the different steps of the ascent of the soul. Artwork is a personal drawing by the author.

Page 122: The obelisk and its reflection. Artwork is a personal drawing by the author.

Page 124: Dome of the Capitol. Personal photo by the author.

Page 128: Square and compass in the 1st Degree. Artwork is a personal drawing by the author.

Page 128: Square and compass in the 2nd Degree. Artwork is a personal drawing by the author.

Page 128: Square and compass in the 3rd Degree. Artwork is a personal drawing by the author.

Page 134: Mason marks found on old stones of the White House, Washington DC. Artwork is a personal drawing by the author.

Page 135: Symbolic representation of the Pelican and the Rose–Cross. Artwork is a personal drawing by the author.

Page 141: One of the representations of the Rose Cross. Artwork is a personal drawing by the author.

Page 145: The cube and its development in the cross. Artwork is a personal drawing by the author.

Page 145: Valentin Andreae Arms. Artwork is a personal drawing by the author.

Page 146: Qabalistic Order of the Rose–Cross. Artwork is a personal drawing by the author.

Page 146: The unfinished pyramid and its development in the cross. Artwork is a personal drawing by the author.

Page 187: The cube and the pronounciations of the name of God (from the Bible). Artwork is a personal drawing by the author.

Page 189: The triangle and the letter G in its Greek shape. Artwork is a personal drawing by the author.

Page 197: Structure of the well in the Royal Arch Degree in the Scottish Rite. Redrawn by the author from the book "The True Masonic Chart". Authorization of the *Scottish Rite Library*.

Page 200: The Tetragrammaton. Artwork is a personal drawing by the author.

Page 202: Representation of the Rose Cross symbol in a plate from Khunrath. Heinrich Khunrath. Amphitheatrum sapientiae aeternae [Hamburg: s.n., 1595]. From the Duveen Collection. By courtesy of the Department of Special Collections, Memorial Library, University of Wisconsin-Madison.

Page 205: Pentagram and the invocation direction. Artwork is a personal drawing by the author.

Page 205: Symbolic representation of the Rite Rose–Cross developed in this part of the book. Artwork is a personal drawing by the author.

Page 218: Representations of an initiation in the Mithraic Mysteries. From the book "Mithra, ce dieu mystérieux" by Martin Vermaseren, Editions Sequoia, 1960.

Page 218: Mithra and Sol. From the book "Mithra, ce dieu mystérieux" by Martin Vermaseren, Editions Sequoia, 1960

Page 220: Symbolic representation of the 32nd Degree called the "Camp". Artwork is a personal drawing by the author.

Page 221: Symbolic representation of the ninth pointed star, center of the symbolic representation from Kircher. Artwork is a personal drawing by the author.

Page 221: Detail of the frontispiece of a book from the Qabalist Athanasius Kirche. Free European source called *European Cultual Heritage Online.*

Page 223: Frontispicce of a book from the Qabalist Athanasius Kircher. Free European source called *European Cultual Heritage Online.*

Page 225: Representation of the Hermetic Cross from old documents in the Rite of Heredom. Artwork is a personal drawing by the author.

Page 251: The Washington Monument as symbolic axis (gnomon) of the city. Artwork is a personal drawing by the author.

Page 255: Symbolic structure of the Library of Congress. Artwork is a personal drawing by the author.

Page 256: Pavement of the Great Hall of the Library of Congress. Personal photo by the author.

Page 257: General view of Capitol Hill. Personal photo by the author.

Page 259: Capitol Hill and the cardinal directionss. Artwork is a personal drawing by the author.

Artwork in the Appendices were all drawn by the author.